Y0-BCR-106

InTerneT Homework Helper

Classroom Connect - Prentice Hall

Educator's Internet Companion

Child Safety on the Internet

Family Internet Companion

Internet Homework Helper

Internet Homework Helper

by The Staff of Classroom Connect

Tim McLain, Senior Writer

Gregory Giagnocavo, Editorial Director

Dorissa Bolinski, Editor

Internet made easy in the Classroom™

Classroom Connect
Lancaster, Pennsylvania
Email: connect@classroom.net
URL: http://www.classroom.net

Library of Congress Cataloging-in-Publication Data

Internet homework helper / by the staff of Classroom Connect . . . ;
  Gregory Giagnocavo, editorial director; Dorissa Bolinski, editor.
    p. cm.
    ISBN 0–13–259557-5 (alk. paper)
    1. Homework—Computer network resources.   2. Internet (Computer
network) I. Giagnocavo, Gregory, 1953– . II. McLain, Tim, 1970– .
III. Bolinski, Dorissa   IV. Classroom connect.
  LB1048.I55   1996
  371.302'81dc20   96–33447

Cartoons: Brad Veley	*Acquisitions editor:* Mary Franz
Design and layout: John Svatek	*Editorial assistant:* Noreen Regina
Indexer: Kim Conlin	*Production supervision:* Mary Sudul
CD-ROM Production: Nathanael Waite	*Cover design:* Talar Agasyan
and Jay Walters	*Cover design director:* Jerry Votta
Project Manager: Les Miller	*Copyeditor:* Isaac Mozeson
	Manufacturing manager: Alexis R. Heydt

Copyright © 1997 by Wentworth Worldwide Media, Inc.,
            1866 Colonial Village Lane
            Lancaster, Pennsylvania 17605

Published by Prentice Hall PTR
Prentice Hall, Inc.
A Simon & Schuster Company
Upper Saddle River, New Jersey 07458

The publisher offers discounts on this book when ordered in bulk quantities.
For more information, contact Corporate Sales Department, Prentice Hall PTR,
One Lake Street, Upper Saddle River, NJ 07458. Phone: 800-382-3419;
FAX: 201-236-7141; email: corpsales@prenhall.com

All terms mentioned in this book that are known to be trademarks
or service marks have been appropriately capitalized.

All rights reserved. No part of this book may be reproduced or utilized
in any form or by any means, electronic or mechanical, including
photocopying, recording, or by any information storage and
retrieval system without written permission of the publisher.

Printed in the United States of America

10 9 8 7 6 5 4 3 2 1

ISBN 0-13-259557-5

Prentice-Hall International (UK) Limited, London
Prentice-Hall of Australia Pty. Limited, Sydney
Prentice-Hall Canada Inc., Toronto
Prentice-Hall Hispanoamericana, S.A., Mexico
Prentice-Hall of India Private Limited, New Delhi
Prentice-Hall of Japan, Inc., Tokyo
Simon & Schuster Asia Pte Ltd., Singapore
Editora Prentice-Hall do Brasil, Ltda., Rio de Janeiro

ConTenTs

Preface

Your friend, the Internet

Spend a bit of time on the Internet, and you may start
to feel that it takes on qualities much like a best friend.
It's available to spend time with, is glad to help you,
introduces you to others, tells you the latest news, likes
to play games, is glad to share what it has with you,
and is intensely loyal. Well, okay, the intensely loyal
part is a bit far-fetched. But get to know it well, and the
Internet can certainly be a helpful "friend" when it
comes time to do research and homework assignments.

In fact, the Internet can actually make learning fun—really.

In my job I travel around the country talking to students, parents, and teachers about how great the Internet is as a tool for learning. That's actually a lot of fun for me, since I truly believe that the Internet is just about the greatest piece of technology ever invented.

I think you'll feel that way too after you discover all the great information online, and experience the thrill of communicating with other people all over the world. There are more than 30 million Internet users worldwide. So, no matter what you're interested in collecting, talking about, or finding out about, you can be sure there are hundreds of others with the same interests and the same problems—homework or otherwise—as you.

I know you don't want a lecture on how to do your homework. No problem—that's up to you. I can tell you this, though—you'll actually enjoy tackling homework assignments—and get them done in record time—using the Internet. This is going to sound hard to believe, but there is so much terrific and helpful information online, that there's no way you could get to use even 10% of it in an entire year.

But, oh, what you can find! Get the lowdown and background on all those famous, but dead, artists by going to the Louvre museum in France. Check out the biographies and written works of famous writers you need to learn about—and read the related comments of other students and teachers. Get help with math, chemistry, and physics problems—finding just what you need by doing a lightening fast keyword search. University, government and research lab databases are only a few keystrokes away. And the best part of all—it's free.

So don't hesitate another moment. Become the best student you can be—impress your teacher and your parents and most importantly yourself. It only takes a little extra effort to get the most out of the Internet and to get all the help you need.

After all, that's what friends are for.

Gregory Giagnocavo
Email: jgg@classroom.net

P.S. I know you're really busy. But since you'll be saving so much time using the Internet to help you with your homework, how about sending me some email. Let me know how you're doing and how the Internet helped you. I get hundreds of email messages a week, but I promise I'll do my best to answer each and every one.

About The auThor

As Senior Internet Writer for *Classroom Connect,* Tim
McLain has much experience helping people learn to
use the Internet. Now 25, he has been surfing the Net
for almost 10 years. He thanks his dad for inciting his
interest in computers by buying him a Commodore Pet
2000 computer way back in 1977. In addition to his role
as Senior Writer for *Classroom Connect,* he contributes
material for their books, CD-ROMs, and Web site as well
as hosting their popular video series. Tim also travels
the country giving workshops to teachers who want to
incorporate the Internet into their curriculum.

What can the Internet do for me?

As a student today, you have a distinct learning advantage
over your parents, as well as people who were in school
just a few years ago—you can use the Internet.
The Internet provides easy access to the largest body
of knowledge ever assembled. It can help you
do research, write better papers, and can make
learning more interesting. This book will tell you
how to best take advantage of this exciting new resource!

Bring the Internet into your life—NOW!

I'm sure you know that *not* being on the Net is way uncool. Soon, not being on the Internet will be equivalent to not having a telephone or TV. In business, not having an email address on your business card is like not having a fax number. (Remember that when you start a little business to work yourself through college!)

Employers and college recruiters want high school graduates with computer and Internet experience. Knowledge of computers and the Internet helps many people get (and keep) their jobs.

You can find all kinds of information on the Internet, and it's not all just text. Pictures, sounds, video clips, software—all these can help you with homework. You can access computers with information on the topics you're studying in your English, science, social studies, math, history classes, and more.

If you don't like computers, or if you're nervous learning new software, don't worry. The tool you'll use most to get around the Internet is very, very easy. It's called an Internet browser. The most popular browser is called Netscape Navigator—and you can get it free on the Internet! (You can find out more about browsers in Appendix A at the back of this book.)

The Internet will never replace the library, but it can take your research one step further. You can get info from the original sources. You can get info that's just minutes or hours old. You can ask questions of people all over the world to bring your work to life.

How do I get on the Internet to use what I learn in this book?

To get on the Net you basically need three things:

1. A Windows or Macintosh computer.
2. A modem, which the computer uses to dial into the Internet.
3. Access to a telephone line.

Once you have these items, you need to get access to the Internet. People get connected to the Internet in one of the following ways. (The percentage beside each indicates the proportion of Internet users who access the Net through each method.)

- Internet Service Providers (55%).
- America Online (25%).
- Prodigy (5%).
- Other commercial providers (15%).

America Online and Prodigy are called *commercial online services.* They're businesses that allow millions of users to access the really big computers at their headquarters. You dial into them with your computer's modem. (Read Appendix A for more about modems.) You pay a monthly fee and sometimes an hourly charge to access the service and its information. They offer lots of extras, such as access to newsmagazines, to make it easy for members to find information.

Unfortunately, commercial services offer slow and somewhat cumbersome Internet access. Still, you can use them to surf the Net using Internet browser software. To get to the browsers, type the keyword **Web** on America Online or the jump-word **Web** on Prodigy.

The best and most common way of getting on the Net is through an Internet Service Provider, or ISP. ISPs are businesses that connect you directly to the Internet at high speeds—no fuss, no muss, but no frills either. They don't offer any extras like the commercial services. But they can be *cheaper* because they usually have no hourly charges.

How would you suggest I hook up to the Net?

Most Net veterans recommend you get online through an Internet Service Provider. You'll get direct, high-speed access to the Internet through a local phone number, usually for a flat monthly fee of less than $20—with no hourly charges.

BONUS! → *The CD ROM included with this book contains online access software for a national Internet Service Provider that you can use to hook up to the Net right away. You also get Netscape Navigator browser software and some free access time!*

If you're really new to the online world or if your parents have an America Online or Prodigy account, use that service to give the Net a try.

Ask your parents to switch to an ISP later. Switching will save them lots of money and save you lots of time hunting down the homework information you need!

This is just the short version of how to connect to the Net. Read "Internet Basics" (Appendix A) for all the info you need to get online.

About this Book
Do I have to be a Net Head to understand this book?

No way. Maybe you've only sent one or two email messages at school or just watched your teacher click through a Web site. Not to worry— this book was written with you in mind! If you are a Net Head, you'll also pick up a lot of inside tips on searching and multimedia.

If you've never used a computer or really don't know anything about the Internet, read Appendix A to learn about Internet basics. You'll find all the information you'll ever need, including:

- Internet history.
- How to get connected.
- How to use each of the Internet's six main navigation tools—email, World Wide Web, gopher, file transfer protocol (ftp), telnet, Usenet newsgroups, and Internet Relay Chat (IRC).

If you're saying "Yikes! What in the world are those?" then be sure to read Appendix A—ASAP!

Introduction

Does the planet really need another Internet book?

Um, yes. Because none of the other books tackle the Net with students in mind. This book satisfies many needs of student Net users. It teaches you how to:

- Track down homework-helping information from the Internet—FAST.
- Figure out whether what you find on the Net is worthwhile information.
- Properly cite the online information you find in your bibliographies.
- Turn your Internet information into a multimedia presentation.
- Create your own Web pages.
- Get connected to the Net and start surfing ASAP.

No other book has successfully done any of these things for students like you!

How to use the Internet addresses in this book

The addresses for Internet sites in this book may look a little different from what you've seen. Here's why.

Just a couple years ago, you had to use different kinds of software to get to different parts of the Internet. You used email software to send email, gopher software to visit gopher sites, and ftp software to go to ftp computers. It was tough, and it kept a lot of people away from the Net.

Today, you only need one kind of software to do anything you want on the Net—a browser. The Internet browser combines all that software into one single navigation tool. Now, getting around on the Net is easy!

You'll see sites listed simply as URLs (an Internet address) that you can access through any Internet browser. Here's how they look:

Type of site	Browser address
Email	URL: mailto:user@internet.edu
File transfer protocol	URL: ftp://ftp.netscape.com
Gopher	URL: gopher://ericir.syr.edu
News	URL: news:k12.chat.teacher
World Wide Web	URL: http://www.classroom.net

Netscape, America Online, and Prodigy Internet browsers

Netscape Navigator and Microsoft Internet Explorer are the most popular browsers, but there are others. The commercial services also have their own browsers. Each browser looks a bit different, so we've used different browsers to take the "screen captures" (pictures of Internet sites) scattered around the book.

The world @ your fingertips

Use Internet Power to improve your mind and school work . . . and then have fun!

You probably know that the Net is filled with all kinds
of fun information about your favorite things,
but do you know that it can also help you
do your homework and other school assignments?
In this chapter, we'll tell you:

✹ Why the Internet is a powerful learning tool.

✹ How it can help you with your school assignments.

The Net is a powerful tool

The Net is cool—everybody knows that. Your friends tell you it's the place to hang out and chat with guys and girls from around the world. Your favorite bands, TV shows, and movies have Internet sites, and you can find info about *anything* you're interested in.

Besides being a fun place to hang out, the Net is also a very powerful tool. It gives you the power to find information that can make your school assignments fantastic! And it gives you the power to find people who can help you answer research questions or other problems. It won't give you more brain cells, but it will make you exercise them a lot more—and that makes you smarter. You might even earn more A's!

When you sit down to use an Internet-connected computer, you can instantly link to two things:

- Excellent information on more than five million computers around the world.
- As many as 30 million people who use the Net in 160 countries.

Thanks to easy-to-use Internet browser software (like Netscape Navigator), these millions of computers and people are only a mouse click away!

OK, so you're impressed. But, um, how do you find the stuff you need to solve your homework problems TONIGHT?

We'll tell you. The *Internet Homework Helper* will give you—junior high and high school students—insider tips that help you use this huge network of people, computers, and information to solve your homework assignment problems!

But really . . . how can the Internet help me with my homework?

If you haven't used the Net, it's hard to see how it can make a big difference in your schoolwork. Maybe you've used the Net only for fun—hey, that's not a crime!

Check out these examples of how the Net can improve your schoolwork.

Subject English.

Assignment Define words and phrases from Shakespeare.

Internet Advantage You can use a search engine to immediately find modern definitions of Old English terms.

Description Your teacher gave you a two-page sheet filled with Old English words and the names of Shakespeare's plays and poems in which they appeared. Your job is to write a

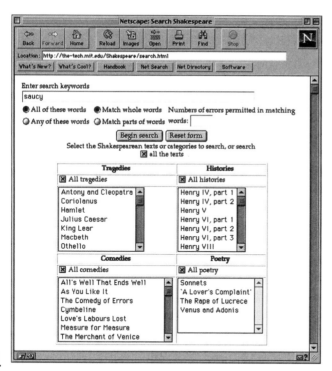

modern definition for each term. Rather than wade through pages and pages, you visit the Complete Works of William Shakespeare Web site and use its searchable Old English dictionary! Just enter an Old English word into the search field and the modern definition appears. You finish your assignment, which could have taken you hours, in less than 15 minutes!

URL: http://the-tech.mit.edu/
Shakespeare/search.html

Subject General Research.

Assignment Complete research paper in time for deadline.

Internet Advantage You can ask a reference librarian for help at any time.

Description You waited until the last minute to do your research paper. Now your teacher won't budge on the deadline. You already found five sources in the school library, and now you go online and use a search engine to do a search for *libraries* and *reference*. It turns up a link to the free "Ask a Reference Librarian Service" at the Internet Public Library. You fill out an online form and ask for help in tracking down sources (both online and print) for your paper. In 12 hours you get a response via email. Cool! The librarian found more than 80 sources that will help you find the information you need. And, best of all, most of them are on the Net. You get the paper done in record time and have nearly twice as many entries in your bibliography as everyone else!

URL: http://www.ipl.org/ref/QUE/

Netscape: IPL Reference Question Form

N

Back Forward Home Reload Images Open Print Find Stop

Location: http://www.ipl.org/ref/QUE/RefFormQRC.html

What's New? What's Cool? Handbook Net Search Net Directory Software

the Internet Public Library

Reference Question Form

Reminder:

We are not able to perform lengthy research. However we can provide brief answers to factual questions or suggestions for locations and sources which might help to answer your question.

NEW: Before you ask a reference question, please check to see if your question is in the Frequently Asked Reference Questions list. You could save yourself, and us, a lot of time.

| IPL Reference Question |

Contact Information: Tell us about yourself.

Please make sure that your e-mail address is correctly entered, so that we can respond to your question. (Example: fluggly@aol.com) If you do not enter a valid Internet e-mail address, we will not be able to respond to your question.

Type in your name: John Q. Student
Your e-mail address: john@redrose.net
Your location (City, State/Country): Redmond, Washington/USA
Not needed after (date): 10/1/96

The Subject Area of the Question: (click to see list -- choose one)

| Environment |

Subject Chemistry.

Assignment Convert data from
English to metric.

Internet Advantage You can
find free software to do metric conversions.

Description As a take-home test,
you've been given a two-sided sheet with data.
Your job is to convert the data into metric

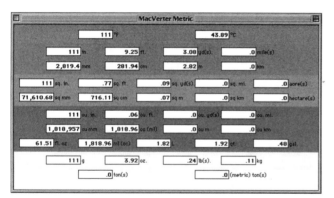

measurements. You go online and use a search engine. A quick search of the Internet for the words _metric_ and _convert_ reveals a link to a free number-conversion program called MacVerter. You retrieve—or _download_ in Netspeak—the program to your Macintosh computer in less than two minutes and run it. Wow! Just plug in the English number you want to convert, and the software converts it into more than two dozen metric equivalents. Your homework is done in a flash!

URL: ftp://ftp.classroom.net/wentworth/
Internet-Software/Mac/MacVerter.sea.hqx

Subject History.

Assignment Describe an artifact from the time of the Russian czars and place it in its time in Russian history.

Internet Advantage You can find an online exhibit of artifacts of the czars with historical background.

Description Your job is to write a five-page research paper describing a major artifact still in existence from an era of the

Russian czars. You have to describe the historical background surrounding it. You go online and do a keyword search of the Internet using the keywords Russia and Czars. Your search returns a link to an exhibit on the World Wide Web called Treasures of the Russian Czars.

You visit the site and click on the Czar Timeline to find a timeline full of historical events and links to artifacts. One click on a small picture of a tapestry portrait of Peter the Great and you've found your artifact. Using the online document as one of your sources, you write the paper and lay it out using a word processor. You set the image of the tapestry in the center of the page. You print the paper on your color printer at home for the final killer effect!

You've uncovered a unique source of information about your topic, and you got bonus points for turning a black and white research paper into a colorful presentation!

URL: http://www.times.st-pete.fl.us/Treasures/

What do you think?

Now . . . how can you NOT use the Net for your homework?

Well, in the rest of the book, we'll show you how to do all this and more. Read on to discover "the Internet way" to do homework and learn all about it.

Chapter 2

The Internet way to do homework

Ten steps to get started using the Net

So, you're ready to try using the Internet
for your next homework assignment.
Before you do, you'll need to learn a
few helpful steps. This chapter will give you:

* Ten steps to doing homework on the Internet.
* Tips for getting organized.
* Suggestions to make your homework
assignments more interesting and creative.

Make the Net work for you

OK. You're connected to the Net and you're ready to roll. But before you go online to do your homework, remember the Internet is simply another tool you can use to do your assignments. It won't do your homework for you or totally replace your teacher, a library, or a good textbook!

Also, the information-gathering skills you use everyday are now more useful to you than ever. The Net is so big and has so much stuff that you'll need to decide what Internet information is valuable and what isn't. Still, the Net is an awesome resource you'll use time and time again. Listed below are ten steps for making the Internet work for you.

Ten Steps to Doing Homework on the Internet

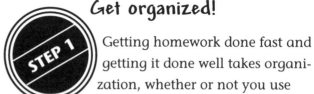

Get organized!

Getting homework done fast and getting it done well takes organization, whether or not you use the Net. Below are some hands-on tips for getting organized.

• Do your homework at the same time every night. This helps you finish it on time and lets you set aside time to use the Internet.

- Make sure your homework space is quiet and has tons of light. Have supplies, including your computer, close by. A study area doesn't have to be fancy. A desk in the bedroom is nice, but the den or a corner of the living room works great, too.

- Turn off the TV. Force yourself not to call your friends during homework time. Of course, you can call a friend about an assignment. If you live in a small or noisy household, ask if other family members can do something quiet during your homework time.

STEP 2   Read the assignment

You're organized and ready to work. Now, read your assignment(s) carefully. Be sure you understand what is required of you and what subject areas the homework covers.

STEP 3   How much time do you have?

The Internet can help you complete both long-term research projects and short-term overnight assignments. But if it's easier and faster to use a book or magazine to complete your work, use them! Don't spend time searching for information on the Net if you can find it faster and more easily somewhere else.

STEP 4 — Is the Internet the best tool for your assignment?

If you're writing a paper, the Internet can definitely deliver sources of information that will make your work better. But if your teacher asks you to define a list of words scattered throughout a textbook chapter you're reading for next Monday's class, using the Internet isn't the best way to complete the assignment.

STEP 5 — Which Internet tools will help you most

You can use these Internet tools in all kinds of ways, for all sorts of homework assignments. Below are just a few of the things that you can do.

Communicate with people one-to-one

Your assignment is to debate an issue with a family member, a classmate, or anyone you choose. You can use email to complete the assignment by debating with a student from another state, another country, or even another continent! Peers, experts, and many other people are willing to help you. These people are like online penpals, so they're called keypals.

Track down the most up-to-date information

The Internet is full of up-to-the-minute news reports from hundreds of newspapers worldwide,

Where to find Keypals

Keypals.com
URL: http://www.keypals.com

thousands of up-to-date databases, and even satellite images taken every hour of every corner of the globe! You can find this information on the World Wide Web, gopher, and Usenet newsgroups. And Internet directories and search engines can deliver tons of the latest information.

Research a specific topic

You can find information about any topic you're researching, such as life in space or American politics. World Wide Web and gopher sites are good places to start looking. In the Usenet newsgroups, you can ask questions of a space shuttle astronaut or a political science professor.

Do a multicultural or global assignment

Do more than just practice your French with a classmate. Use the Internet to strike up a live conversation with a student your age in France! Use the Web to find a French speaker, then use email to try your French with a native speaker. Once again, go to the Keypals.com site mentioned earlier to find someone you can write to.

Compare and contrast information

Use Usenet newsgroups to follow the discussions about issues you have to research. You'll find plenty of debates on the pros and cons of gun control, the similarities and differences between the works of two writers, and so on.

Sites with up-to-date info

Electronic Newsstand
URL: http://www.enews.com

Electric Library
URL: http://www.elibrary.com

Satellite Images of the Earth
URL: http://rs560.cl.msu.edu/weather/

The Internet Way to Do Homework

Where to find experts

Ask An Expert!
URL: http://www.keypals.com/
pitsco/ask.html

NASA Usenet News
URL: news:sci.space.shuttle

Political Usenet News
URL: news:soc.politics

Where to find clip art

Multimedia & Clip Art
URL: http://www.itec.sfsu.edu/
multimedia/multimedia.html

Where to post surveys

IECC Surveys
URL: http://www.stolaf.edu/
network/iecc/

Critical thinking and analysis

The Net is full of people who can help you think more critically about your assignment. After you finish a paper about the history of flight, post it to the aeronautics history Usenet newsgroup and ask the experts to critique it. Use their constructive criticism and turn a so-so paper into an A+ affair!

Information gathering from experts and others

Say you have to interview a famous local person for an assignment. Why focus only on your local area when you could interview Peter Jennings or George Lucas via email?

Find art work or computer graphics

The Net is home to millions of pieces of clip art and scans of works of art. One click of your mouse brings these images right to your computer. If you use them in your paper, just remember to credit the original creator of the images. If you're allowed to turn the assignment into a multimedia presentation using Hyper-Card, PowerPoint, or HyperStudio, the Internet will be a life saver!

Conduct a survey or questionnaire

Say you want to use a questionnaire to collect data. You can type it into your computer and post it to places online where the audience you want to reach gathers. You'll be amazed at the number of responses you get back overnight!

STEP 6

Which directories and search engines can best help you?

You should use several Internet search directories to "mine" the Internet for the best and most complete information. Simply look over your assignment, decide which "key-words" will give you the best search results, and use them in your search.

Sometimes you'll use email or Usenet news-groups to solve your homework problems. But most of the time you'll be searching for Web sites that have the information you need. To do that, you'll need to use Internet directories and search engines.

Some search engines are broken down into long lists of sites, called directories. Directories such as Yahoo and TradeWave Galaxy organize sites into categories you can browse. They're great for looking for information by clicking on cate-gories, such as Science, then Biology, then DNA. Start with the directories when you're looking for a site. If they don't help, turn to the search engines.

To use the Net's search engines, you first have to type in keywords that describe the information you're hunting for. Then the search engines go out on the Net to find the sites that match your keywords. So start thinking about the "key" words which describe your homework assign-ment.

Internet search engines and directories

Yahoo!
URL: http://www.yahoo.com

Excite
URL: http://www.excite.com

Alta Vista
URL: http://www.altavista.digital.com

Take a look at your assignment(s) again. Read the instructions out loud to yourself. What are the keywords that jump out at you? Write them down. Here's an example.

Assignment The Language of Shakespeare.

Description Elizabethan language may seem very different from modern-day English, but if read out loud, its meaning becomes clearer. Your teacher lists some of William Shakespeare's most famous passages, and asks you to read them and then "translate" them into modern-day English, using slang and modern grammar.

Keywords Shakespeare, Elizabethan, English, translate.

Alta Vista returned these results when the keywords from the assignment were entered.

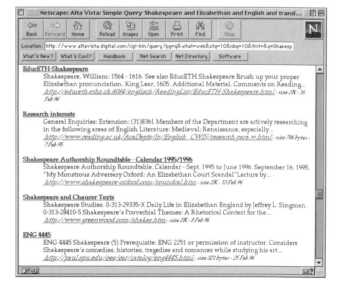

Search engines work best when you give them very specific keywords. They help the engine return to you only those sites that most closely match the keywords you've given it. For example, using the popular Alta Vista search tool with the keywords for the Shakespeare assignment brought more than 150 results, including those in the screen capture on page 24.

Develop a search strategy

STEP 7

Once you've got your keywords, decide how much time and how many search engines you want to use. You should run your keywords through at least five search tools—three Web search engines (such as Alta Vista, Lycos, and Savvy Search), Veronica (to search through gopher sites), and DejaNews (to hunt through the contents of Usenet newsgroups). Don't forget that you'll need to give yourself some time to visit at least some of the sites the search engine returns to you.

Go online and find what you need!

STEP 8

You've gone through each of the previous steps. You've got your keywords. You've created a killer game plan to tackle your homework as quickly and efficiently as possible. Now it's time to fire up your modem and get started!

Force yourself to stay focused while you're online. Sure it's fun to surf the digital waves all night with no purpose, but it won't help you complete your assignment. Use a timer if necessary. Give yourself an hour or so to find the information you need. If the timer runs out and you still haven't found the info yet, turn off the computer and look elsewhere. An hour of searching is more than enough time to discover whether or not the Internet will help you!

STEP 9

Critically judge the information you find

If your Internet search returned a few sites that look like they might be useful, it's time to use your information literacy skills. Before you use information from a site for your assignment, take a critical look at it to determine whether the information is authentic and valid.

Why should you do this? Because anything can be published to a worldwide audience in seconds via the Net. This "information" could read like something from your textbook. But it could also contain inaccurate, unsubstantiated, or misleading facts.

The Internet has no "information police." Gone are the editors and proofreaders of the real world who question, sometimes rewrite, and check the validity of information in an author's work. In the real world, it's only after this time-intensive editing process does a book, newsletter, or magazine get published. This is not so with the Net. As you retrieve information from the Net to do your homework, think about whether it's "good" information that you can trust.

STEP 10 — Cite the Internet information you use to do your homework

OK, so you've found helpful information online for your assignment. Go ahead and use it! But be sure to cite the online sources in your bibliography. See Chapter 7 for a full discussion of this, along with samples to show you just how to cite your sources.

Congratulations! The Internet has helped you finish your homework—doing a better job in record time.

Where to go to find what you want

How to use the Internet's directories and search engines

The Internet is like a huge ocean of information.
Now that you're ready to begin surfing
the Net for your homework research,
you'll need to know the best way to find stuff.
This chapter will teach you about:

✹ Using Internet directories and search engines.
✹ Developing keywords to help in your searches.
✹ Great searching tips.

Directories and search engines

Finding stuff on the Internet is getting easier all the time. Two tools—directories and search engines—will help you find anything you need, 24 hours a day! Many people get directories and search engines confused. Aren't they the same thing? Actually, no. A directory is a man-made list of links organized by topic or category, while a search engine is software backed up by lots of very powerful computers. Many large sites have search engines that help you quickly find the information on their sites. That's why many directories, such as Yahoo, also have search engines.

Some sites, such as Alta Vista, exist solely to provide you with access to their very powerful search engine software and computers. They want to help you quickly find whatever you need on the Internet. So the Alta Vista site is actually described as a "search engine," since that's the only reason it exists. And you can use it for free!

Keep it simple—try a directory

Nobody likes to do more work than they have to. That's why a directory should be your first stop when you need to find something on the Internet. Directories are sites you can visit that have thousands of other Internet sites organized by category. They're easy to click through and find what you want.

The people who run the directories make it their mission to check out Web sites. They only include worthwhile sites in their directories, saving you the effort of wading through lots of weak sites in your quest to find valuable ones. They've already organized the Web so you don't have to search for a needle in the huge Internet haystack. Looking for movie reviews? Just go to Yahoo, click on Entertainment, then Movies, then Movie Reviews, and you'll find all the reviews you will ever need.

Let's use a directory!

To give you a feel for how directories work, we'll take a quick tour through one of the most popular ones, Yahoo. Feel free to follow along on your computer if you want.

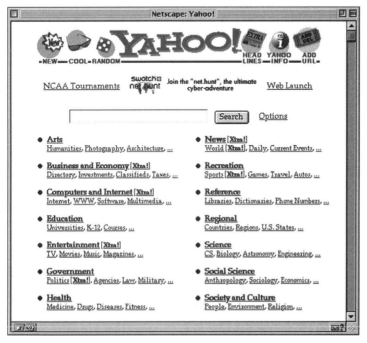

This is Yahoo!, one of the most popular directories on the Internet.
http://www.yahoo.com

Let's pretend I'm doing a paper on the Seven Wonders of the Ancient World. I've had trouble finding anything about the Colossus of Rhodes, not to mention a couple others. So I went to Yahoo and scanned the categories on the home page. Under **Arts** I saw **Humanities.** History is a humanity, so I figured that's where I would find it. I clicked on Humanities and got this page. Then I clicked on History and got the screen below.

Wow! Look at all those categories. This is a great place to go for any kind of history research. See the number in parentheses next to the name of each category? Each number tells you how many sites are listed in that area. (The 17th Century has 4 and World History has 32.) The first column has a category called Ancient History. That's got to be the place where I'll find what I need.

Bingo! The list on this page includes one called the Seven Wonders of the Ancient World.

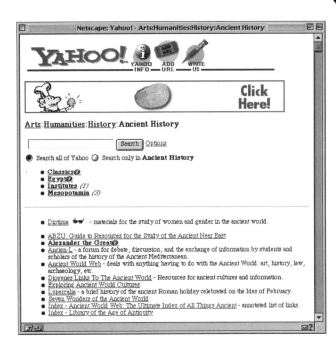

I clicked on it and saw this. Fantastic! I clicked on the picture of the colossus and found the screen on the following page.

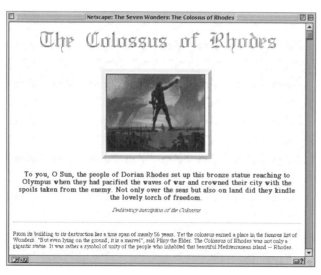

This is great material for my assignment! But before I use it in my paper, I've got to make sure the site is "cool." That is, does whoever built this site seem to know what they're talking about?

So I went back to the home page for Seven Wonders, and I looked at any background information I could find. From the award logo on the page, it's obvious that Point Survey likes the site, so that's one good sign. I clicked on copyright, but that didn't tell me much about the author.

Then I clicked on the author's name at the bottom of the page. That brought me the info on this screen.

This guy seems legit. And all his contact info is there in case I have any questions about his site. My search has ended! Yahoo!

One more thing about Yahoo and the other directories—some of them include search engines for their sites. These search engines allow you to search only the contents of that particular directory, rather than the entire Internet. Go back to Yahoo's home page, and you'll see the search engine at the top of the page. You'll also find it on their other pages, thus allowing you to search only the category that you're interested in, such as History.

If you don't find something helpful at Yahoo, you can try one of the other directories on the Web. The next section provides a list of the more popular directories, along with a brief description. Check each one out, give it a test drive, and bookmark it if you find it useful. Note that some directories, Magellan and iGuide! for example, include a review of each site to save the time and effort of visiting it to judge for yourself.

Netscape: Alaa Ashmawy

Alaa Kamal Ashmawy

Postdoctoral Fellow
Geosystems Engineering
Georgia Institute of Technology

School information

School of Civil and Environmental Engineering
Georgia Institute of Technology
Atlanta, GA 30332

Office: 114-D (Geotechnical Building)
Phone : (+1) 404-894-2284
Fax : (+1) 404-894-2281
E-mail: ashmawy@geosystems.gatech.edu

Home information

2550 Akers Mill Rd., Apt F-27
Atlanta, GA 30339-3212

Professional information

Where to Go to Find What You Want

Meet directories that can help you

GNN Select
http://www.gnn.com/gnn/wic/wics/index.html

GNN Select lists sites by subject, much like Yahoo. Topics include Arts and Entertainment, Education, Government and Politics, Humanities, Science and Technology, and more. Before you access a site, GNN gives you a brief description. GNN also lists its 50 most-accessed sites so you can quickly visit the most popular ones.

Here's GNN's downside. It isn't updated often enough and it offers too few entries. It's great if you have time to browse, but skip it if you're in a hurry. Here's a time-saving tip: Click on the All Entries link and allow the list of sites to scroll into your browser. Then click on your browser's Find button to enter a keyword for what you want.

iGuide!
http://www.iguide.com

iGuide! resembles an online magazine more than it does a directory. It offers weekly articles and news features in addition to its directory of sites.

Sites are reviewed on a scale of one to four, four being the highest. Some reviews are in-depth and include sound and video clips. iGuide! claims it's the "definitive guide to the Internet." Maybe it's not that good, but it's not too shabby either.

Magellan
http://www.mckinley.com

Magellan's writers review and rate thousands of new sites every month. The list for each site includes its name, rating, a partial or full description, and a link labeled Review, which identifies the creator(s) of the site and their email address.

You can browse Magellan's categories or use its powerful search engine, which connects you with a growing number of yet-to-be reviewed sites (currently a million and a half). This is an excellent directory for students, as it reviews sites for inappropriate content. A site with a "Green Light" next to it means that it has been found to be free of "adult" material. Magellan isn't noted for its speed, so expect to wait a little for your search results.

Pointcom
http://www.pointcom.com

The folks at Pointcom peruse the Web daily
and decide which pages are the best of the
best—the top 5% of the Web. You won't miss
Pointcom's little "5%" sign on pages on sites all
over the Net. (Do you remember the Seven
Wonders of the Ancient World site that we
searched earlier in the chapter? It has a
Pointcom 5% sign.)

Reviewers rate each site on a scale of 1–50, with
50 being the best. Categories include content,
presentation, and experience. It doesn't cover all
subject areas, so don't use Point for an extensive
search on a particular subject. Use Point if you
feel like browsing or are looking for sites a cut
above the rest.

Shareware.com
http://www.shareware.com

If you're seeking software (graphics, drawing, software calculator, games, and so forth), then Shareware.com, a directory of sites with software, should be your first stop. Shareware.com offers searching through its index of nearly 200,000 shareware software titles. A search for math software uncovered more than 100 shareware programs for the Macintosh alone!

Shareware software isn't free. Instead, each program's author expects you to pay for the program if you find it useful. Try it for a few days, but if you want to keep it, then you should strongly consider paying for it.

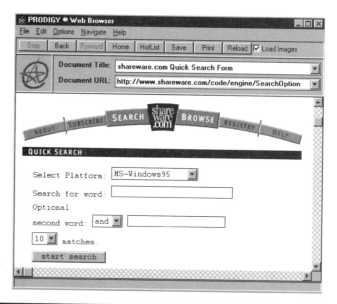

Similar Sites

Snoopie   http://www.snoopie.com

Jumbo   http://www.jumbo.com

TradeWave Galaxy
http://galaxy.einet.net

Galaxy is a list of sites (with a search engine) that is broken down by subject area. Government, Humanities, Reference, Science, and Social Science are just a few of the categories you can choose from.

Galaxy's directory represents only a small portion of the Web, so don't use it for serious searching. Forget hunting through Galaxy's topical list of sites unless you have lots of time! Instead, click on the Search link at the top of the page and enter your keywords.

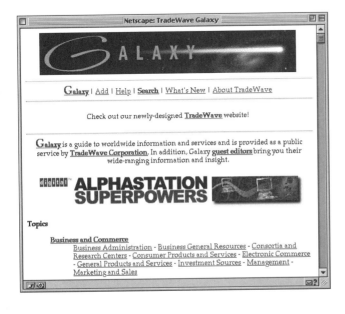

WWW Virtual Library
http://www.w3.org/hypertext/DataSources/
bySubject/Overview.html

Think of the WWW Library as an online library card catalog, with new categories always being added. The Library is maintained by volunteers, schools, and universities. Each volunteer gathers links on a specific subject, such as nursing or zoology. Topics range from the obscure, such as aboriginal studies, to the everyday, such as gardening.

You can view the listings by subject, Library of Congress classification, statistics, or just by the ten most popular subjects. Visitors are encouraged to add their favorite entries. The categories lean toward the academic, however.

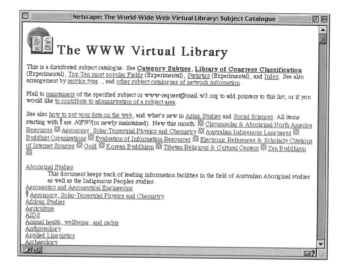

Yahoo!
http://www.yahoo.com

This is the directory that gets all the media attention, and with good reason! It's the largest and most popular directory on the Web. The categories are arranged in hierarchical order for easy searching.

Other directories, such as GNN Select and Tradewave Galaxy, try to mimic Yahoo but can't compete with its well-organized directory. It enables you to track down good information from its long lists rather quickly.

You can also enter your keywords into the search field to find specific information faster. Yahoo's popularity does have a down side—It can take up to six months to add a new link, so its directory is usually several months behind the rest. Links also aren't updated often enough, resulting in some links that just don't work.

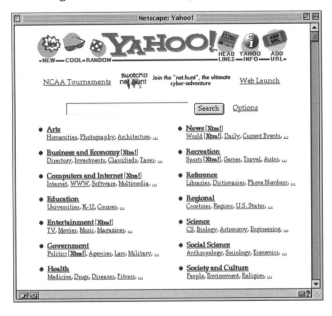

If directories don't help—use a search engine!

So you tried a couple of directories and you couldn't find what you need. Now it's time to do a "power search" of the entire Internet with a search engine. Search engine sites exist to help Internet users find what they need on the Net. They're very powerful, fast, easy to use, and—unlike your local library—open 24 hours a day!

How do you use a search engine? Simple. A site with a search engine will have an empty rectangular field with space for you to type. (It's usually near the top of the Web page.) You type in a series of keywords related to the subject you want information about.

After you type in your keywords, look for a gray button with the word **Search** or **Submit** next to the empty field you typed into. Click on it (sometimes you don't even have to click on it— just hit your return key), and the engine searches the Internet for pages with all or most of your keywords. In seconds, the search engine fills your computer screen with a list of Internet sites you can visit to see whether their information satisfies your request.

Here's why keywords are so important

Search engines have millions of references to information that you can search with keywords, but your search will only be as good as your keywords. What does this mean? Read about the following assignment to find out.

Assignment Write a three-page research paper on DNA this weekend answering these two simple questions:

1. What is the basic structure of DNA?

2. How does it replicate itself?

Description Use this information to start your information quest to complete this assignment: The basic structure of DNA is the double helix. The double helix is formed from two individual strands that complement each other perfectly. Amazingly, DNA is made of only four main building blocks, referred to as A, T, G, and C. An A block always pairs with a T block and a G block always pairs with a C block. This remarkably simple structure makes it easy to see how DNA is replicated. DNA can be copied to make a related molecule called RNA.

After reading the teacher's assignment, you can use a highlighter to pick out the words and concepts that seem most important.

Keywords DNA, RNA, double helix, and replication are all from the assignment, but you remember a few more concepts that you talked about in class—chemistry, genetics, amino acid, and translation—and so you add them to the list.

The search engines use these keywords to seek out specific references to the information you're looking for. This can take from 5–30 seconds. Then, the engines return the related links to you in an ordered list. Here's an example of what happened when we used these keywords for a search using the Inktomi search engine.

Result
Look at the list of sites Inktomi returned. The sites near the top most closely match your keywords. They received the most *hits* to your keywords, which means they received the highest score in terms of being the most relevant links to your search. Those near the bottom are less likely to be what you wanted, but they matched your keywords in one way or another.

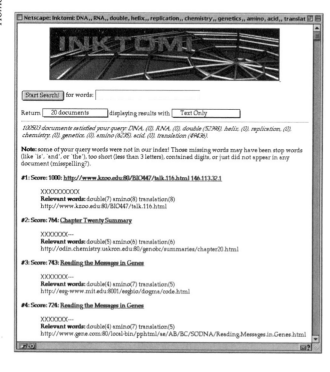

Note that the item at the top of the list scored 1000 hits. That's the highest score an item can receive, and that means it's probably the best link to the information you need—but not always. In this case, it looks as if links three and four would be a better starting point.

Try the links at the top first, and work your way through the rest. Just like the rest of the Internet, trial-and-error will make the most of your search results.

How fresh is the information in these search engines?

It's very fresh! Virtually all of the search engines update their database of Net sites at least once a month. The addresses of Internet sites change, new ones appear, and some disappear. For a search engine to be effective, it has to keep up with these constant changes in the millions of pages of info on the Net.

How does it do that? Each search engine deploys thousands of Internet "spiders," software that crawls all over the Internet. They visit old and new sites and record what they find. These records are quickly sent back to the search engine and added into its master index. When you do a search, you're searching the search engine's master index.

Not all search engines are equal. Each engine competes for the title of the largest index to the freshest Internet information. That's why it's important to use several search engines when doing your research. Don't rely on one engine to find what you're looking for. Visiting three or four engines brings the best results.

Let's try a search engine!

Search engines are incredibly easy to use. They're so fast you'll wonder how you got by without them. Let's do a quick search of the Net using the Alta Vista search engine (our favorite, 'cause it's fast!) to show you how it's done.

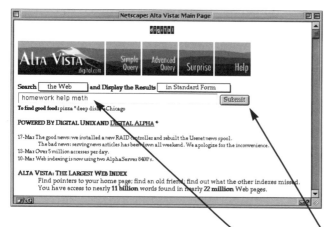

1. Start your Internet browser and go to Alta Vista's home page.

   http://www.altavista.digital.com

2. You'll see a lot of stuff on the home page, but the most important area is the blank box near the top. That's where you enter your keywords to search Alta Vista's index. It has a Submit button next to it.

3. Let's do a search for the words **homework help math**. Remember, the more specific your keywords, the more likely the search results will include the material you need. Click Submit to begin the search.

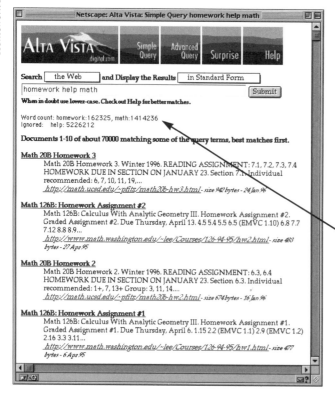

4. The results appear a few seconds later. Look at the top of the results. In small type, you can see that the engine actually found the word **homework** 162,325 times in its index. It found the word **math** 1,414,236 times! Yikes!

Thankfully, you can only see the first ten results of our search. But 7000 more are waiting to be viewed. Our first task is to scan through the first few hits to see whether we got what we wanted out of the search.

Just follow each link by clicking on it. It will take you to the site and allow you to view what's there. If you want to return to the search results, just hit your browser's Back button a few times until you see it again.

If you aren't satisfied with the results, you could put new keywords in the search box, click Submit again, and see if you come closer to your goal.

Search engine reviews

Now that you know the basics of how to use an Internet search engine, it's time to review each of the major engines currently available online.

Use these reviews to hunt down the search engines that will provide you with links to the information you're looking for—whether it's raw data, documents, graphics, software, or sound and video clips.

As noted underneath the screen captures for the search engines discussed below, each of the captures was done through the "eyes" of the Netscape Prodigy, or America Online Internet browsers.

There are so many search engines. Where should I start?

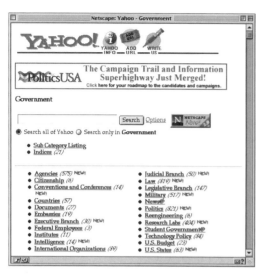

If you're in a hurry to find online information for your assignments, access the Yahoo and Tradewave Galaxy sites first. These search engines are different from the others because they offer an easy-to-browse, "topical" menu. Clicking on each topic brings up an on-screen listing of sites they've come across that are related to the topic. A quick scan of this list will reveal some helpful information right away. The screen capture on the left shows what this looks like via Yahoo. As you can see, these are the main-level topics for Government

As you can imagine, clicking on topics can be much faster than plugging in keywords and waiting for search results to come back. Still, you should read over the reviews that follow to see which of the other engines will be of most use to you. Also, check out Chapter 4 to find out how to maximize your time online to find the information you need!

Where to find it

Classroom Connect Reviews and links to Internet search engines

URL: http://www.classroom.net/classroom/search.htm

Keep up-to-date on the latest search engines!

Finally, keep in mind that new search engines come online virtually every month. What's hot this month may be passé in a few short weeks. So, to stay abreast of the latest search tools, be sure to visit the Internet Homework Helper searching page at *Classroom Connect's* Web site. Reviews and links to the latest searching tools are continually added to keep you up to date!

Alta Vista

URL: http://www.altavista.digital.com

Searching services offered

World Wide Web and Usenet newsgroup
postings.

Amount of indexed Internet documents

50 million Web pages and one million Usenet
newsgroup postings from 13,000 individual
groups updated once every 24 hours.

Pros

Alta Vista's super-huge index is updated every
four days, which means that your search results
will be fresher than any other search engine
currently available. Also, the Alta Vista search
engine is run on an AlphaServer 8400 computer,
one of the fastest machines currently available
from Digital, the company hosting the service.
We tried eight different searches through the
engine over the course of one day, and the
results always came back in less than five
seconds. Wow! Not only is this
engine comprehensive and fast,
it also contains no ads—unlike
many of the other search
engines.

Cons

If you're in a hurry to find good
links to help you with your
homework, then Alta Vista is a
dream come true. However,
there is very little opportunity to
custom-tailor your search.

Where to Go to Find
What You Want

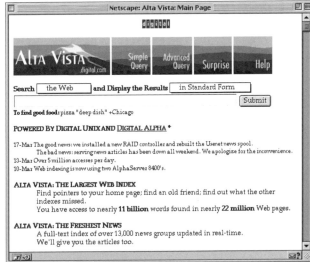

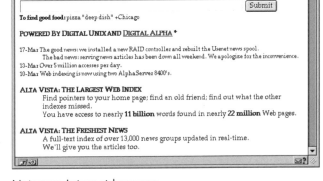

Netscape Internet browser

Search tips

Note that you have two optional drag-down menus at the top of the screen. The first menu allows you to search either Alta Vista's Web or Usenet newsgroup index for the keywords you enter into the search field. The second menu allows you to tell Alta Vista to return the results in Standard, Compact, or Detailed mode.

Search results example

A keyword search for **algebra equations high school homework** returned 20,000 results! That sounds like a lot, but the first five links on the list were incredibly on target.

Archie
URL: http://hoohoo.ncsa.uiuc.edu/archie.html

Searching services offered

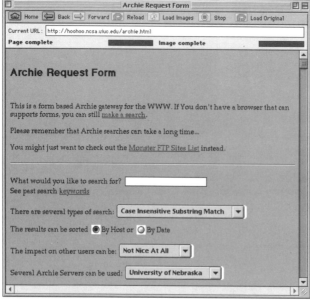

America Online Internet browser

Locate free programs and graphic files stored in ftp sites worldwide. Essentially, ftp sites are publicly accessible, online hard drives whose owners choose to make available to all Internet users. All programs or graphics on these hard drives can be retrieved to *your* hard drive.

Amount of indexed Internet documents

50 million individual computer files stored in six million public ftp sites.

Pros

If you know the filename that you're looking for (or even part of it), then Archie is your knight in shining armor! The Web page interface to Archie makes it simple to select different search options.

Cons

Archie has always been slow, somewhat cumbersome to use, and sometimes less than accurate. Still, it's the only game in town when it comes to looking for programs and graphics on the Internet by filename.

Search tips

Be creative with the keyword you use to search for files. For instance, if you're looking for a graphic of President Bill Clinton, don't type in Bill Clinton as your search words. Archie only understands filenames. So, try **clinton.gif** (gif means it's a graphic) or simply **clinton** instead. Always leave Archie in **Case Insensitive Substring Match**, and set the impact on other users to **Not Nice At All**. If Archie keeps telling you that it's busy, try searching on different Archie Servers. Try one near the bottom of the list— they're not used as much as the others.

Where to Go to Find What You Want

Similar sites

ftpSearch
URL: http://ftpsearch.ntnu.no/ftpsearch

Jumbo
URL: http://www.jumbo.com

Snoopie
URL: http://www.snoopie.com

DejaNews

URL: http://dejanews.com/forms/dnquery.html

Searching services offered
Usenet newsgroup postings.

Amount of indexed Internet documents
DejaNews updates its index to Usenet's 13,000 message bases twice every day, resulting in an index to roughly one million individual messages.

Pros
DejaNews is very fast and extremely comprehensive. Reading Usenet news postings through DejaNews also gives you incredible flexibility, including the ability to click on the name of the person who's posted each message and send a reply directly through your browser! All Internet users can post messages to Usenet groups, which allows students from around the world to contact thousands of experts in their field. If you're doing a long-term search, then use DejaNews to track down experts in the field you're writing about. Send them your questions!

Cons
You have to be very specific with your keywords when using this service or your search results will be useless.

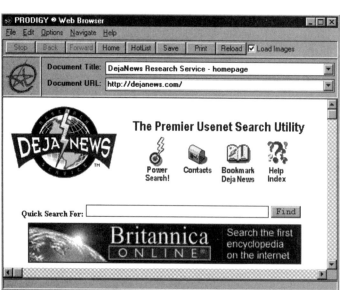

Prodigy Internet browser

Search tips

Like most other search engines on the Net, DejaNews is strictly self-service. All you have to do is access the site, enter some keywords in the search field, click Find, and go to town!

Search results example

A keyword search for **biology red blood cells** uncovered more than a thousand Usenet postings on the topic, many from groups like bionet.biology.cardiovascular, bionet.journals.contents, and misc.health.aids. Very helpful indeed!

Similar sites

Sift

URL: http://sift.stanford.edu

Excite

URL: http://www.excite.com

Searching services offered

World Wide Web pages, 50,000 reviews of Web sites, Usenet newsgroups, and classified advertisements.

Amount of indexed Internet documents

1.5 million Web pages, 50,000 Web site reviews written by 30 professional journalists, one million Usenet articles from 10,000 newsgroups, and a small database of national U.S. classified ads.

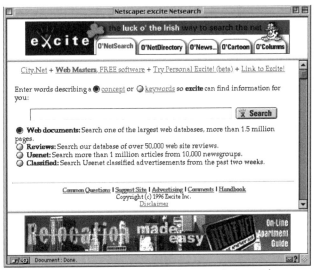

Netscape Internet browser

Pros

Very fast. Returns not only links to the information you're looking for, but also rates each link by a 0–100% score (100% being the best) and gives a small description of where each link goes. Best of all, Excite allows you to do concept searches for online information.

Cons

Excite is riddled with ads—some of them quite large that will slow down your searches.

Search tips

Note that Excite allows you to select either a *concept* or *keyword* search. Be sure to click the Concept button! That will allow you to type in plain-English searches like **President Clinton's policy on Bosnia** and get very focused results in return. Keyword searching works well, but concept searching is much more intelligent and finds better results more quickly.

Search results example

A concept search for **Russian Czars and Peter the Great** returned an incredible 1000 hits. Concept searching truly makes Excite one of the best search engines on the Net.

GNN Select

URL: http://www.gnn.com/gnn/wic/
        wics/index.html

Searching services offered

World Wide Web sites.

Amount of indexed Internet documents

Links to about 10,000 individual Web sites.

Pros

GNN Select isn't a search engine per se, because you can't enter keywords to hunt through a database of links. However, it is a categorized listing of sites by subject area. So if you're looking for information on math, just click on the Education link, then the Math link. A huge list of sites appears, which you can hunt through.

Cons

Not updated enough, and it doesn't link to enough sites. GNN Select really isn't a search engine because you have to hunt and peck your way through its lists of sites to find what you want. If you've got some time to look around for the links you need, go for it. Otherwise, I'd recommend bypassing GNN Select entirely.

Search tips

Your best bet is to click on the All Entries link. Allow the entire list of sites to scroll into your browser, and then click Find to hunt through the list for what you want.

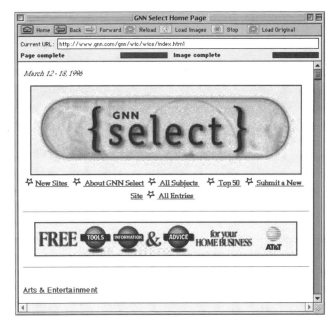

America Online Internet browser

Similar sites

Yahoo, which contains thousands more links than GNN and is fully keyword-searchable, does a much better job in breaking out its indexed sites by category.

With Tradewave Galaxy and GNN Select, it feels like a burden to look through their lists of sites. When you hunt through Yahoo, however, you feel like you're having fun—yet you're still finding the links you need to get your homework done!

InfoSeek
URL: http://www.infoseek.com

Searching services offered
World Wide Web pages, World news headlines, Usenet newsgroups, World Wide Web FAQ files.

Amount of indexed Internet documents
Not revealed.

Pros
InfoSeek offers a completely new approach to finding information, called *search-in-context.* When you do a keyword search, this feature provides you with a list of the direct matches to your search *and* points you to a set of closely related topics. No other search engine offers such a service.

InfoSeek is also quick, while not revealing the size of its searchable database. It returns links that are helpful and fresh. It also has built-in *word stemming,* meaning that when you search for a keyword such as quilt, it automatically

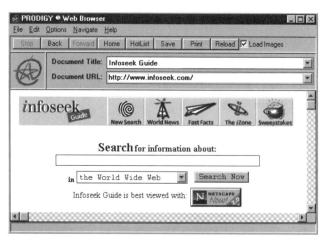

Prodigy Internet browser

also looks for quilting, quilted, etc. This engine also uses the most advanced searching "intelligence" to date, meaning that, as of this writing, it's the best tool for finding the most relevant online information that matches your keywords.

Cons

InfoSeek charges for usage after 100 search results. (But those 100 hits are a great start!) To make full use of InfoSeek, you'll need to use the service through Netscape browser software. It's Search-In-Context feature works much better this way, and makes your search results much easier to scan. Contains advertising.

Search tips

Be sure to capitalize all proper names and locations. Place double quotes (" ") around words that must appear next to each other in your search, as in "Renaissance art." Finally, use brackets to find words that appear within 100 words of each other, such as words you would expect to see in the same sentence or paragraph. For example, to find safety tips for using chemicals, type [chemical safety].

Search results example

A search for **Congress "Legislative Branch" Bills** resulted in 100 of InfoSeek's best results being returned in less than ten seconds. Also included in the results were 20 links to related listings of information (the Search-In-Context feature at work!), including Campaign Trail, Library of Congress, Legislative, and History of the United States. Very nice!

Inktomi
URL: http://inktomi.berkeley.edu

Searching services offered
World Wide Web pages.

Amount of indexed Internet documents
1.2 million Web pages.

Pros
Inktomi is one of our favorite search engines. It's lightning fast, and the results are almost always right on target. There's also no advertising.

Cons
Inktomi doesn't give you an opportunity to customize your search, but this isn't much of a detriment. If you're looking for fresh links to Web information fast, Inktomi should be your first stop.

Search tips

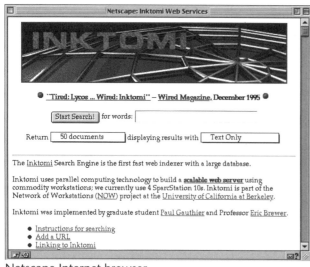

Netscape Internet browser

Inktomi's interface is simple. Just put spaces between the keywords you're searching with (you can enter up to 10), select how many returns you want, and click Start Search. Don't use any numbers or symbols. Words shorter than three letters or very common words—such as **is**, **and**, or **the**—are ignored. The system will also remove common endings, such as **ing** and **ed**, from your words and search for matches that share the same root. For example, "watching" will match words like watch, watched, and so forth. Use **+berkeley** to indicate that the word "berkeley" must be in the document, and use **-berkeley** to indicate that it must not.

Search results example

A search for **Shakespeare plays poems prose** found more than 91,000 documents which matched my query. Whoa! However, the first 20 or so results were more than enough to satisfy the requirements of even an in-depth assignment covering this topic.

Lycos

URL: http://www.lycos.com

Searching services offered

World Wide Web pages, World Wide Web site reviews, Usenet newsgroups, gopher and file transfer (ftp) sites.

Amount of indexed Internet documents

10.75 million links to information on the Web and on gopher and ftp sites.

Pros

Lycos offers quick searching of one of the largest Internet link indexes currently in existence, and is second only to Alta Vista

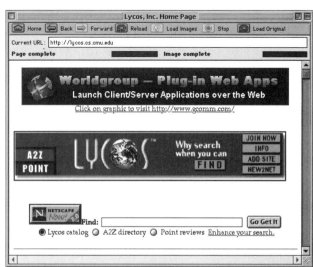

America Online Internet browser

in this regard. The Lycos catalogue is refreshed every three days. Search results include a useful abstract of the information found at each link, and, if available, a short review of the site. One of the best features of Lycos is that it has indexed millions of graphic images and free software available on ftp sites worldwide! (If you're looking for pictures or programs on the Net, try Lycos first, then Archie.)

Cons

Cannot perform a Boolean search. (See Chapter 4 for an in-depth explanation of what this is.) Can't search for combinations of words and phrases, and you can't view your search term in the context in which it was found.

Search tips

Doing a regular keyword search is a breeze. Enter your keywords, click Go Get It, and you're done. If you'd like to customize your search, click on the Customize Your Search link. The next screen that appears will allow you to set different search options (match all terms, match any term, match two terms, etc.), and select how good the match should be to qualify as a valid result (loose, fair, good, close, strong). You can also select the maximum number of returns (10–40) and list the results in standard or detailed form.

Search results example

A search for **weather hurricanes** returned links to 133 sites which were chock full of the information I needed.

Magellan

URL: http://www.mckinley.com

Searching services offered

World Wide Web sites, many with accompanying reviews.

Amount of indexed Internet documents

1.5 million Web sites, more than 50,000 Web site reviews.

Pros

Magellan is an online directory of reviewed and rated Internet sites. Perform a search or explore Magellan topics and you'll instantly go to a list of sites in your area of interest. As the Internet expands, so does Magellan. Its writers review and rate thousands of new sites every month from every geographical corner of the world. Magellan's powerful search engine also categorizes and connects you with an ever-growing number of yet-to-be-reviewed sites (currently a million and a half). Magellan also allows you to search for all sites, or just Green Light sites. Green Light sites have been found to be free of "adult" material.

Cons

With so many excellent searching options, doing a simple search can sometimes be confusing. Magellan also isn't noted for its speed, so expect to

Prodigy Internet browser

wait a little for your search results to return. Contains advertising.

Search tips

After you give Magellan keywords to search for, it will give you a list of search results, or *hits*. Each hit shows the name of the site, its rating, a partial or full description, and a link labeled Review. Click on the name of the site to go to the site. Click on Review to see a complete review and more information, such as producer, audience, contact name and email address, and how the site scored in Magellan's ratings. To pare the hit list down to exactly what you're looking for, enter text in the search box and click on Focus Search.

Search results example

A search for **business macroeconomics auto industry** came up with 850 links, all of which contained site reviews and a synopsis of what information is available. Too cool! The reviews make it easy to find the sites with the best information for your current assignment.

Similar sites

Excite NetDirectory
URL: http://www.excite.com/Subject/

PointCom
URL: http://www.pointcom.com

Starting Point
URL: http://www.stpt.com

NlightN

URL: http://www.nlightn.com

Searching services offered

World Wide Web pages, news wire stories,
reference resources, and hundreds of private and
public databases.

Amount of indexed Internet documents

Not revealed.

Pros

NlightN gives you access to mountains of electronic and printed information—indexing the
World Wide Web, reference works, news wires,
and hundreds of important private databases—
at fast speeds. The databases include Library of
Congress, National Library of Medicine, Mer-
riam-Webster, Film Literature Index, Magazine
Articles Summary, and Reader's Guide to Periodic Literature.

Cons

To make use of most of the search results you
receive from this engine, you'll have to pay.

Although doing a search is free,
much of the results link you to
for-pay services and databases,
for which you must sign up and
pay a fee in order to gain
access. Some results costs as
little as 10 cents each; others are
more expensive.

Netscape Internet browser

Search tips

NlightN allows you to locate data stored in hundreds of places on the Net, all at the same time. With other engines, you're limited to searching one database at a time; with NlightN, you enter the word or phrase you want to learn more about, without having to know where information is located. Thus, your choice of keywords is paramount with this engine. You must be as descriptive as possible to garner the best results.

Search results example

A search for **current events Bosnia** turned up about 500 *authoritative links*—including 173 in the Information Database, 2 articles in the current News Briefing, 179 articles in the Archived News, and 15 Web sites in the WWW Internet Index. Not too shabby!

Okra net.citizen Directory Service

URL: http://okra.ucr.edu/okra/

Searching services offered

Email addresses for Internet users worldwide.

Amount of indexed Internet addresses

More than 3.5 million individual users were listed in the database as of this writing.

Pros

OKRA will help you find email addresses of your friends, organizations, and experts in thousands of fields—no matter where they live on the planet. Just type in part of their name, and Okra does the rest. You can add your friends and family to the database with ease, thereby making it easy to find one another if you lost an address.

Cons

None. Well, okay, maybe the graphic on the home page is a little bit too big for users with slow modems, but otherwise, I couldn't find any drawbacks to this engine.

Search tips

Essentially, there are two functions provided: submitting a query and adding or deleting from the database. Primary differences between this database and most others are that OKRA does not require any registration for using the service, and its data comes from a variety of different sources.

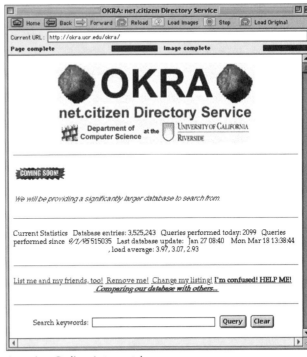

America Online Internet browser

Similar sites

411
URL: http://www.four.com

Switchboard
URL: http://www.switchboard.com

LookUp!
URL: http://www.lookup.com/
 lookup/search.html

Who, Where?
URL: http://www.whowhere.com

Research-It!

URL: http://www.iTools.com/research-it/
research-it.html

Searching services offered

Dictionary (English and computing), thesaurus, acronyms, quotations, French and Japanese translators, French conjugator, anagrams, King James Bible searches, world map searches, CIA world factbook search, U.S. area code and 800 number directory, global currency converter, stock quotes and symbols, zip-code locator, andtracking of UPS and FedEx packages. Wow!

Amount of indexed Internet documents

None.

Pros

Research-It! offersso many helpful resources that it's incredible that they've assembled them all in one place. Each search tool is integrated right onto a single Web page. Just enter your search terms into each field for each tool, click Look it Up!, and the results appear a few seconds later. No ads.

Prodigy Internet browser

Cons

Unless you use Netscape to access this site, it's difficult to use the tools. Netscape makes full use of the site's Web frames to present the tools in easy-to-use formats all on one page.

Search tips

Try them all, they're a blast!

Open Text Index

URL: http://www.opentext.com:8080

Searching services offered

World Wide Web pages.

Amount of indexed Internet documents

Total amount not revealed. However, the Open
Text Index is updated continuously, adding and
updating more than 50,000 Web pages per day.

Pros

A fast search engine to tons of Web pages. Open
Text has been a leader in the full-text indexing
software business for years. The strength of their
search engine software lies in its ability to
search extremely large databases at blazing
speeds. It also understands the structure of
documents. When the World Wide Web came
along, the firm thought it would be cool to see if
their software would run on it. And guess what?
It does!

Cons

Be careful of your keywords
with this engine! Since Open
Text actually indexes every
single word on Web pages, it's
easy to turn up thousands of
hits to information you don't
want. Contains advertising.

Search tips

Always click the All of These
Words button before doing a

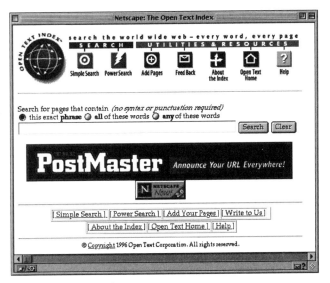

Netscape Internet browser

search. If you started your search too generally by entering, say, **computer**, you can refine it by searching for the word **computer** in the title of Web pages and the word **software** in the subject. Or try searching for **computer and bill gates but not microsoft.** Open Text allows you to search for a single word or a group of words; search for a phrase of any length; search for combinations of words and phrases; link your search terms with Boolean operators (and, or, but, not); search only titles and headings of pages; and search for pages similar to the first.

Search results example

A search for **frog dissection anatomy** turned up 105 excellent results! Each result also contained a Find Similar link that allows you to go to sites with information very similar to that found by your search.

Savvy Search
URL: http://guaraldi.cs.colostate.edu:2000/form

Searching services offered

Links to more than a dozen other Internet search engines, which are searched in real-time directly through this service. How do they do that? SavvySearch sends your keywords to Alta Vista, Excite, Inktomi, Lycos, Open Text, WebCrawler, Yahoo, and more! Amount of indexed Internet documents: Nearly a billion. Since SavvySearch references all of the major search engines, you can add all of their links together and get a number pretty close to one billion.

Similar sites

Internet Sleuth
URL: http://www.isleuth.com

Mother Load
URL: http://www.cosmix.com/motherload

MetaCrawler
URL: http://www.metacrawler.cs.
       washington.edu:8080/hpme.html

Search.com
URL: http://www.search.com

Pros

SavvySearch makes it easy for a student to do a search of multiple search engines to obtain the best possible results in the least amount of time. You see, SavvySearch is a *meta-search tool* designed to simultaneously send your query to multiple Internet search engines and return the complete set of results. SavvySearch offers the advantage of a single location and common user interface for querying many diverse data-bases.

Cons

Your search may take several minutes to process, since Savvy-Search accesses so many search engines using your keywords. It's impossible to custom-tailor your searches, since your key-words are blasted out to each search engine at the same time. Each engine, for the most part, has unique ways of customizing your search if accessed directly.

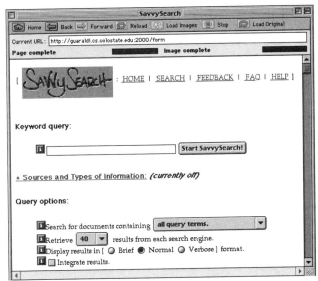

America Online Internet browser

Where to Go to Find
What You Want

Currently, there is no option for case sensitivity or specification of words you do not want in your results.

Search tips

Enter keywords related to your information need in the box labeled Query. This exact query is forwarded to the search engines queried by SavvySearch. Small words—**the**, **it**, **for**—are typically ignored. There is no need to insert **and** and **or** between words, as this is done automatically.

Shareware.com

URL: http://www.shareware.com

Searching services offered

Shareware.com offers searching through its index of nearly 200,000 Shareware software titles.

Prodigy Internet browser

Amount of indexed Internet documents

None.

Pros

If your homework assignment could benefit from using a piece of software (graphics, drawing, software calculator, etc.) then Shareware.com should be your first stop. It makes it easy to track down the software you're looking for and makes Archie look like some kind of old, out-of-date cartoon character! (Um, I think he already is!)

Cons

Shareware isn't free software. Instead, each program's author expects you to pay for the program if you find it useful. However, feel free to use it for a few assignments, and if you want to keep it, then strongly consider paying for it. Includes two advertisements per page.

Search tips

Select the kind of computer you use (Mac or Windows), limit the files returned to 100, enter a search word, and click Start Search. A few seconds later, links to the software you were looking for are displayed. Click on each link to download the program right to your computer.

Search results example

A search for **math** turned up more than 100 Shareware programs for the Macintosh! Many would be of good use to high school students, including a Geometry proof analyzer, graphing software, and copious Calculus programs.

Similar sites

Snoopie
URL: http://www.snoopie.com

Jumbo
URL: http://www.jumbo.com

TradeWave Galaxy

URL: http://galaxy.einet.net

Searching services offered

World Wide Web pages, gopher documents, and telnet resources.

Amount of indexed Internet documents

Links to about 15,000 individual Web sites.

Pros

TradeWave Galaxy is the only engine that lets you search for telnet information. Galaxy employs professional information specialists to organize and oversee the classification process. The Web is much harder to classify than paper publications because people frequently lump unrelated information together or leave out important details like contact information. These professionals help solve such problems. For the most part, Galaxy is a categorized listing of sites broken down by subject area. So if you're looking for information on Biology, just click on the Biology link under Science. A huge list of sites appears, which you can hunt through.

Cons

Although Galaxy allows you to search for telnet information, you'll rarely, if ever, want or need to do this. It's not updated enough, and it doesn't link to enough sites. Galaxy's index includes only

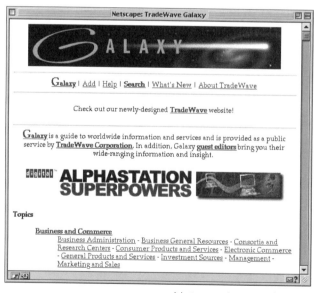

Netscape Internet browser

those pages that are actually submitted to the engine by human beings. Although its hosts periodically re-index sites that Galaxy links you to, it still represents a minuscule portion of the Web.

Search tips

Forget hunting through Galaxy's topical listing of sites, unless you have lots of time to spare! Instead, click on the Search link at the top of the page and enter your keywords. If you want to customize your search, click on the Gopher or Telnet button to search for those resources in addition to Web pages.

Search results example

A search for **Mark Twain literature** netted 20 documents, all of which seemed to be on target as general Twain resources.

Veronica

URL: gopher://futique.scs.unr.edu:70/11/veronica

Searching services offered

Files located in file transfer (ftp) sites worldwide.

Amount of indexed Internet documents

Thousands of gopher documents that are stored on more than 6,000 gopher servers worldwide.

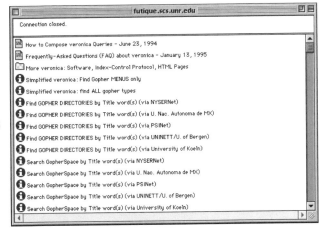

America Online Internet browser

Pros

Veronica is your direct search tool to gopher sites. Until 1992, gopher sites were the most popular sites on the Net. These menu-based wonders were home to all of the Net's largest databases. Then the Web came along, and much of the information in gopherspace was moved onto the Web. Still, there's plenty of good information available on gopher sites around the world—you just have to be patient and let Veronica do the leg work for you.

Cons

Searching through gopher sites with Veronica can sometimes be worse than getting your teeth drilled! There are five main Veronica sites which contain similar indexes to gopher sites. All of these servers are usually busy between noon and 6 P.M., so you'll quickly develop carpal tunnel syndrome hitting the ol' Reload button in your browser to keep sending your keywords to each server. Since much of the information stored on gophers is moving rapidly onto the Web, many of your search results may not function, or may simply point to Web sites instead.

Search tips

Reload button—use it! After you send your initial query to one of the Veronica servers, chances are you'll get a *server busy* error in return. Keep hitting Reload until your knuckles turn blue. The faster and harder you click your mouse, the more likely it is that you'll get through! Be sure to use Boolean searching to better focus your search. (See Chapter 4 for more info.) Also, note that you can either search gopher directory entries or search by title words. Use both methods when doing your searches to guarantee the best results. Remember that many of the other search engines index gopherspace as well. Consider using one or a few of those engines in addition to Veronica to search this diminishing part of the Net.

Search results example

A search for **Gulf and War not Iraq** resulted in a 10-minute wait (and a tired mouse hand clicking the Reload button), but then—paydirt—two screens worth of links to gopher documents. Unfortunately, most returned errors when I clicked on them. (Oops! Looks like both Veronica and Archie should consider retiring from the Internet business!)

WebCrawler

URL: http://www.webcrawler.com

Searching services offered

World Wide Web pages.

Amount of indexed Internet documents

100,000 Web pages.

Pros

Run by the folks at America Online, WebCrawler provides you with a lightning fast search of a representative

America Online Internet browser

sample of the Web. It's database is far from the largest, but WebCrawler's creators didn't want to make it the largest index on the Net; they just wanted to create a lean-and-mean database that found results quickly and easily. If you're really in a hurry, then WebCrawler is guaranteed to satisfy your on-the-run information needs.

Cons

WebCrawler is so fast because its index to the Web is so teeny tiny! Keep this in mind if you need to do any serious searching for information. (In other words, if you're looking for comprehensive links to information, don't use WebCrawler.)

Search tips

Note that you can select whether to find **all** or **any** of your keywords in WebCrawler's index, and set the number of returns—from 10 to 100. Combine these choices with some very specific keywords and you've got yourself a successful, quick search of a small sample of what the Web has to offer.

Search results example

A search for **Holiday Customs December** located 198 documents. Many would certainly be of use to a student doing research into the customs of people around the world during the holiday season.

Yahoo!

URL: http://www.yahoo.com

Searching services offered

World Wide Web pages.

Amount of indexed Internet documents

Not revealed.

Pros

This is the search engine that gets all the press, and with good reason. Think of Yahoo as an enormous listing of good sites broken down by category. (NetHeads call it a searchable, browsable hierarchical index of the Internet.) Unlike the other engines that try to mimic Yahoo (GNN Select and Tradewave Galaxy), this guy actually makes it a quick affair to track down good information formatted in big lists. You can also enter your keywords into the search field to quickly find what you need.

Cons

Yahoo may have lots of links, but there certainly aren't links to a vast majority of the information on the Web. Also, it can take up to six months to get a new link added to Yahoo, so think of this engine as being several months behind the rest of the engines. The results of a search are hard to read, since the category where every result was located is

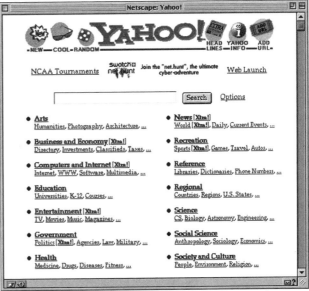

Netscape Internet browser

listed with each hit. This makes it hard to browse the results.

Search tips
Use the search feature. You have no real options, though, besides entering a few keywords and entering Search. In this case keep your keywords to a minimum. Yahoo isn't designed to work on long strings of keywords. Try a general search to see what comes up, and expand it from there until you get what you need.

Search results example
A search for **current events news** found 32 links to online news sites. Not too shabby for less then five seconds of searching time!

Similar sites

iGuide!
URL: http://www.iguide.com

In conclusion . . .

Hopefully, you will find this review of search engines helpful when trying to decide which ones to use for your homework assignments. Now that you know the pros and cons of the major search engines, it's time to get searching.

Now it's time to give some of these directories and search engines a try. Develop a list of keywords for a current homework assignment, and go to town!

Become an
Internet super-searcher

Boolean what? Searching tips from the Net gurus!

Now that you've had a thorough overview
of Internet directories and search engines,
we'll tell you how to refine your searching skills.
This chapter will teach you about:
✹ Narrowing your search results to get
the best information possible
for your specific homework assignment.

Super searching tips

Chances are you've probably done a few searches using the search engines reviewed in the last chapter. How'd you do your first time out? You probably got tons of results, but many were links to stuff you didn't want. You may have searched through the results anyway and found a few tidbits you could use; kind of like finding uncut diamonds among tons of fool's gold! Don't be discouraged. Fact is, this is a normal state of affairs for the beginning Internet explorer.

So how do you find just what you want? Easy!

Just take a few minutes to look over this chapter, learn the tricks of the trade from some of the Internet's searching gurus, and then master a little-known technique called Boolean searching.

Boolean searches and wildcards, oh my!

There's not much to Boolean searching, really. It's simply a matter of using **and, or, not**, two parenthesis ( ), and an **asterisk ***, between and around the keywords in your searches. These words and characters are known as *Boolean operators.*

For instance, placing the word **and** between multiple keywords is a good first step in narrowing your search. It will look for information that contains all of your keywords, even if they're not right next to each other, for example:

industrial and pollution biology and molecular

Search engines vary, but most assume that there's an **and** between your keywords even if you don't type it. Read the instructions for each engine to see how it handles this and other Boolean operators. Still, it couldn't hurt to type it between your keywords just to be sure this basic Boolean search works!

Next, try an **or** between some of your keywords. This will take your Boolean search to the next level, and force the engines to return even more specific hits. Be careful though! Placing an **or** between keywords in a random way may produce unpredictable results.

For instance, here's an example of a good search using **or** between keywords:

Cal or Ripkin and baseball and Orioles

Here's an example of a bad search using **or** between keywords:

soviet or union

The first example will net dozens of links to the information you were looking for; the second will produce thousands of random hits with links to everything from the United Auto Workers Union to Lenin. Now it's time to try the word **not** between some of your keywords. Just like the **or** operator, if **not** is used properly it has the power to turn ordinary keywords into a "Ginsu knife" of a search, as in this example:

england not london

In this case, the engine will search for all links containing the word **england** but not the word **london.** You can see how this would cut down on the number of hits and increase the likelihood that you'd get just the links you'd want to use!

Putting parenthesis or quotes around a set of keywords forces the engine to match the entire word or phrase as it stands (and not each individual word in the phrase):

"carpal tunnel syndrome" treatment

The quotes will force the engine to link the words **carpal tunnel syndrome** together exactly as they are, and return links only to information that is relevant to all three words together, along with the word **treatment.**

Get wild

Now it's time to try a wildcard search. An asterisk (*) at the end of a keyword will match anything. For instance, if you try **quilt*** it will pull up links to information that contain quilt as part of the word, for example: quilt, quilts, quilting, quilted, or quilter. You can also add the asterisk to the end of any of the keywords you're looking for and in any order.

Note that using these operators may produce different responses, depending upon the engine you're using. If you get some wacky results, consult the engine's help screen or FAQ (frequently asked questions) file for more information.

Move to the next level of Internet searching!

In most cases, adding these simple Boolean operators to your search will help you find what you're looking for much more quickly and efficiently.

Still, if you really want to become an expert, here's an example from Alta Vista's search tips page that will take you to the next level.

Let's say you went to the Alta Vista engine:

http://www.altavista.digital.com

and entered these three words as your query:

american indian language

Result *Word count:* indian 395,185, language 2,048,030, american 2,654,433. 100,000 documents. Yikes! Alta Vista found links containing as many of these words as possible, in both upper and lower case. This search is much too broad! It produces pages containing **american** and **American** having nothing to do with American Indians. In addition, it produces pages about **languages** in the African subcontinent.

Become an Internet Super-Searcher 4

Strategy Make clear how you want the query to be handled. In other words, link **american** and **indian** together as a phrase. Also, so that the plural of **language** is found, use an asterisk as a wildcard.

To continue, try the same keywords again with some Boolean operators around some of them:

"american indian" language*

Result *Word count:* american indian 30,000, language* 2,050,463. 20,000 documents found. The documents found are now much more relevant to information about American Indian languages, enabling you to refine your search further. Unfortunately, there is no way to limit subsequent searches to just the results of the previous search. You have to construct progressively narrower keywords. For example, suppose you want to know specifically about the *ojibwa* language.

Strategy Require that the word *ojibwa* and its variants *ojibway* and *ojibwe* be included in the search. Since this is an American Indian word, you could now omit **american indian** from the search.

So, let's try it one more time! Add the * operator to turn the keywords into wildcards, and a +, which forces that word to be present in the search results which are returned. (The + is unique to Alta Vista.)

language* +ojibw*

Result *Word count* ojibw* 3,625; language* 2,050,463. 1,000 documents found.

Observation Bingo. Now you got exactly what you were looking for!

Take this example and try it out with the other search engines. You'll be surprised at how well it works.

Searching Tips

Here are some other important searching tips to help you become a professional Net spelunker. These tips were culled from dozens of Web sites and conversations with more than a dozen Internet searching experts.

* If you're in a hurry, Alta Vista, Savvy Search, and Yahoo should be your first research stops on the Net. They're fast, easy-to-use, and updated frequently.

* Another tip if you're in a hurry—set the search tools to return the smallest number of results, say 10. This can usually be set using pull-down menus of each of the engine's home pages. That way the search takes less time, and you still get a good sampling of the best results.

* Always remember that the Internet is not a be-all, end-all information resource. (*All* of the experts agreed with this tip!) Your school library, an encyclopedia, or even your textbook should also be used as sources of information for your "overnight" homework and long-term assignments.

* The search engines are busiest from about 9 A.M. till 6 P.M. If you can do your research early in the morning or later in the evening, do it! If not, don't be discouraged. You'll just have to wait a little longer for search results to get to you.

* A great way to start any search for information on the Internet is to read a FAQ, or Frequently Asked Questions, file about the topic. Thousands of FAQs are freely available online; they cover just about any topic you can name. Although each references an individual newsgroup, FAQs also contain pointers to other sources of information on that topic, both online and off. You can find hundreds of FAQs at the following site.

    URL: ftp://rtfm.mit.edu/pub/usenet/

* Don't limit your search to just one area of the Internet. While many of the search engines hunt out links to your keywords in Web sites, gopher sites, and Usenet newsgroup postings, many do not. Familiarize yourself with the reviews of search engines in Chapter 3 to see what areas of the Internet

are searchable using each tool. Be sure to use at least three of the engines to do a preliminary search. Time permitting, try others in turn until you've found everything you need in at least three areas of the Net, such as the Web, gopherspace, and Usenet postings.

* Some of the engines allow you to use the word **near** in your searches. Let's say you were doing a short biography on the life and times of Albert Einstein. Searching for Albert Einstein will turn up thousands of links related to his work, his life, his research, and so forth. To find documents specifically related to his life, try searching for **Albert near Einstein.** (**Near** is sometimes called a *proximity operator.*)

Dealing with searching errors

Don't get frustrated when you click on a search result and get some kind of an error. There are many reasons why this may have happened:

• The Internet computer serving the information may be down at the moment.

• Access restrictions may have been introduced at the server since the last time the engine indexed its information.

• The server may be so overloaded that you can't get in for the moment. Try again in a few seconds!

- Your Internet Service Provider or commercial online service may be having problems with their Internet lines. Call Technical Support if the problem persists.

- The information may have been renamed or removed by its owner since the last time the engine indexed its information.

- Capital letters in a search will usually force an exact case match. For instance, submitting a query for **MacinTOSH** will search only for matches of **MacinTOSH**. (Don't be surprised if there aren't any hits using this keyword!)

Sometimes you'll go searching for something on the Net that you know is there, but the engines can't seem to find a link to it. There may be many reasons why this occurred, such as:

- Some servers specifically request that they not be visited by spiders from search engines, and most of the engines will respect that request.

- The page you are looking for is new. Search engines are constantly searching the Net for new pages to add to their indexes, but it is likely that they will not find a new page (or new version of an old page) for at least a few days.

- Sometimes an engine knows of the existence of a Web page because it has found a link to it, but every time it tries to retrieve the page to index it, the connection times out. This means there is heavy congestion at the server or the server is not online at that moment. (Meaning it probably crashed or went down for repairs/updates.)

- The information is behind something called a firewall. Some information is stored on corporate Internet computers that are not publicly accessible, and the engines cannot access them. Likewise, any pages that require additional "work" beyond following a link (such as Web pages that require filling out a form, or registering, or providing a password) cannot be indexed.

Using mailing lists to find information

If you have a few weeks or even just a few days to get an assignment done, try subscribing to some mailing lists or try reading and posting to several Usenet newsgroups to obtain information. (You'll find more information in Appendix A on how to track down these Internet resources.)

Think of these mailing lists as worldwide discussion groups. You can post questions to experts in hundreds of fields and ask for help from people around the world!

Your Internet Service Provider or commercial online service hosts virtually all of the Usenet newsgroups and will let you read and post to them all.

If you're in a hurry, here are some quick ways to find mailing lists

Email to: listserv@cunyvm.cuny.edu

Type **list global /keyword** in the body of your message. Be sure to replace the **keyword** with a subject area like **biology** or **history.** This auto-mated system will return a list of mailing lists that fit the keyword you give it.

- Publicly Accessible Mailing Lists Archive
  URL: http://www.neosoft.com/internet/paml
- Tile.Net Index of discussion groups
  URL: http://www.csn.net/tile/listserv/

Try it out!

Try the Boolean search tips listed in this chapter on your next homework assignment, and see if you don't dig up more concise information about the topics you need. You're on your way to becoming an super-searcher!

Chapter 5

Virtual searching tours

In their own words—how four students search the Net!

Are you still a little shaky when it comes
to searching the Net? Follow along
with the four example homework
assignments in this chapter, and you'll learn:

* How to get sources for an English paper from the Internet.
* That downloading software from the Internet may
  help you complete homework assignments.
* What to do when you get an "error" message
  when trying to access a Web site.

Net Searching on your own . . .

Imagine if you were forced to learn how to drive a car all on your own. Your Dad drives you out to the mall parking lot, hands you the keys, and says, "Here are the keys. Get behind the wheel and start drivin'!" Man, that's pressure! Chances are both your nerves *and* the car (what's left of it) will need some work after you bounce off the light poles and finally realize what each pedal does!

With a little help from your "wired" friends

It's the same with searching the Net. Without some help, you may be a bit clueless about where to start and which online search tools to use to find the information you need. To help you get a better handle on how to best use the Internet to do your homework, follow along with the "wired" students in this chapter as they use the Net to get their assignments done in record time.

At the end of each of the searching tours in this chapter, you'll find a detailed listing of the places they went and the things they did during their search for the information they needed. These searches are pretty basic ones, but they're still killer examples of how Internet search engines can help you get all of your homework done in record time, no matter what the subject area.

Mark Twain Research Paper

Student grade level: High School (10th grade)

Assignment The first project in your American Literature class is writing a five-page research paper about the life and times of Mark Twain. Focus on several of the major events in his life which affected his work, or simply on one of his major works. You must list a minimum of seven sources of information in your bibliography. A maximum of three sources may be from the Internet. Be sure to cite them as discussed in class.

Deadline Three weeks.

Three weeks! Now Ms. Steinburg's done it. My grades in this class are less than stellar, and now she has to throw this paper on us at the last minute! Three weeks to write a five page paper. No way!

Well, my literature textbook has some stuff on Twain, so that's a start. The card catalog in the library had some of his books and two entries in the encyclopedias. Some of the books looked like good references, but when I went looking for them, most had already been checked out by other people in my class! Well, that's four sources. Not enough. I guess it's time to hit the Net and see what I can turn up there.

The Net should be a no-brainer. My dad's been all over me about learning how to use it. We got a new PowerMac with a modem a few weeks ago, and Dad hooked it up to Fast.Net, the local Internet provider in town. He got a copy of Netscape when he signed up and has been hogging the machine just surfing around!

Come out, come out wherever you are!

Well, I think I know what I want to write about. The stuff I got out of the library focused on Twain's life and how it affected his work. I think I'll look online for some background on his life and then search out essays and stuff that focused on how those events affected his writing.

Hmm. 8 P.M. Dad said the Net should be a little less busy now. OK, I click on the little phone icon under the Apple Menu to get online.

I click the big Open button. The modem dials a number, and then it starts screeching! Weird. A few seconds later it says something about hand-shaking, then logging in, and then the hands join together. I'm in! Then I click the Netscape Navigator icon. The welcome screen pops up. Cool! This isn't so bad after all.

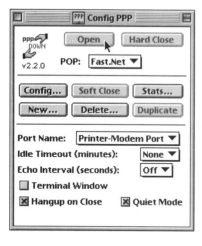

Then a window opens, and nothing happens. It's blank. Where do I start! Well, there's a little button there at the top marked **Net Search.** That should be a good place to start.

One click, and a few seconds later, I'm in!

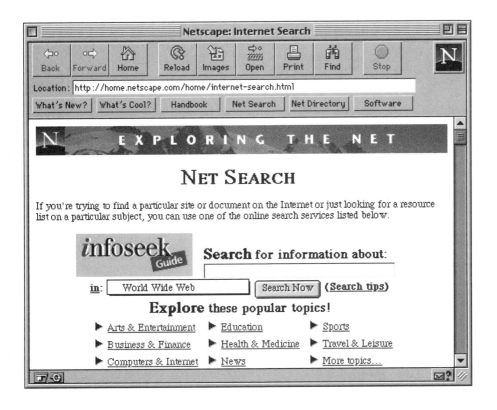

OK, by the address in the Location window it looks like I've jumped to Netscape's Web site at home.netscape.com. It also looks like these guys like the InfoSeek search tool! I click in the box beside the InfoSeek logo, and type **Mark Twain** as my keywords, and hit the big **Search Now** button.

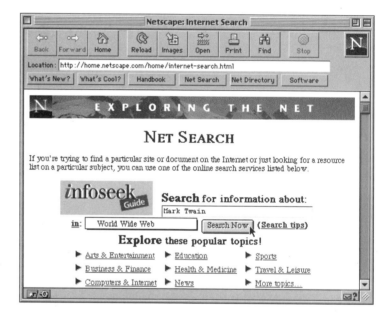

The little comets fly behind the big N there in the top right hand corner, and then, whamo, results!

Wow, that was pretty fast! Let's see what I got. Hmm. . .

The first two results won't help me much! But the third one looks pretty good, and that **Related Topics** link marked **Twain, Mark** on the left-hand side looks interesting. OK, I think I'll start with that third search result that reads **Literary Works—Mark Twain.**

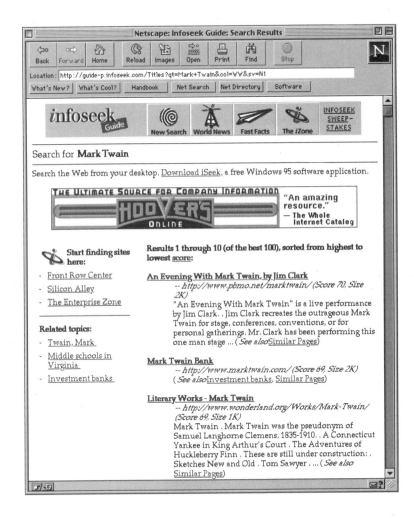

One click of the ol' mouse over those words (hey, my arrow turned to a hand when I did that! Cool!) and . . .

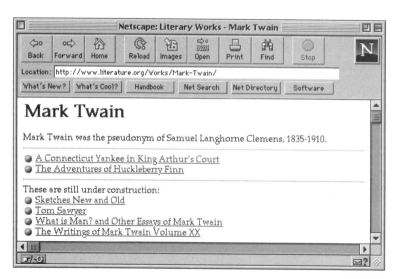

Great! This stuff is on a Web server called www.literature.org. I'm not interested in the online versions of *A Connecticut Yankee in King Arthur's Court* and *The Adventures of Huckleberry Finn*. I've already read *Yankee,* and I managed to check *Huck Finn* out of the library! But the links near the bottom sound like they could get me somewhere. I'll click on **Sketches New and Old**—looks like there could be some personal essays there.

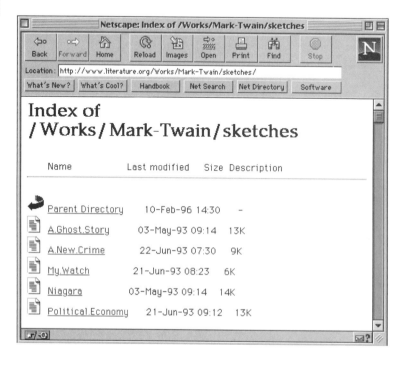

I was right! There are only five here, but they look pretty interesting. Think I'll start with **My Watch.** Click!

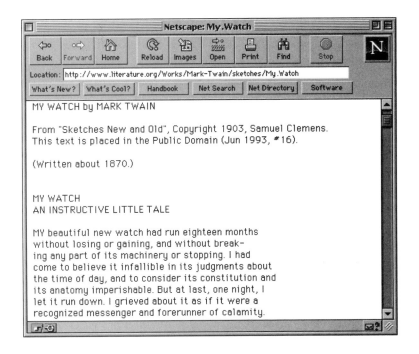

Netscape: My.Watch

Back Forward Home Reload Images Open Print Find Stop

Location: http://www.literature.org/Works/Mark-Twain/sketches/My.Watch

What's New? What's Cool? Handbook Net Search Net Directory Software

MY WATCH by MARK TWAIN

From "Sketches New and Old", Copyright 1903, Samuel Clemens.
This text is placed in the Public Domain (Jun 1993, #16).

(Written about 1870.)

MY WATCH
AN INSTRUCTIVE LITTLE TALE

MY beautiful new watch had run eighteen months
without losing or gaining, and without breaking any part of its machinery or stopping. I had
come to believe it infallible in its judgments about
the time of day, and to consider its constitution and
its anatomy imperishable. But at last, one night, I
let it run down. I grieved about it as if it were a
recognized messenger and forerunner of calamity.

Wow! Here's a story that's part fact and part fiction about Twain's experiences in getting a watch fixed. It's riddled with social commentary and even a personal reflection on what his Uncle had to say about life in general. Great stuff! That's one new source!

Okay, I hit Print and out it comes. Next, I've got to cite it so I can put it in my bibliography. According to how we were taught in class, this citation should satisfy Ms. Steinberg.

> Twain, Mark. My Watch. [Online]
> Available http://www.literature.org/
> Works/Mark-Twain/sketches/My.Watch,
> September 13, 1996.

Virtual Searching Tours

I click the **Back** button once to return to the list of essays, and read through them all. The "New Crime" essay is really killer! It's a long essay about recent crimes in Twain's day, and his thoughts on how the laws of that time were flawed in dealing with the criminals.

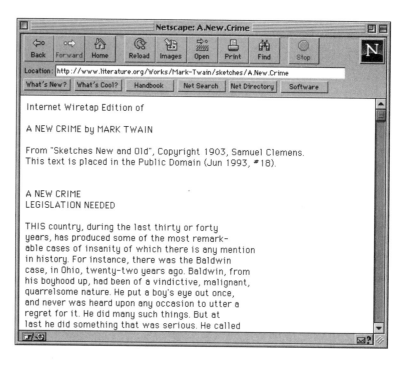

His last line says it all, and makes for great fodder for my paper: "Really, what we want now, is not laws against crime, but a law against INSANITY. There is where the true evil lies." Great stuff!

Twain, Mark. A New Crime. [Online] Available http://www.literature.org/ Works/Mark-Twain/sketches/ A.New.Crime, September 13, 1996.

Only one source left. Not too bad! Less than 20
minutes of searching and I'm almost home free.
OK, I hit the **Back** button three times until I get
to the InfoSeek search-results screen again. Hey,
my keywords **Mark Twain** are still in the window at the top!

On the left hand side, there's that **Related Topics**
link again marked **Twain, Mark.** Sounds great.
One click on those words, and. . .

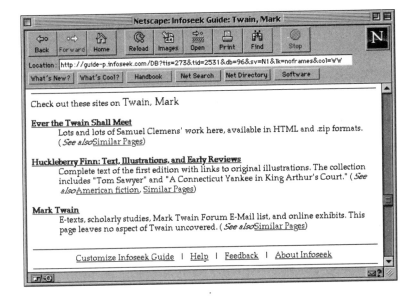

Three new links here. And again, it looks like
the third one may "net" the best results—**Mark
Twain.** A click of the mouse, and. . .

Wow! It's hard to know where to start on a page that's so packed with stuff! All of the links look great.

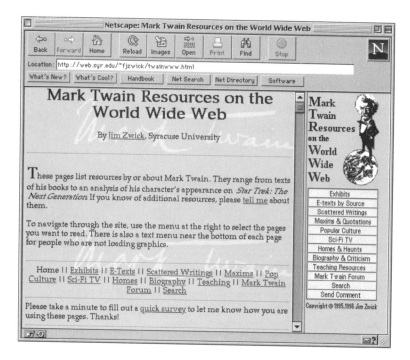

The **Scattered Writings** link has twice as many essays as the last site I was looking through!

And the **Culture** link, well, you'll have to check it out for yourself! All done. The Internet was a huge help!

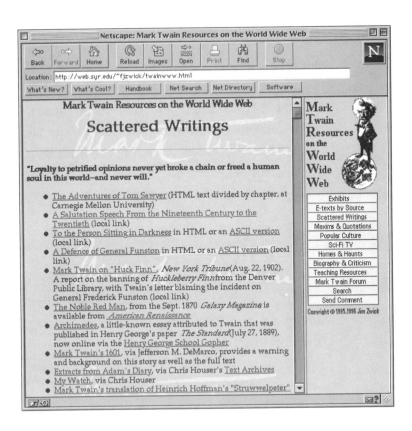

Netscape: Mark Twain Resources on the World Wide Web

Location: http://web.syr.edu/~fjzwick/twainwww.html

Mark Twain Resources on the World Wide Web

Scattered Writings

"Loyalty to petrified opinions never yet broke a chain or freed a human soul in this world—and never will."

- The Adventures of Tom Sawyer (HTML text divided by chapter, at Carnegie Mellon University)
- A Salutation Speech From the Nineteenth Century to the Twentieth (local link)
- To the Person Sitting in Darkness in HTML or an ASCII version (local link)
- A Defence of General Funston in HTML or an ASCII version (local link)
- Mark Twain on "Huck Finn", New York Tribune (Aug. 22, 1902). A report on the banning of Huckleberry Finn from the Denver Public Library, with Twain's letter blaming the incident on General Frederick Funston (local link)
- The Noble Red Man, from the Sept. 1870 Galaxy Magazine is available from American Renaissance
- Archimedes, a little-known essay attributed to Twain that was published in Henry George's paper The Standard (July 27, 1889), now online via the Henry George School Gopher
- Mark Twain's 1601, via Jefferson M. DeMarco, provides a warning and background on this story as well as the full text
- Extracts from Adam's Diary, via Chris Houser's Text Archives
- My Watch, via Chris Houser
- Mark Twain's translation of Heinrich Hoffman's "Struwwelpeter"

Mark Twain Resources on the World Wide Web

| Exhibits |
| Exhibits |
| E-texts by Source |
| Scattered Writings |
| Maxims & Quotations |
| Popular Culture |
| Sci-Fi TV |
| Homes & Haunts |
| Biography & Criticism |
| Teaching Resources |
| Mark Twain Forum |
| Search |
| Send Comment |

Copyright © 1995,1996 Jim Zwick

Mark Twain Searching Tour

Netscape Net Search
URL: http://home.netscape.com/home/internet-search.html

Literary Works—Mark Twain
URL: http://www.literature.org/Works/Mark-Twain/

Mark Twain Sketches
URL: http://www.literature.org/Works/Mark-Twain/sketches/

Mark Twain Resources on the World Wide Web
URL: http://web.syr.edu/~fjzwick/twainwww.html

Math homework

Student grade level: High School (12th grade)

Assignment Worksheet 15. Differential equations. Solve these equations by hand or with a TI 85 calculator. Note that the final three questions are extra credit. They involve creating a differential equation given a solution.

Deadline Next school day.

Math and I don't get along—period—and this differential equation stuff has me bogged down! This worksheet is just too much. Two sides no less; 15 problems. Overnight. Mrs. Kuharr truly has no mercy!

This year, my school switched over to intensive scheduling and cross-curriculum teaching. It's been pretty hairy making the switch, but it has brought some pluses: calculators in math classes, for instance.

Calculators in the classroom!

Our math text is full of hints and tips for using Texas Instruments graphing calculators to help solve problems, and Mrs. Kuharr lets us use them quite a bit in class. My parents gave me a TI 85 for my birthday. They even threw in a cable and the "Link" software so I could hook it up to our Pentium PC, though I haven't tried doing that quite yet. I haven't had a reason to, really. Well, perhaps it's time to use it now. These equations take hours to work through by hand. My buddy Mark says there's tons of TI 85 software on the Net I can retrieve and transfer to my calculator using the Link.

I just got the new version of the America Online software along with a magazine I bought yesterday, so I'll upgrade my home PC to the new version and get on the Net that way. Mom and Dad use AOL to email my sister who's a senior at Rutgers University in New Jersey. Installation was pretty simple. The America Online software even detected that I had an old version of its software on the hard drive and copied all of our information over to the new version. Nice touch! One click of the **Sign On** button, a few squeals from the modem, and I hear the familiar "Welcome" come out of the speaker. I hit **control-K**, type **Web** as my keyword, and AOL's Internet browser screen pops up.

I remember reading that America Online hosts the WebCrawler search engine. Maybe that's a good place to start. I click in the little box at the top of the browser (just below the **Back** and **Forward** buttons) and type in its URL,

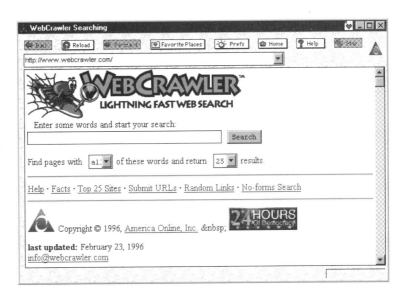

http://www.webcrawler.com. I press enter, and it brings up WebCrawler about 20 seconds later. (Man, using the direct Internet access at school is much faster!)

OK, no time to mess around! I'll try going right for what I want. I type **TI 85** in the search box and click the **Search** button.

Pretty raw results! Just links to sites, but the first two look great! I click on **TI-GRAPH LINK** at the top of the list.

It's Texas Instrument's Web site for the TI Link software. No actual programs here though. So, one click on the **Back** button and I'm back to my search results.

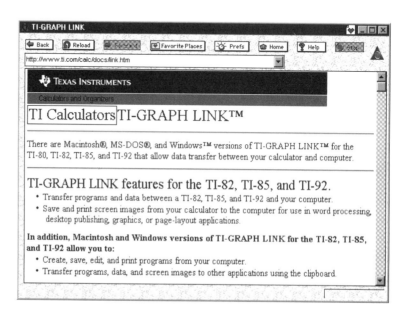

A little further down on the list is **TI-85 Programming Information.** I click on that to continue.

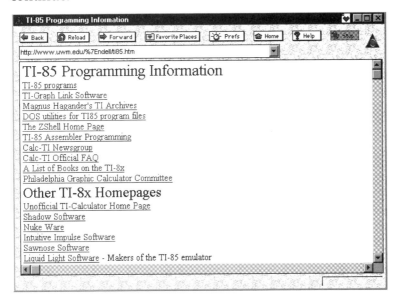

Awesome! Looks like some of these links could be of use. I've heard a lot about what's available on the **Unofficial TI-Calculator Home Page—** like links to the programs I need to get this assignment done! One click on those words, and, well, this is a first.

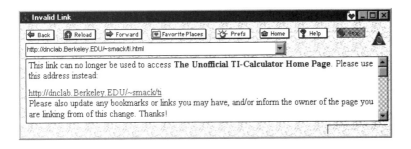

Looks like they've moved the site. I click on the link to go to the new location.

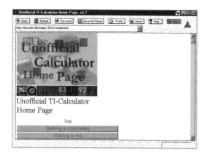

Phew! Here we go. A quick scroll downwards reveals a link to the programs I need! **Getting TI resources on the Net.** Click!

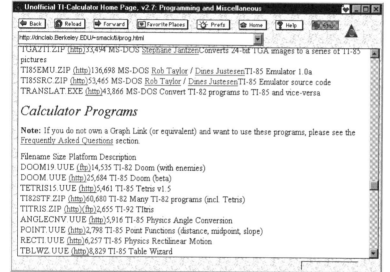

There are two programs for the calculator that deal with differential equations. A quick download to my PC, some fumbling around with the Link, and they're up and running on my TI 85. Two hours later, I'm done with the assignment *and* I think I'm getting a better handle on this stuff. Really!

Math Homework Searching Tour

WebCrawler
URL: http://www.webcrawler.com

TI GRAPH LINK
URL: http://www.ti.com/calc/docs/link.htm

TI Programming Information
URL: http://www.uwm.edu/%7Endell/ti85.htm

Unofficial TI-Calculator Home Page
URL: http://dnclab.Berkeley.EDU/~smack/ti/

Getting TI Resources on the Net
URL: http://dnclab.Berkeley.EDU/~smack/ti/getnet.html#net

Debate research

Student grade level: High School (11th grade)

Assignment Debate 3. This time
around, we'll divide the class in half and debate
the Death Penalty issue over a two-day period.
In reality, a worldwide debate over the pros and
cons of this ultimate punishment has been
raging for decades. You're a member of the
Debate Group #2. As such, you are to conduct
independent research on the drawbacks or
"cons" of the Death Penalty.

Next Monday you and your anti-death penalty
team will have the entire class period to compare the information you've collected to begin
preparing for the debate. Copies of your independent research must be turned in at that time.
You may use the Internet as a source of your
information. It's a hotbed for political advocates
on both sides of this issue.

Deadline Next Monday.

The death penalty. Mr. Bennett sure likes to
choose the hot topics for my debate class. Worst
of all, I'm not sure how I stand on the death
penalty issue. Mr. Bennett has taught us that the
best debaters are those who are highly knowledgeable and personally committed to the views
of one side of an issue. I hardly know anything
about this topic, let alone which side to take!

Well, here's a start. Included with the assignment are five pages of background material on the pros and cons of the penalty. This is good material, but all of us get to see it, which means both teams know the basics of each others' argument, so we've got to go beyond it. I've got to get more information on my own.

The library media center is home-base for the Internet in my school. If what Mr. Bennett says is true, I should have no trouble tracking down some good stuff for my side. I have a study period next, so I think I'll spend it surfing the Net for as much as I can find about the anti–death penalty view.

Hmm. Interesting. Looks like Ms. Soja, the library media specialist, has made the Savvy Search site the default home page for all ten of

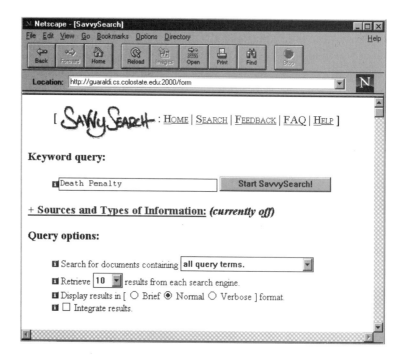

the Pentium PCs here in the library. No one's
around and all the screens show this page. Good
choice! A lot of my buddies have started and
finished their online research in less than an
hour thanks to the Savvy Search engine! OK,
death penalty it is. I type that into the search
field, click the **Start** button, and, well, wait. The
hourglass sits there, and the comets fly behind
the N in Netscape . . .

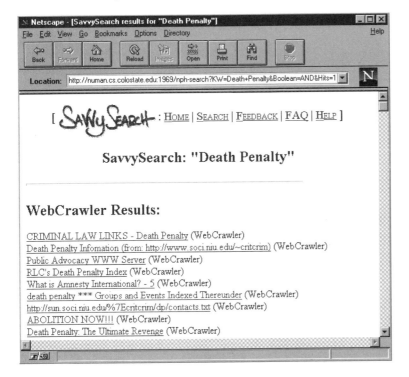

There we go! It took more than a minute to
return these results. Oh yeah, I remember why
now! Savvy Search sends my keywords to about
ten different search sites and then displays all
the returns to me all at once—too cool! But it
does take some time. (Still, it's less time than
visiting each search site and running the search
one at a time.)

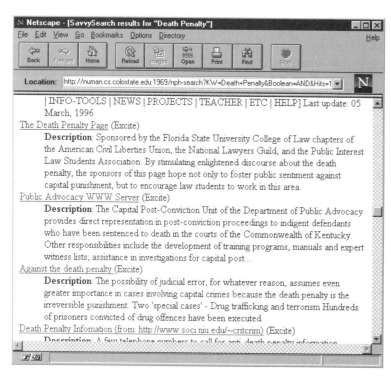

There's certainly a ton of good stuff here! I scroll down a little bit, and then these links appear.

The Death Penalty Page. Designed to foster public discussion about the issue. Man, that's just what I need! There's got to be some arguments from those against the penalty. I click on those words to link to the information.

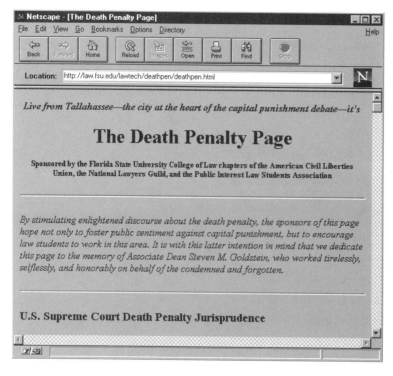

Lots of stuff on the issue—pro *and* con! I print it all out to the printer in the corner. Wow! Not only does it have a point-by-point list of the positives and negatives, but also links to other similar sites. Now I can clearly see how the other team will argue their case (if they get research as good as this), and how we can rebut all of their arguments.

This is way too much good stuff for less than five minutes searching the Net! The final straw will be statistics on the issue from a Web site in England. (I can tell that by the .uk on the end of the address when I put my cursor over The Facts & Figures on the Death Penalty link.) Talk about getting a global perspective! The death penalty has been banned over much of Europe, and the description of the site says it contains background information on why it's been abolished there. I click on the link, and. . .

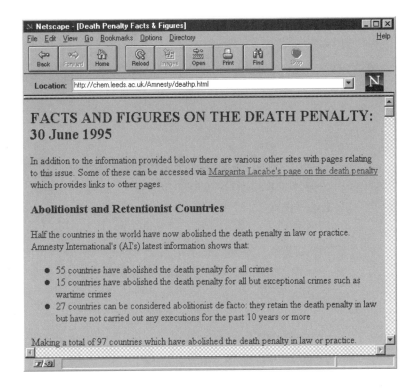

Sure enough! Here's it is. Statistics and background information. Print, print, print! I know the other team won't be able to find as up-to-date information as all this, and dig up stuff about how other countries (and continents!) deal with the issue.

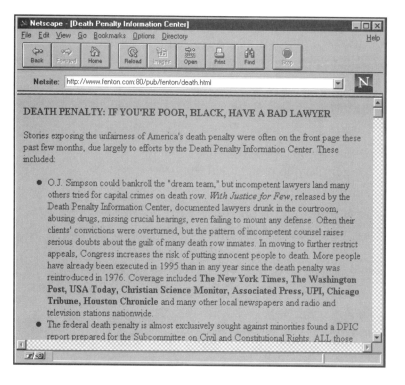

Then again, I hope they won't come down here and get the same stuff I did! So, I need a little bit more then. I click the Back button a few times until I return to the original search results. A little further down is a link to strictly anti–death penalty info via the Death Penalty Information Center link.

Great! I print it. Very cool! Well, maybe one more link. I click the **Back** button and end up back in the search results again. I follow one final link to **ABOLITION NOW: Abolish the Death Penalty.** Wow! This is all I need to do some serious damage to the other team. Cool!

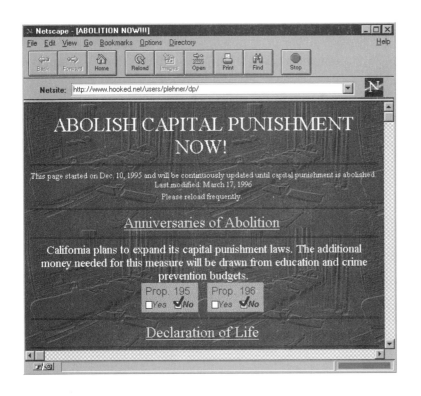

Debate Searching Tour

Savvy Search
URL: http://guaraldi.cs.colostate.edu:2000/form

The Death Penalty Page
URL: http://law.fsu.edu/lawtech/deathpen/deathpen.html

Facts & Figures on the Death Penalty
URL: http://chem.leeds.ac.uk/Amnesty/deathp.html

Death Penalty Information Center
URL: http://www.fenton.com:80/pub/fenton/death.html

Abolition Now
URL: http://www.hooked.net/users/plehner/dp/

Social Studies homework

Student grade level: Junior High School (9th grade)

Assignment National Statistics. Fill in the blanks on this double-sided worksheet with the necessary statistics (population, total land area, natural resources, state of the government) for each country.

Your textbook and the library are good places to start to track down this information. Other sources of the information will be accepted, but all must be cited. Bonus points will be awarded to the student(s) who find the most up-to-date information in the class.

Deadline Next school day.

Find country statistics to put in these 25 blanks. No problem!

I've seen tons of this stuff on the Internet. I did a three-page report on the Bosnian War last quarter, and I found all the fresh statistics I needed in the CIA World Factbook—available only on the Net!

If I remember right, I found the Factbook using the Inktomi search engine. I didn't write down the exact address for the Factbook, so I guess I'll have to search for it again.

I fire up the ol' Mac Performa in the living room, dial into the Net (with my new 28.8 modem!), and load up Netscape. Under Book-marks, there's trusty Inktomi, which links me right to http://inktomi.berkeley.edu in less than a second! Not bad for eight o'clock on a week-night.

I quickly type the keywords **CIA World Factbook** into the search window, click **Search**, and. . .

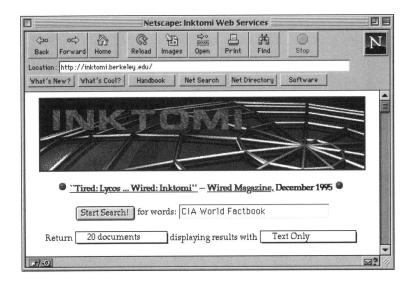

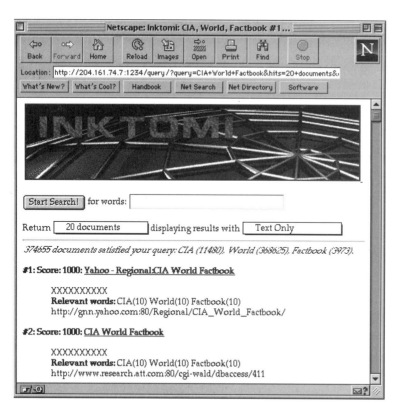

Looks good so far! The first search result, **Yahoo—Regional: CIA World Factbook**, should bring me right to it. Click!

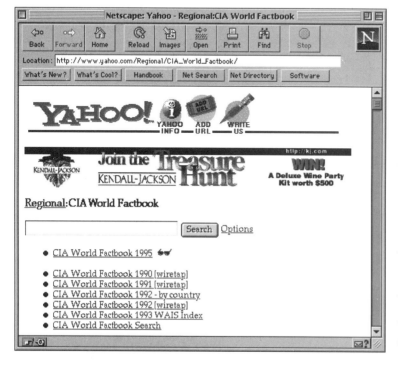

Wow! The 1995 version is online now. The last time I used it, only the 1994 version was online. Bonus points, here I come! Just one click on **CIA World Factbook 1995**, and. . . nothing. Just a spinning cursor and a "Contacting host, waiting for reply . . . " message at the bottom of the screen. Ho hum. Then all of a sudden . . .

What's this? Oh well, I'll try again. And again. And again. By now, nearly five minutes have gone by. Guess they're having problems there at the main

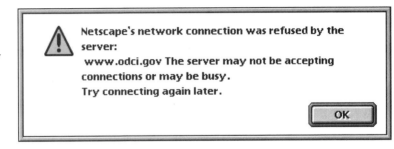

Netscape's network connection was refused by the server:
 www.odci.gov The server may not be accepting connections or may be busy.
Try connecting again later.

OK

CIA Web server tonight. But there's got to be a way to get to that new information!

I press the **Back** button to see what else Inktomi comes up with, and all of the results link right to the main CIA server—the one that's out of service right now! OK, keep calm. How about another search engine. Maybe it'll have a different link to the '95 Factbook.

Alta Vista sounds good. That's up under the **Bookmarks** menu, too. This time I'll force it just to look for the 1995 version of the Factbook. I type it in, click **Submit**, and wait a few seconds.

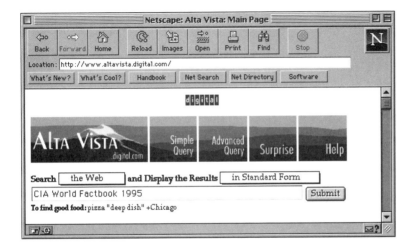

The results appear! Uh-oh, lots of links to the server that's down again. But a little further down, right in the middle of the screen, something looks interesting.

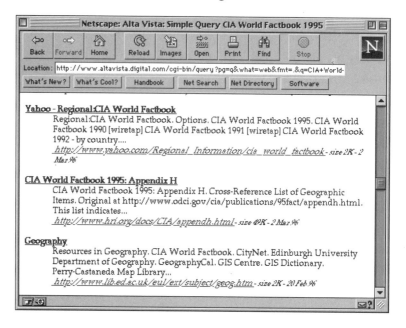

See that link right in the middle of the page? **CIA World Factbook 1995: Appendix H**. Notice that at the bottom of the paragraph it shows exactly where the link goes to—a Web server called www.hri.org.

Cool! That's not the CIA's Web server that I tried to connect to before. These guys must be hosting the Factbook on their server for some reason!

It's also just a link to the Appendix, but that's OK. It's at least a foot in the door. I can fix that in a second. So, I click on the link to follow it.

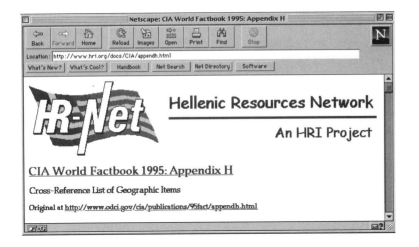

Looks great, but I want the main index to the book. No problem! Take a look up in the **Location:** field at the top of the browser screen. The location it's currently referencing is http://www.hri.org/docs/CIA/appendh.html—this Appendix. But I want to back up to the table of contents.

So, I simply click up in the **Location:** field at the end of the address, and hit **Delete** until the address reads just http://www.hri.org/docs/CIA/—that should back me up and give me the table of contents.

I hit return, and. . .

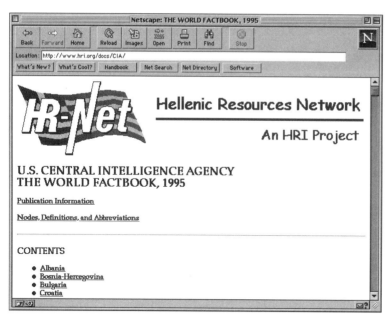

Here we go! Note the main **CIA** subdirectory in the **Location:** field that we just backed up to. It brought up the main table of contents to the site, which is also known as the home page. Now it's time to get some work done!

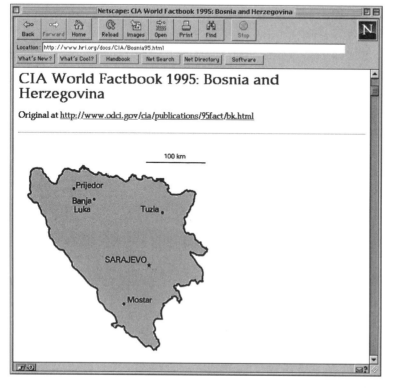

The first set of questions relate to Bosnia, so I scroll down and click on the word **Bosnia**.

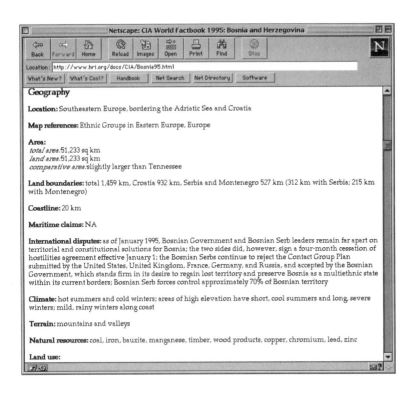

Netscape: CIA World Factbook 1995: Bosnia and Herzegovina

Back Forward Home   Reload Images Open   Print Find   Stop   N

Location: http://www.hri.org/docs/CIA/Bosnia95.html

What's New? What's Cool? Handbook   Net Search Net Directory Software

Geography

Location: Southeastern Europe, bordering the Adriatic Sea and Croatia

Map references: Ethnic Groups in Eastern Europe, Europe

Area:
total area: 51,233 sq km
land area: 51,233 sq km
comparative area: slightly larger than Tennessee

Land boundaries: total 1,459 km, Croatia 932 km, Serbia and Montenegro 527 km (312 km with Serbia; 215 km with Montenegro)

Coastline: 20 km

Maritime claims: NA

International disputes: as of January 1995, Bosnian Government and Bosnian Serb leaders remain far apart on territorial and constitutional solutions for Bosnia; the two sides did, however, sign a four-month cessation of hostilities agreement effective January 1; the Bosnian Serbs continue to reject the Contact Group Plan submitted by the United States, United Kingdom, France, Germany, and Russia, and accepted by the Bosnian Government, which stands firm in its desire to regain lost territory and preserve Bosnia as a multiethnic state within its current borders; Bosnian Serb forces control approximately 70% of Bosnian territory

Climate: hot summers and cold winters; areas of high elevation have short, cool summers and long, severe winters; mild, rainy winters along coast

Terrain: mountains and valleys

Natural resources: coal, iron, bauxite, manganese, timber, wood products, copper, chromium, lead, zinc

Land use:

All of the entries start with a map, and then below it the statistics are listed.

These are the freshest statistics I've seen. Even a detailed account of the current state of the conflict. Great stuff!

More than a third of my assignment is done in no time. I click **Back** to return to the table of contents, and then keep clicking on the name of each country I need to find statistics for. In less than 15 minutes I'm all done, and I'm pretty sure I'll have the freshest statistics in the class. Cool!

Social Studies searching tour

Inktomi
URL:http://inktomi.berkeley.edu

CIA World Factbook
URL: http://www.hri.org/docs/CIA

Keeping Track

As you search the Net, make notes of your experiences. Keep track of strange glitches you run into and how you solve them. Also keep track of any short-cuts or helpful hints you discover. Then share your experiences with your friends. They'll be glad you did!

Chapter 6

What to do with what you find online

Not all Internet information is equal: Judging the good from the bad!

By now you have a good idea of the extent
of information available on the Internet.
Now it's time to separate the worthwhile information
from the worthless. This chapter will help you:

✹ Think critically about what you find on the Internet.

✹ Use steps to evaluate online information.

✹ Understand shareware, freely distributed
software found on the Internet.

The bountiful Internet

Internet experts estimate that 500 million computer screens worth of information are transmitted across the Internet each week. That means that millions of photographs, computer graphics, sounds, video clips, multimedia files, and pages of text are transmitted over the Net every seven days. Wow!

Thanks to the Internet, you now have more information available to you than at perhaps any other period in the history of the world. Once you've been on the Net for a few weeks, you'll find yourself retrieving tons of resources to your computer—from incredible photographs to include in your social studies report to the latest Internet programs to help you surf the Net faster and more efficiently. The Net is truly a dream come true for news junkies, writers, researchers, and, of course, *students* the world over.

However, this freely accessible repository of information does pose some challenges to student researchers.

Information Highway potholes

Here's the main problem: On the Internet, anyone can publish anything to a worldwide audience in seconds. This "information" could read like an entry from your textbook but, in reality, could contain inaccurate, unsubstantiated, or misleading information.

No "information police" exist on the Internet. In most cases, there are no professional editors and proofreaders as in the real world who question, sometimes rewrite, and always check the validity of information in a writer's work. In the real world, a book, newsletter, magazine, or article is published only after a thorough editing process.

So, as you read and retrieve information from the Net do to your homework, how do you know that what you're looking at is "good" information you can trust? Truth is, it's sometimes difficult to be sure.

Question your sources

Just as you should be wary of information in printed, real world material, be careful of what you accept as fact on the Internet. Even popular news magazines like *Time, Newsweek,* and *U.S. News & World Report* sometimes contain biased and sometimes blatantly inaccurate information.

It's the nature of the beast. No human being can write from a completely unbiased point of view. Our beliefs, emotions, and unique backgrounds all influence us when we write something. Often without knowing it, we choose words and facts which are organized in such a way as to bias it to fit our view of the world. You're more likely to find biases on the Internet than in a magazine or newspaper because no editorial staff checks the content of Web sites.

In addition to concerns about the quality of the information you retrieve from the Internet, there are a few other issues you need to be aware of:

- The *proper attribution of information.* How do you cite the information you find on the Internet in your research?
- Intellectual property issues—better known as *cut, paste, plagiarize.* How do you properly integrate information you find on the Internet into your work without plagiarizing?
- Software piracy, or *don't copy that floppy.* How can you be sure you're not breaking copyright laws when using software downloaded from the Net in your assignments.

This chapter will help you understand and deal with these potholes on the Information Highway. In the end, you'll discover that a sharp eye and a few extra steps are all that are required to get past these problems!

Think critically about information

How information literate are you? Can you think critically about the information you include in your research?

We live in a high-tech, fast-paced, information-intensive society. We often form opinions based on mere glimpses of facts related to important issues. The mainstream media bombards us with fast-paced news capsules that may, over time, paint a picture that's sometimes different from the true situation.

In the end, though, we should be highly critical of the information we take in every day. We shouldn't just rely on sketchy television sound bites to be our sole source of information about the world. Unfortunately, this is about all the information many of us can process due to our busy schedules.

In the end, all of us tend to view information from TV, newspapers, magazines, and online sources less critically than we should.

The Internet has the power to open in-depth, meaningful learning opportunities to people worldwide. But, sadly, the Internet may increase the likelihood that people will be satisfied with a general, surface knowledge of our world and the people in it.

Jamie McKenzie, author of *Grazing the Net: Raising a Generation of Free Range Students,* thinks that "the rich information resources to be found in cyberspace (the Internet) are both a blessing and a curse. Unless students have a toolkit of thinking and problem-solving skills which match the feasts of information so readily available, they may emerge from their meals bloated with techno-garbage, information junk food or info-fat. We must teach students to graze and digest the offerings thoughtfully in order to achieve insight. We must guide our students to become info-tectives."

How to separate the good information from the bad

The Internet provides an incredible opportunity for free expression, but it also gives unscrupulous and irresponsible people a large stage to speak from. False, incomplete, or inaccurate medical, legal, and scientific information can be found on a variety of Web pages on the Net, not to mention in Usenet newsgroups.

To make things even more complicated, a lot of people use the Internet to post their political views or satirize those in power. At first glance, some sites could easily be mistaken for "official" Web sites, because they often mimic the page layout and even Net address of the original.

People often create parody pages of famous people, like politicians and celebrities. Someone has posted a fake *Bob Dole for President* page, and it looks virtually identical to the real site, right down to it's address. Note the differences in the last three letters of these Web addresses, though.

URL: http://www.dole96.*org*
URL: http://www.dole96.*com*

Which is the "real" site?

Sometimes these online parodies are very funny. The problem is that some are so similar to the "real" site that it is hard to know what's true. That could create problems if you begin assuming that the president plans to paint the White

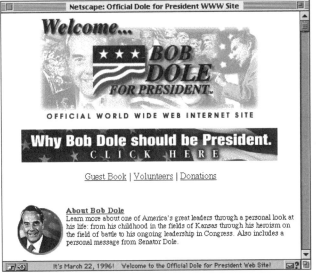

This is the fake Bob Dole '96 Web site:

URL: http://www.dole96.com

The two look strikingly similar, but this first site is a spoof. Note that there's no warning label telling us that this page is a fake! Many "spoof" Web sites prefer not to mark themselves as such. This creates a dilemma for everyone using the Internet to search for quality information.

This is the real Bob Dole '96 Web site:

URL: http://www.dole96.org

House green or that Bob Dole favors legalizing drugs—just because you found a parody Web site! The key is to be a little cynical about everything you read online, perhaps more than you are when you receive information from other media sources like TV, radio, or newspapers. Be sure to gather material from a variety of sources. If you have doubts about information from the Net, ask someone you know who's an expert in that area for feedback—your teacher or parents, for instance.

Remember—and this is very important—not everything you read on the Net is true! To become a knowledgeable, well-rounded person, it's important to be curious, ask questions, doubt information, and to look at information in different ways.

Checklist for evaluating online information

Here are some questions you should ask yourself to help you evaluate the online information you uncover on the Internet.

What is the source of the information?

Chances are, an Internet site created and maintained by a recognized institution is more reliable than one created by a private citizen or a special interest group. This also holds true for the information each site provides. It's perhaps more likely that a university, hospital, or museum will be unbiased, while a private citizen or special interest group may tend to lean one way or another on sensitive issues.

How can you tell whether you're reading information that's posted by an organization or an individual user? In most cases, a legitimate information provider will have a straight-forward online address, such as:

http://www.information.com

On the other hand, an individual user may have an online address reading something like this:

http://www.abc.org/~smith/position.html

The ~**smith** part of the address gives it away. Chances are an individual named Smith has put personal Web pages in this directory, and made their contents available to the world.

Why is this information online?

Authors of online information have a reason for putting it there. Is the purpose to inform and educate Internet users about a particular topic, or is there some kind of hidden agenda involved? Again, keep in mind that there are many special interest groups who use the Internet as a soap box for their opinions.

Who wrote the information, and what is the writer's point of view?

This is perhaps the most important question you need to answer about the information you find online. Material that's written by an expert who's well-known in his or her field is likely to be okay. If you've never heard of the author or the information wasn't well-written, chances are you should do more research into his or her background before accepting the information as factual. Go to a search engine and type in the person's name. What comes up? Do they seem to be highly knowledgeable about the topic? What else have they published? Check the library to see if this person has published anything in the real world. Have they been known to write "questionable" things in the past on this same topic?

Do the links to other sites reveal any biases of the author?

Following the links web-site authors place on their pages is one of the best ways to discover more about the author, and may reveal the author's biases (or lack of biases). For instance, pretend you were reading an online essay about racism in America. The point of view of the author may seem to be that of an unbiased researcher. However, clicking on a link marked Related Organizations brings up a list that features White Power and Skinheads Online. This may reveal that the author wrote the piece from a racist point of view. Use this example to more closely scrutinize the links an online author may include in his or her information.

How recent is the information?

New information is not necessarily any more accurate than old information, but this is still an important question to answer. If you're doing a report on the current state of the former Soviet Union, steer clear of any information that was put online before 1993. As a general rule of thumb, look very carefully at the information you retrieve from the Internet, note the date it was put online, and then ask yourself if it's really relevant to your assignment.

How often is the site or information updated?

This is a question you can usually answer by reading over the home page or main menu of the site you're using as a source of information. Messages like "Last updated September 1, 1996" are prevalent on home pages across the Web. The creators of these sites know that the more up-to-date their information is, the more likely that users will return week in and week out. If the site you're using as a source has no such message, keep looking to see if anything else on the site has a date affixed to it. If you can't find any, the site may not have been updated for quite a while.

How does this site compare with others that deal with the same subject matter?

You're sure to find several sources of online information which seem to be reliable and pass the scrutiny of the questions already posed above. As a final check, search the Internet to see if other authors refer to the sources. If several do, chances are it's probably good information. Also, search for related documents to see how the authors' perspectives compare to one another. Don't forget traditional resources such as textbooks, journals, and other print resources.

Might a commercial online service be a better source for this information?

Not just anyone can provide content on the main areas of America Online and Prodigy. For instance, AOL forms agreements with select "content providers" who can provide quality information to the service. Subscribers to America Online and Prodigy can be reasonably sure they'll find something to help them with their homework. Which online option service would you prefer—the Internet, which may offer one online magazine comprised of one or two screens of text with some graphics thrown in, or would you choose a commercial online service that offers hundreds of periodicals in dozens of fields that can be searched for the information you need? Because of its sheer size, complexity, openness, and global scale, the Net is an entirely different animal from a commercial service. There's not much we can do to reduce the amount of clutter on the Net, but Internauts can take measures to ensure that the information they obtain from the Net is valid and useable in their homework. Answering the questions in this chapter is a good start!

Once you've answered all of these questions, you'll have a good idea about whether or not the information you find is reliable and should be cited as a source in your homework.

Cut, paste, plagiarize?

The Internet makes it easier than ever to retrieve information, but it's also easy just to copy other peoples' work found on the Net and put it into your papers. Copying other peoples' work word-for-word and not citing where it came from is called plagiarism.

It's very easy, and sometimes tempting, just to copy information from a Web site into your word processing document.

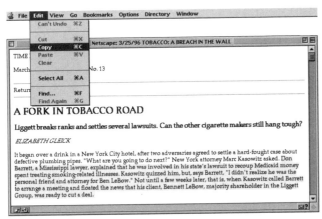

Copying information from a Web site right into your paper is plagiarism! It's tempting to hold down your mouse button and swipe across a block of text in, say, an online *Time* magazine article, click Copy, then. . .

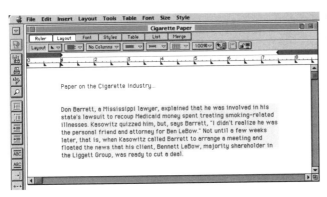

go to your word processing document and hit Paste. Though it's easy to do, using someone else's work in this manner and calling it your own is unethical. If you do wish to use portions of someone else's work you need to put quotes around it, properly attribute it in your paper, and then list the source of the information in your bibliography.

Make it easy for your teacher to check your online citations!

In the old days, teachers who suspected something was amiss in your paper could easily check the sources you used since they could assume that most of your research came from the school library or a local library. Because of the Internet, this isn't the case anymore. Worst of all, even though you may have properly cited your online material, the information may have moved or been taken off the Net before your teacher had a chance to check the sources.

While this problem will never go away, it's important to properly cite your online material so your teachers have a quick way to check your sources. If you don't make it easy for them to check, chances are they won't allow you to use the online sources to support your research and may ask you to rewrite the paper.

What's the solution to this problem? Printed copies of all of the online material you cite in your bibliography! Your teacher may need these printouts as proof that the original material existed. (See Chapter 7 for information on properly citing online resources.)

Don't copy that floppy!

One of the reasons the Internet is so popular is that you can locate and download "shareware"—freely distributed software that you can try before deciding to pay for it. Many shareware titles are excellent homework helpers! Yet this privilege is abused by many people who download shareware programs and use them frequently without ever registering or paying for them.

As a rule, think of all computer media this way: Treat each program or document as a single copy of a book which only one person can read at a time. Similarly, only one computer can access the software or document at once.

All computer programs on the Internet fall into one of five categories, each with different rules of use and distribution: commercial, shareware, postcardware, freeware, and public domain. It's important that you understand the differences. You should "do the right thing" by paying for this software if you find it useful and decide to keep using it. And keep in mind that downloading or copying software from unknown or questionable online sources can put your computer at risk for viruses or other problems.

Commercial programs

Commercial software has the most restrictions and cannot legally be copied or redistributed without the author's or publisher's permission. If you make illegal copies of commercial software you can face lawsuits, fines, or worse. Making a backup copy in case the original is lost or damaged is permitted. Before making copies of software or installing it on multiple computers, check the software license agreements that come with them. Some are more restrictive than others.

Shareware

Authors of shareware programs don't charge initially for the software. They generally ask for a donation or registration fee if you like the program and plan to use it. If you pay the fee, you may receive printed documentation or a notice of updates. If you don't pay, you can still use the software, but most programs will continue to display a welcome screen noting that the software is copyrighted by the author and can be freely redistributed but not sold.

Postcardware

Some of the software on the Internet is postcardware. The programmers don't ask for money but, instead, want you to send them a postcard as "payment" for the program so they can track who is using their software and where. In most cases, the authors retain full copyright and allow anyone to make copies. They do ask that it not be sold without their consent.

Freeware

Freeware is software that can be freely used and distributed. The author retains the copyright, but encourages you to freely copy and distribute the program at no cost.

Public Domain

Many software authors—including universities and government agencies—dedicate some of their work to the public domain, which is free to use by anyone. These programs are not subject to any copyright restrictions and can be copied and redistributed freely.

Where to find it

Microsoft Software Piracy Information
URL: http://www.microsoft.com/Piracy/

U.S. Copyright Office
URL: gopher://marvel.loc.gov:70/11/copyright

Copyright FAQ
URL: http://www.cis.ohio-state.edu/hypertext/faq/usenet/Copyright-FAQ/top.html

Brad Templeton's 10 Big Myths About Copyright Explained
URL: http://www.clarinet.com:80/brad/copymyths.html

Intellectual Property Rights
URL: http://www.isa.net/project-open/proprights.html

Microsoft, one of the world's largest software publishers, offers lots of information about software copyrights and piracy. Several Web sites also offer more information about copyright issues and the continuing problem of software piracy.

A rule of thumb for The Net

Remember, when using the Internet, a good rule of thumb is to not believe everything you read. Not everyone who posts information on the Net is out to confuse you with wrong information, but you should be aware that some information can be misleading. Use your head and think like a critic!

Chapter 7

How to cite online resources in your bibliography

Give credit where credit is due

In the previous chapter, we talked a little
about the idea of avoiding plagiarism
by citing all the sources you use in a homework
assignment. In this chapter you'll learn:
* How to cite online resources, such as email,
gopher, ftp, telnet, Web sites, Usenet
newsgroups, and Internet Relay Chat.

How to cite online resources in your bibliography!

Just as you need to cite all the books and periodicals you use to support your research, you need to cite online sources of information as well. Below is the latest "preferred" way to cite online information in your bibliographies. Follow each style as listed so that your teachers can return to the sites you've used and check the information.

Also, be sure to keep printed copies of all of the online material you cite in your bibliography. Sometimes your teacher will not be able to link to the sites where you obtained the information, and will need your printed proof of the original information to declare your citations valid.

Electronic Mail (Email)

Structure
Author of email message. Subject line of the message. [Online] Available email: student@address.edu from author@address.edu, date of message.

Examples
Reynolds, Robert. Nile Research Project results. [Online] Available email: student1@smallvillehigh.edu from ert@informns.k12.mn.us, February 3, 1996.

Lowmiller, Russell. Hubble Space Telescope image enhancement techniques. [Online] Available email: student2@exeter.high.edu from btaylor@hst.nasa.gov, January 23, 1995.

Gopher

Structure

Author. Title of gopher item. [Online] Available gopher://address/filename, date of document or download.

Examples

U.S. Department of Agriculture. Agriculture Statistics for 4th Quarter 1995. [Online] Available gopher://agri.usda.gov/Department of Agriculture/Latest Statistics for 1995/4th Quarter Folder, January 28, 1996.

Chalmers, Andrea. Bosnia: A Country in Transition. [Online] Available gopher://nywer.net/Today's News/World News/Bosnia-Herzegovina, February 5, 1996.

File Transfer Protocol (FTP)

Structure

Author. Title of item. [Online] Available ftp://address/filename, date of document or download.

Examples

Herman, Wayne. Networking in the Information Age. [Online] Available ftp://194.335.23.10/pub/research/internet/network.txt, May 5, 1996.

Barrell, Tarquin. Shakespeare and his Muse. [Online] Available ftp://ftp.guten.net/gproject/texts/english/bard/research/muse.txt, March 25, 1996.

Telnet

Structure

Author. Title of item. [Online] Available telnet: address, path, date of document or download.

Examples

Brady, Robert. Map of Iraqi Troop Movements for 1/9/96. [Online] Available telnet: fedworld.gov, Government Information/ CIA/Maps/Latest Maps/Iraq, January 10, 1996.

Sanford, Fred. Statistical Weather Data for Wisconsin, January 1996. [Online] Available telnet: weather.machine.umich.edu, Weather Data/January 1996/States/Zooms/Data/ Wisconsin, February 25, 1996.

World Wide Web

Structure

Author. Title of item. [Online] Available http://address/filename, date of document or download.

Examples

Weiser, Dan. Guidelines for better writing. [Online] Available http://www.usa.net/~weiser/ home/better-writing.html, January 9, 1996.

Wickenheiser, Ed. The Cold War Revisited: A Splintered Germany. [Online] Available http://usa.coldwar.server.gov/index/cold.war/ countries/former.soviet.block/Germany/ germany.html, March 5, 1996.

Usenet Newsgroups

Structure

Author. Title of item. [Online] Available usenet: group, date of post.

Examples

Soja, Julie. Educational Insights 1995. [Online] Available usenet: k12.ed.research, December 27, 1995.

Kinyon, Melissa. How to Build a Better Mouse-trap. [Online] Available usenet: sci.tech. inventions.mousetrap, January 16, 1996.

Internet Relay Chat (IRC)

Structure

Name of online speaker. [Online] Available IRC: telnet (site address), IRC channel name, date of session.

Examples

McBane, Lisa. [Online] Available IRC: telnet world.sensemedia.net:6677, #egypt, March 8, 1996.

Frappe, François. [Online] Available IRC: telnet france.irc.edu:1234, #france, January 23, 1996.

Web sites offering more information about citing electronic sources.

MLA Citation Guide
URL: http://www.cas.usf.edu/english/walker/mla.html

Citing Computer Documents
URL: http://neal.ctstateu.edu/history/cite.html

Williams College Library Web
URL: http://www.williams.edu:803/
    library/library.www/cite.html

The Internet is a great research tool for all your homework assignments. Just remember to cite any sources you find online.

Chapter 8

Turn online information into a multimedia presentation

Collect online images and sounds for killer class projects

Many students are learning how to create multimedia presentations instead of traditional research papers. Although this may sound scary and difficult, it's not as bad as it seems. In this chapter, you'll learn how to:

* Collect and save all the cool stuff you find on the Net—like sound, pictures, and video.
* Cite the multimedia files you save from the Net.
* Create different types of multimedia presentations.

Using the Net to make your assignments really cool!

By now you've searched the Net high and low for information you could use in your home-work assignments. Along the way, it was impossible not to notice all of the colorful images, sounds, and even video clips that are available on Net sites around the world.

All these multimedia items are simply computer files stored on the Net. You can easily capture these files to your computer, which gives you the potential to turn your everyday assignments into interactive, colorful presentations or projects! Many teachers now allow their students to create multimedia presentations instead of writing traditional research papers, so this information may save you a lot of work *and* a lot of time; time that might be better spent researching the Net for more sources and more multimedia files for your presentations.

What kinds of multimedia presentations are we talking about?

The sky is the limit. Whatever you see on the Internet can potentially be retrieved to your computer for use in your presentation—including images, sounds, and video clips. So, when you look through NASA's Galileo Probe Web site and view online images of the probe and ani-mated video clips of its mission, don't think of these files as simply part of the Web! In this chapter, you'll learn how to copy these files to your computer, and which programs can help you take these files and turn them into killer multimedia classroom presentations in no time.

Currently, only Netscape allows you to capture multimedia files using the methods outlined here. If you're accessing the Internet via America Online or Prodigy, you can't capture anything directly through their browsers. (However, remember that AOL users will soon be able to use the Netscape browser. Contact AOL directly for more information about this.)

Before you begin to retrieve multimedia files to your computer, it's best to create a new directory (or folder) on your computer called *multimed* or something. Store all of the items you capture in this location for easy reference later on.

How to collect images

You can save almost any image you find online in a few easy steps. First, access the Web page that contains the images you want to retrieve. Second, place your mouse arrow anywhere on top of the image you want.

If you're a Macintosh user, click and hold down your mouse button. If you're a Windows user, click and hold down your right mouse button.

A small menu will appear, as in the example on the next page. (This menu is identical on Mac and Windows computers.)

Turn Online Information into a Multimedia Presentation

```
Netscape - [http://images.jsc.nasa.gov/images/pao/AS13/1007...]
File  Edit  View  Go  Bookmarks  Options  Directory                    Help

 Back  Forward  Home      Reload  Images  Open  Print  Find      Stop

Location:  http://images.jsc.nasa.gov/images/pao/AS13/10075537.jpg        N
```

Back
Forward

Open this Link (none)
Add Bookmark for this Link
New Window with this Link
Save this Link as...
Copy this Link Location

View this Image (10075537.jpg)
Save this Image as...
Copy this Image Location
Load this Image

Next, scroll down to the **Save this Image as . . .** item, and let up on your mouse button. You'll then be able to save the image to your hard drive. The image you save looks exactly the same as the one you see on the screen.

Here's how to capture images if you surf the Web via a commercial online service. Both Macintosh and Windows users can obtain inexpensive (or even free) programs which can take snap shots of your entire screen, or just a small part of it.

Window users need look no further than Paint Shop Pro, a shareware program available on the Internet. It allows you to capture both the entire screen or just a portion of it (that is, the graphics you want on a Web page), all by clicking and dragging your mouse across what you want.

URL: ftp://ftp.classroom.net/wentworth/
    Clip-Art/.utilities/IBM-PC/PSP30.ZIP

Mac users have three choices. First, if you page through your user's manual you'll find that all Macs have a built-in screen capture utility. Hitting **Apple-shift-3** takes a snapshot of everything on your screen and saves it as a PICT graphic file, Picture *X*, on your hard drive. If you'd prefer to capture just a small portion of your screen, such as a single window of any size or just a small graphic in your Web browser window, download a copy of PIXs from the Net.

URL: ftp://ftp.classroom.net/wentworth/
    Internet-Software/Mac/PIXs.sit

How to retrieve sounds

This is easy. Access the Web page that contains the sound(s) you need. Place your mouse arrow on top of the link to the sound file. If you're a Macintosh user, click and hold down your mouse button. If you're a Windows user, click and hold down your right mouse button.

A small menu will appear, as in this example. (This menu is identical on both Mac and Windows computers.)

Drag down to the **Save this Link as . . .** item, and let up on your mouse button. The sound will then be downloaded from the Web site right onto your hard drive!

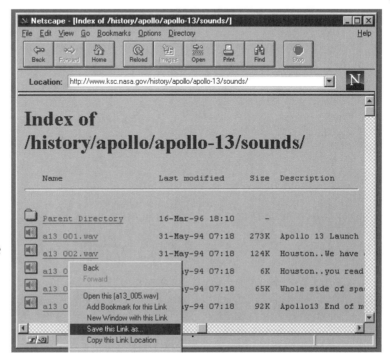

How to capture video clips

This is simple, too. Just access the Web page that contains the video clip(s) you want. Place your mouse arrow on top of the link to the video clip. If you're a Macintosh user, click and hold down your mouse button. If you're a Windows user, click and hold down your right mouse button.

A small menu will appear, as in this example. (This menu is identical on both Mac and Windows computers.)

Draw down to the **Save this Link as** . . . item, and let up on your mouse button. You'll then be able to save the video clip file to your hard drive. The clip will then be downloaded from the Web site right onto your hard drive!

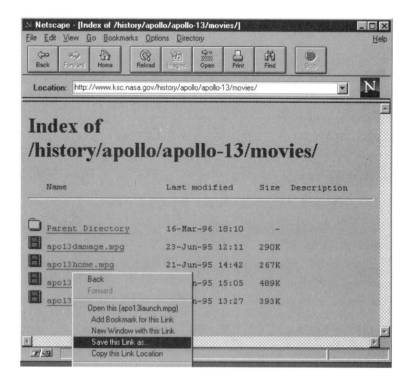

Citing the multimedia files you retrieve from the Net

Properly citing the multimedia files you retrieve from the Net for use in your presentations is extremely important. Think of the files just as you would normal print documents you reference in your research. A person or an organization created these multimedia files. As such, they need to be cited in bibliographic form. When you give your multimedia presentation, your teacher may very well ask you for this bibliography. Citing the files is pretty straightforward. Here are three examples to get you started.

Online images

Structure
Description or title of image. [Online Image] Available http://address/filename, date of document or download.

Example
Hubble Space Telescope just before release in the Space Shuttle's Payload Bay. [Online Image] Available ftp://explorer.arc.nasa.gov/pub/SPACE/GIF/s31-04-015.gif, October 1, 1996.

Online sounds

Structure
Description or title of sound. [Online Sound] Available http://address/filename, date of document or download.

Example

Reflections on Apollo. [Online Sound] Available ftp://town.hall.org/radio/IMS/NASA/100394_nas a_01_ITR.au, September 25, 1996.

Online video clips

Structure

Description or title of video clip. [Online Video Clip] Available http://address/filename, date of document or download.

Example

Shoemaker-Levy Comet enters Jupiter's atmosphere and breaks up. [Online Video Clip] Available ftp://ftp.cribx1.u-bordeaux.fr/astro/ anim/sl9/ breakingup.mpg, March 5, 1996.

Software to bring it all together!

After a few hours of hunting around, you'll be amazed at the number of multimedia files you've retrieved for use in your presentation. Now that you have your raw materials on your hard drive, it's time to put them all together!

There are dozens of software packages that allow you to take the elements you've downloaded from the Net and assemble them into a classroom presentation. Let's take a look at the best of these software packages and briefly describe the types of files they can be used with.

If you need to purchase one of these packages, just visit your local computer store or call

MicroWarehouse at (800) 367-7080 for Windows software or MacWarehouse at (800) 622-6222 for Macintosh stuff. They always seem to have the best deals on software! You can also visit them on the Web for the latest on prices and availability at:

URL: http://www.warehouse.com

Also, the CD-ROM included with this book has demos of several of these programs, and lots of ready-to-use multimedia files.

Your word processor

No matter which word processor you have on your computer (WordPerfect, Microsoft Word, ClarisWorks, etc.), chances are it has the ability to bring in images, sounds, and maybe even video clips. You can then place these multimedia files inside of the assignment you're typing up, and then turn it in on diskette to your teacher.

If you have a word processor that's called *SomethingWorks* (as in ClarisWorks or WordPerfectWorks) you're definitely in luck! These "Works" programs have a word processor, drawing, painting, and even a spread sheet and modem program all built into one. That means they can definitely allow you to import multimedia files and use them to create a presentation. Most "Works" programs also have a built-in slide show feature, which allows you to create screen after screen of information and then play them back one at a time.

Turn Online Information into a Multimedia Presentation

Keep in mind that if you plan on bringing your presentation to school to show to the whole class, be sure that your teacher has the same word processor available. If they don't, you could be out of luck! All word processors are different, so consult your user's manual for more information on using multimedia files inside of your documents and whether what you create can be loaded onto your teacher's computer if he or she has a different word processor.

Microsoft PowerPoint (Mac & Windows)

As a student, you don't have the time to spend hours learning how to put a multimedia presentation together. So, consider using PowerPoint as your tool for this task. It's easy to use and very powerful. You can import any images, sounds, and video clips you retrieve from the Net into it, and create a colorful slide presentation in seconds. Many businesses use PowerPoint to create presentations for their new product lines or sales demos; even the O.J. Simpson

This is the kind of presentation you can create with Microsoft PowerPoint.

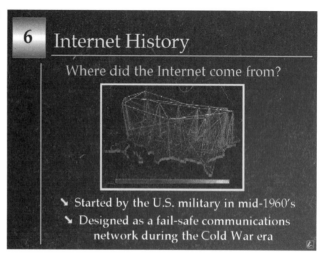

prosecution team used PowerPoint during their closing remarks to be sure that everyone could follow along with their arguments.

Another plus of PowerPoint is that it's completely cross-compatible, meaning that you can create a presentation on your Windows machine and play it back in your teacher's Macintosh, and vice versa.

If you're a Mac user, you'll probably have to purchase a copy, but it isn't cheap at $275. If you're a Windows user, your computer may have come preloaded with the Microsoft Office Suite which includes PowerPoint.

To find out more about PowerPoint (and download a free PowerPoint player and some demo presentations), check out Microsoft's Web site.

URL: http://www.microsoft.com

Astound (Mac and Windows)

One of the most powerful multimedia authoring programs available, Astound allows you to create multimedia slide shows that contain not only files downloaded from the Net, but also flying text, floating images, and sound effects. Astound is not for the technically faint of heart, though. Still, it may be worth learning because it can help you create killer presentations.

One of the biggest downsides of Astound is its lack of cross-compatibility: If you make a presentation on your Mac, you will not be able to

This is the kind of presentation you can create with Astound.

play it back on your teacher's Windows machine, and vice versa. (Bummer!) A true cross-platform version is due in January, 1997.

To find out more about Astound (which costs about $165), visit Gold Disk's Web site.

URL: http://www.golddisk.com

Monstrous Media Kit (Mac and Windows)

OK, this program was created for kids, but don't let that stop you from trying it out! No one but you needs to know that you used it to create your presentation, since you can easily make your slides look hip and trendy.

This software is definitely the easiest to use of the bunch. Load the software and create a new presentation. A blank screen pops up. You want to place a sound? No problem! Click on the large **Sound** button, and it asks you where the sound is on your hard drive. Click the file, and it appears as a button on the card. If you want to place the sound, you just click the button. Same goes for video clips.

BONUS! ────►

Not only is it easy to use, it comes with tons of clip art and sounds. Best of all, it's included on the CD-ROM found in the back of this book! To find out more about the Monstrous Media Kit, visit CyberPuppy's Web site, or send email to info@cyberpuppy.com.

URL: http://www.cyberpuppy.com/mmkinfo.html

HyperStudio (Mac and Windows)

HyperStudio was also designed for use by young students, but it's a little more powerful than the Monstrous Media Kit. It's easy to create slides, link them together, and place text, sounds, and video clips on them.

HyperStudio comes with a CD-ROM holding more than 250 MB of images, sounds, and video clips. Use them in conjunction with the items you download from the Net to produce a killer presentation quickly. The new version (which costs about $125) even allows you to hyperlink from a button or word in your project directly to Internet information. Wow!

To find out more about HyperStudio, visit Roger Wagner Publishing's Web site. A trial version of the software is included on the CD in the back of this book.

URL: http://www.hyperstudio.com

BONUS!

Turn Online Information into a Multimedia Presentation

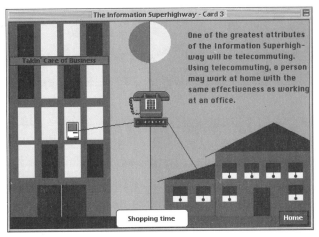

The Information Superhighway - Card 3

Takin' Care of Business

One of the greatest attributes of the Information Superhigh-way will be telecommuting. Using telecommuting, a person may work at home with the same effectiveness as working at an office.

Shopping time

Home

This is the kind of presentation you can create with Hyperstudio.

HyperCard (Mac)

Finally, there's HyperCard. If your school has Macs, chances are you learned how to use this program in one of your classes. Basically, Hyper-Card was the first program that allowed you to create presentations on slides that, when saved, are called stacks. You could then show these slides to the class, or give them to your teacher on diskette for the class to explore.

This program comes free with every Macintosh, so if you're a Mac user, dig it out of the Apple Extras folder on your hard drive and get started! For more information about HyperCard, visit Apple's Web site.

URL: http://www.apple.com

This is the kind of presentation you can create with Hypercard.

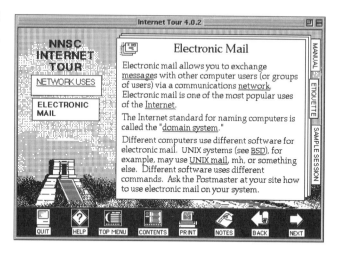

The Digital Chisel (Mac)

A relative newcomer to the multimedia software market, Digital Chisel is making waves in schools around the United States. It's one of the most powerful and easy-to-use educational multimedia authoring software packages available.

Digital Chisel allows you create your own full-color graphics with the built-in paint and draw tools, record and playback your own sounds, "shoot" and record your own color animation, and make power-buttons that can control your project. You can also create speaking text, hyperlinks to online information, and more.

For more information, contact Pierian Spring Software via the Web.

URL: http://www.pierian.com

Go for it!

Now that you know a bit about your options, try your luck at creating a multimedia presentation instead of a typical black and white term paper. You may surprise yourself and your teachers!

Make Web pages @ home or school

Publish your work to the global Internet audience!

Have you ever been surfing the Web, and thought,
"Hey, I know tons about that topic! I wish
there was a way I could add my two cents to the Web."
You're in luck! This chapter will teach you:

★ How to become a Web publisher.

★ The "language" of the Web.

Join the revolution!

It's clear that the World Wide Web offers rich educational resources. From online frog dissection to touring historical sites online, the Web is your interactive link to an entirely new way of learning and experiencing the world. Best of all, you (yes you!) can become a part of this revolution by publishing your school work to Internet users around the globe via the Web.

So, you want to become a Web publisher? No problem! You just need to learn the basics of making a Web page. (It's so simple and fun you'll be amazed!).By weaving your own informative and innovative Web pages, you'll move beyond passive learning and become a global publisher!

What kind of information could you offer the Net community? You name it. Post your research papers for experts to read and critique, poems for all to enjoy, school news, descriptions of your community, and links to favorite Web sites. You may also want to post an electronic portfolio of your school work so that college admittance staffers and employers can take a look.

You should also consider making Web pages out of your research papers or homework. If your teacher has the ability to load up Web pages at school or home, you're in business. Think of it— no more text-only reports! By reformatting your text into a Web page, you can add sounds, video clips, and killer graphics to illustrate your points.

The language of the Web

To put text and graphics onto a Web page, you'll need to use a special language called HTML, or Hypertext Markup Language. It sounds more intimidating than it really is.

The "language" is simply a matter of putting one of about a dozen HTML tags into brackets—like **<title></title>**—around information you want to put on a Web page. These tags help you layout a Web page as if you were doing desktop publishing. You can use italic, boldface, underlined, centered, or large type. You can make headlines, horizontal rules, and bulleted lists. You can even place images, sounds, and video clips on your pages.

How do you work with these codes? Use the simplest word processor on your computer, such as Notepad (Windows) or SimpleText (Mac), and write your document in plain text. (If you use a more complex program such as WordPerfect, you must save the files as plain ASCII text or "text only.") Type the HTML codes around the words you want to turn into headlines, make boldface, or become hyperlinks on your Web page.

When you're done formatting your page, save the file to your hard drive as *webpage.htm* or something similar.

Then start your Web browser software, select Open File, open the *webpage.htm* document, and see how each code produces a different effect on your screen. The first time you try this you'll be thrilled to see your words on a Web page.

The following example of making a Web page will help you understand how Web publishing works. But you don't have to do it this way! Software called Web or HTML editors eliminate a lot of the coding chores. You can even find templates of pages that you simply fill in with your text and graphics. You'll find pointers to this software at the end of the chapter.

Kathleen makes a Web page

The best way to learn how to make a Web page is to follow along with Kathleen as she makes her first page. Kathleen Davidson is a fictitious high school student at Anytown Middle School. She learned about making Web pages by surfing the Net for her homework assignments and looking over an online HTML tutorial. (See the end of this chapter for links to Web tutorials.) Let's follow her footsteps.

Tools Kathleen needed to make her Web page

Kathleen used a computer with a simple text word processor, an Internet browser (Netscape), an HTML/Web publishing primer from the Net, a list of basic HTML codes, and the graphics and text she planned to put onto the Web page.

Before I sat down at my computer, I decided to make a pretty simple Web page to start. I put up a picture of my dad's den along with a para-graph of text. I can always go back in later and change it.

Kathleen's Step-by-step Web page

1. First, I created a new folder (or directory, for Windows users) on my Macintosh computer and named it *Web Page.* I knew I needed to put all the Web pages and graphics I created in the same folder or directory. You'll see why shortly.

2. Then I started my text program, SimpleText. The first thing I typed was the title for the Web page, *Kathleen's Web Page.* Then I typed the HTML tags **<title>** and **</title>** around the text. The first bracket tells the browser to turn this feature (or formatting) on, while the second bracket with the slash says turn this feature (or formatting) off. The text between the title brackets—Kathleen's Web Page—will appear in the title bar at the top of the Web page.

3. I kept the file open and selected Save As from the pull-down File menu to save the file. I named it *home.htm* and put it into the Web Page folder I created earlier. I used the .htm extension so I can tell that the file is in HTML. I'll do all my HTML work to create the page in this one file.

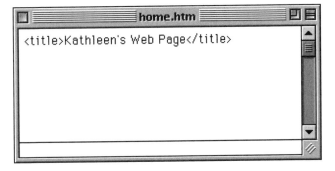

4. Next, I wanted to include a graphic—my dad's den. I scanned it in using Dad's scanner on his Windows machine. The scanner software let me save it as a GIF graphic, one of two graphic formats (the other is JPG) that all Internet browsers can handle. If the graphic were in another format, such as PICT or BMP, I'd have to use a shareware graphics program such as GraphicConverter or Paint Shop Pro to turn them into GIFs or JPGs. I copied the file with the graphic from a diskette onto my computer's hard drive and named the image file *dadden.gif.*

5. To make the graphic show up on the Web page, I returned to my SimpleText document. I typed the name of the graphic file and surrounded it with quotation marks and an image code. The result—**<img src= "dadden.gif">**—is called an *image tag.* To center the image, I surrounded the entire image tag with **<center>** and **</center>**. I made sure the dadden.gif file was in the Web Pages folder because browser programs expect to find graphics in the same directory or folder as the page they're linked from.

6. Next, I created the headline, "Welcome to my first Web Page!" The code for headlines is **<h1>** and **<\h1>** with the numeral representing the relative size of the type—the larger the number, the smaller the headline. I saved the *home.htm* document again so all the codes I'd just typed would be saved to the file. At this point, this is how my Web page looked in SimpleText.

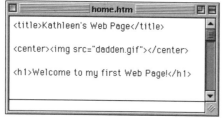

7. I wanted to see how this home page looked so far. To do that, I started Netscape, my Internet browser. (This would also work using America Online or Prodigy's browser.) I selected the File menu, then Open File to view the page. (Why didn't I select Open URL from the list? Because this page isn't really on the Web yet—it's still just a file on my computer.) I went into the Web Page folder and double clicked on the *home.htm* file to open it into Netscape.

8. Wow! Not a bad start! But I noticed that the headline was too big and wasn't centered, so I switched back to the SimpleText program, changed the codes around the headline to **<h2> ** and **</h2> **, and hit Save. I remembered that anytime you make a change you should save the file before viewing it in the Web browser because the browser accesses the last saved version, which won't reflect your most recent changes.

9. I went back into Netscape to check the change I had made. But the headline looked the same. Oops! You have to hit Reload in Netscape to make sure you're viewing the most current version of the page.

10. Next, I typed **<hr>** to draw a horizontal rule across the page this code needs no closing brackets. Then I typed in a practice paragraph. I wrote a paragraph welcoming visitors, which I surrounded with **<p>** and **</p>** to mark it as a paragraph and to put a blank line before and after the text. I wanted to list the features I'm planning to add to my page as a bulleted list (that is, with a dot before each item). So I typed **<li>** before each of the items. To make sure the list was separated from the next section, I typed **
**, which forces a line break to provide more space.

11. Of course, what makes the Web special are its *hyperlinks,* which let users click their way to other Internet sites. I wanted to include some links to other Web sites of interest to visitors to my page. To make a hyperlink, I surrounded the words I wanted to be "click-able" with **<a href=" ">** and **</a>**, and put the Internet address between the quotation marks in the first bracket. I linked my page to the Oakland Unified School District, a great example of what schools are doing with Web technology.

12. I saved the file, went back to Netscape, reloaded the page, and saw the hyperlink on the page printed and underlined in its usual blue color. Great!

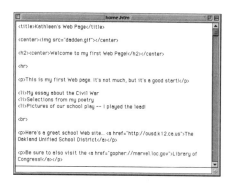

```
home.htm
<title>Kathleen's Web Page</title>

<center><img src="dadden.gif"></center>

<h2><center>Welcome to my first Web Page!</h2></center>

<hr>

<p>This is my first Web page. It's not much, but it's a good start!</p>

<li>My essay about the Civil War
<li>Selections from my poetry
<li>Pictures of our school play -- I played the lead!

<br>

<p>Here's a great school Web site... <a href="http://ousd.k12.ca.us">The
Oakland Unified School District</a></p>

<p>Be sure to also visit the <a href="gopher://marvel.loc.gov">Library of
Congress!</a></p>
```

13. The nice thing about HTML is that I can put any Internet address between those quotation marks, including gopher and ftp sites and newsgroups. So I included a link to the Library of Congress gopher site by typing **<a href="gopher://marvel.loc.gov">**. I could also do ftp links such as **<a href="ftp://ftp.classroom.net">** and newsgroup links such as **<a href="news:k12.chat.teacher">**.

14. I saved the file, switched back to Netscape, hit Reload, and viewed the page again.

15. Way Cool! I saved and closed the *home.htm* document.

To create another page, all I had to do was create a new SimpleText document, type in the text, and save it with a different name such as *nextpage.htm*. To link this new page to my home page, I opened the *SimpleText home.htm* file and added this line:

> Move on to my next Web page by
> **<a href="nextpage.htm">clicking here!</a>**.

The words "clicking here" will become a hyperlink that connects to the *nextpage.htm* file. I'll add more pages later by creating, saving, and linking to new documents.

Putting your pages on the Web

Kathleen knew when she closed her *home.htm* file that the pages weren't "live" on the Internet, but rather stored on her computer's hard drive. To mount Web pages online so other Internet users anywhere in the world can visit them, you must copy the folder or directory with the HTML documents and graphic files onto a specially configured, Internet-connected computer called a *Web server*. The server lets anyone connected to the Net with a Web browser access your pages.

If you're a subscriber to America Online or Prodigy, check out their Web forums for information about personal Web pages. You can place your pages in a special place on the services so that the whole world can see them! If you sign on to the Internet through an Internet Service Provider, chances are you were given a modest amount of free space for Web pages when you signed up. Contact your online provider for more information about free Web page mounting space.

You can send your Web pages to the Web server by sending them via ftp. Make sure all the HTML pages are saved and uploaded as text, and the graphics as raw binaries. Your commercial online service or Internet provider can work closely with you on this to make sure everything works okay!

Basic HTML Tags

Here's a list of the basic tags you can include in your Web pages to accomplish different things—from bolding text to inserting a graphic or sound clip.

<title></title>	Title
<h1></h1> *up to* <h6></h6>	Headline sizes
<center></center>	Centers text
<b></b>	Bold text
<I></I>	Italic text
<hr>	Horizontal Rule
<p></p>	Paragraph
<li>	Bulleted list item

	Break between lines
<image src="name of graphic file">	Graphic or image tag
<a href="Internet address">Name of Site</a>	Hyperlink to another Web page, or to a sound or video clip you want users to be able to play

Essential equipment for weaving your Web

A Beginner's Guide to HTML

Here's an excellent resource for your Web author's toolbox, straight from where it all began—NCSA, The National Center for Supercomputing Applications. (These were the guys who created Mosaic, the first Internet browser.)

URL: http://www.ncsa.uiuc.edu/General/
Internet/WWW/HTMLPrimer.html

Software to help you make Web pages

Instead of typing HTML codes, you can use software known as *HTML editors*. You select a word, sentence, or paragraph, then click on a button or select a menu item to apply a certain HTML code to that selection. Some Web makers find these programs easy to use, while others prefer typing the code. One of the best-known editors is Adobe PageMill, which can help speed up the creation of your pages.

Check out these Web sites to retrieve a copy of Web page creation software to your computer.

URL: http://www.vmedia.com/alternate/vvc/
onlcomp/hpia/software.html

URL: http://www.env.com/tucows/softhtm.html

URL: http://bonnie.mcauley.acu.edu.au/
media/htmled.htm

URL: http://www.enterprise.net/stars/Vlib/
Providers/HTML_Editors.html

Free textures, clip art, and images

Need art for your Web pages? You'll find plenty on the Net! Here are just a few places where you'll find hundreds of free, high-quality textures, patterns, pieces of clip art, and photographic images. *(Also, the CD that accompanies this book contains tons of this material in the HyperStudio demo!)*

URL: ftp://ftp.classroom.net/wentworth/Clip-Art/

URL: http://www.widomaker.com/~spalmer/

URL: http://www.itw.com:80/~imagesys/

URL: http://inls.ucsd.edu/y/OhBoy/icons.html

URL: http://www.csulb.edu/gc/

Maggie's Guide to HTML Authoring Resources

This is a robust site with links to hundreds of other HTML-authoring resources on the Web, including how-to manuals; sound, image, and icon archives; browser and HTML editing software; and more.

URL: http://www.mindspring.com/~mconti/html.htm

Background colors

Here's an extensive list of all the "mysterious" HTML codes used to change the background, text, link, and visited link colors on Web pages enhanced for Netscape.

URL: http://www.infi.net/wwwimages/
      colorindex.html

Web Usenet newsgroups

Learn the ropes of Webmastering by reading posts to these newsgroups. You'll find up-to-date information about Web techniques and innovations and even communicate with professional Web designers.

URL: news:comp.infosystems.www.authoring

URL: news:comp.infosystems.www.authoring.images

URL: news:comp.infosystems.www.authoring.misc

URL: news:comp.infosystems.www.servers

URL: news:comp.infosystems.www.browsers

Graphic converters

These software tools are essential to anyone making Web pages. They allow you to open a graphic in one format and save it in another. You can even take "screen shots"(capture an area on your screen as an image).

- GraphicConverter (Mac)
  URL: ftp://ftp.classroom.net/wentworth/Internet-
     Software/Mac/Graphic.Conv-2.1.5.sit.bin

- PaintShop Pro (Windows)
  URL: ftp://ftp.classroom.net/wentworth/
     Clip-Art/.utilities/IBM-PC/PSP30.ZIP

Web-savvy schools

Visit these two sites to see how schools use the Web's global, multimedia capabilities!

• International WWW Schools Registry
URL: http://web66.coled.umn.edu/schools.html

• ClassroomWeb
URL: http://www.classroom.net/classweb

Give it a try!

Hopefully, this chapter has gotten you interested in the idea of creating your own Web page. Although they look impressive, they're not as difficult to make as most people would think. So go ahead—publish your work for a global audience!

Internet
homework helper
sites

Online sites to help you get
your assignments done ASAP

The following URLs are separated into subject categories. They should come in handy when you're researching various topics for homework assignments.

Art

18th Century French Painting Exhibit
URL: http://dmf.culture.fr
A French art display with everything from Palæolithic cave paintings to the Age of Enlightenment.

Leonardo da Vinci Museum
URL: http://cellini.leonardo.net/museum/main.html
The original "Renaissance Man," Leonardo da Vinci was a great painter, designer, scientist, futurist, andthinker. This site contains many of his famous artworks, sketches, and engineering designs for the future.

Gallery Walk
URL: http://www.ECNet.Net/users/mfjfg/galwalk.html
Through this site you can link to more than three dozen online art galleries around the world—all on the Web!

Art Laboratory
URL: http://www.artn.nwu.edu/index.html
Artists around the world are just beginning to use high-end computers and the Internet to create new forms of visual art. The Art Laboratory Web site is your link to the exhibitions of online artists who are using these sophisticated

electronic tools to create virtual sculptures, photographs, holograms, and paintings. A great site for all high school art students to explore!

DaliWeb

URL: http://www.highwayone.com/dali/daliweb.html
DaliWeb is the official online counterpart to the Salvador Dali Museum in St. Petersburg, Florida. The site is divided into a large main collection and a separate gallery of the Spanish surrealist's early work. More than 94 oils; 100 watercolors; and 1300 graphics, sculptures, and *objets d'art* are deftly reproduced here. It contains not only his artwork, but it also has a biography of the artist.

Internet Movie Database

URL: http://www.msstate.edu/Movies/search.html
Here you can search for movies by title, actor, quote or even by soundtrack! If you're doing research on movies, this is definitely the place to go.

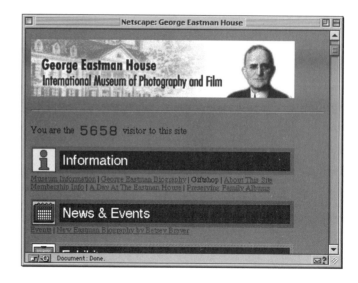

Eastman Museum of Photography & Film

URL: http://www.it.rit.edu:80/~gehouse/

Students taking photography classes will find this site extremely useful. It contains hands-on information about black-and-white photography, George Eastman's biography (he was the founder of the Eastman Kodak Company), and a detailed history of photography.

ArtServe

URL: http://rubens.anu.edu.au

Browse through 6,000 images of art and architecture, mainly from the Mediterranean Basin, which are not available elsewhere. Contents featured are Western Art, megalithic (images from prehistoric ritual monuments in the British Isles), and architecture in thumbnail sketches.

WebMuseum

URL: http://sunsite.unc.edu/louvre

Browse through the works of and learn about
the lives of Leonardo da Vinci and other artists.
Based on the famous Louvre Museum gallery in
Paris, this site allows you to click on famous
paintings and view the works according to the
artists' names or themes. A glossary of painting
styles from baroque to surrealism will be useful
to students of art.

National Museum of American Art

URL: http://www.nmaa.si.edu:80/
    masterdir/pagesub/tourthegallery.html

Contains nearly 1,000 works of art, voice clips,
and more that highlight this interactive art
gallery located in Washington, D.C.

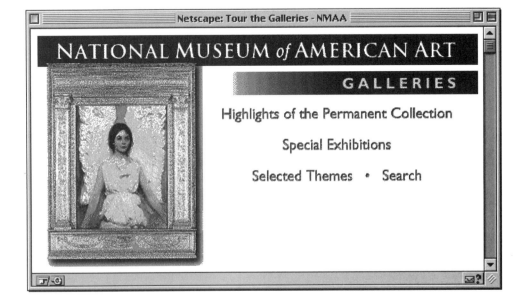

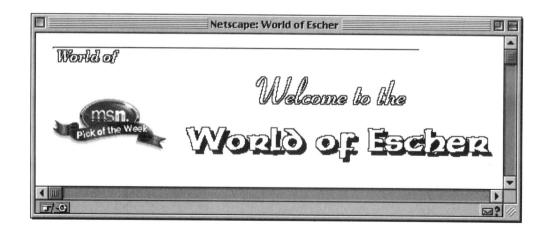

The European Dance Server

URL: http://www.net-shopper.co.uk/dance/index.htm

This site links you with great information on a wide variety of dances and styles, such as ballet, samba, ballroom, tap dancing, jive, and more.

World of Escher

URL: http://www.texas.net/escher

The art and life of M.C. Escher, the Dutch graphics artist whose work continues to fascinate students around the world.

Cezanne

URL: http://www.cezanne.com/eng/

This site contains a selection of Cezanne's works, online 24 hours a day for your use! You'll also find an essay about the artist's life.

Mailing Lists

Paint-L

This list was created for painters of all ages to discuss all aspects of their art, including technical and aesthetic issues. Media can include—but are not limited to—oils, acrylics, and watercolor.

URL: mailto:majordomo@charliek.coe.edu

Type **subscribe PAINT-L** in the body of your message
URL: http://topaz.coe.edu/~pthompso/
　　paintl.html

Student Artist Discussions

URL: mailto:ARTIST-L@UAFSYSB.UARK.EDU
Type **subscribe ARTIST-L <Your Name>** in the body of your message

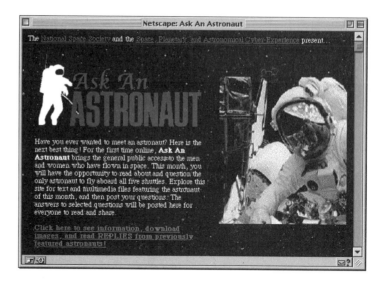

The National Space Society and the Space, Planetary, and Astronomical Cyber-Experience present...

Ask An ASTRONAUT

Have you ever wanted to meet an astronaut? Here is the next best thing! For the first time online, **Ask An Astronaut** brings the general public access to the men and women who have flown in space. This month, you will have the opportunity to read about and question the only astronaut to fly aboard all five shuttles. Explore this site for text and multimedia files featuring the astronaut of this month, and then post your questions. The answers to selected questions will be posted here for everyone to read and share.

Click here to see information, download images, and read REPLIES from previously featured astronauts!

Usenet Newsgroups

URL: news:alt.binaries.clip-art

URL: news:can.schoolnet.arts.drama

URL: news:can.schoolnet.arts.music

URL: news:clari.living.arts

Ask An Expert

If you have questions only an expert can answer, look no further than these Ask An Expert services! From Astronomy to home repair, these experts are on call 24 hours a day, seven days a week.

Ask an Amish Expert
URL: http://padutch.welcome.com/askamish.html

Ask an Antarctic Expert
URL: http://icair.iac.org.nz/~psommerv/
web/askaques/askaques.htm

Ask An Astronaut

URL: http://www.nss.org/askastro/

Ask an Astronomer

URL: http://www-hpcc.astro.washington.edu/
    scied/astro/ask.html

URL: mailto:ask@astro.washington.edu

As an Astronomer II

URL: http://tfnet.ils.unc.edu/ask.html

URL: mailto:starman@unc.edu

Ask the Astronomers and Space Physicists

URL: http://umbra.nascom.nasa.gov/spartan/
    ask_astronomers.html

Ask a Banker

URL: http://www.oba.com/public/public.html

Ask a Bell Labs Expert

URL: http://www.research.att.com/leisure/ask/

Internet Homework
Helper Sites

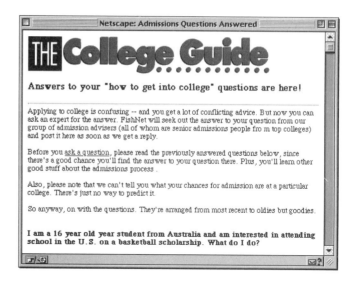

Netscape: Admissions Questions Answered

THE College Guide

Answers to your "how to get into college" questions are here!

Applying to college is confusing -- and you get a lot of conflicting advice. But now you can ask an expert for the answer. FishNet will seek out the answer to your question from our group of admission advisers (all of whom are senior admissions people from top colleges) and post it here as soon as we get a reply.

Before you ask a question, please read the previously answered questions below, since there's a good chance you'll find the answer to your question there. Plus, you'll learn other good stuff about the admissions process.

Also, please note that we can't tell you what your chances for admission are at a particular college. There's just no way to predict it.

So anyway, on with the questions. They're arranged from most recent to oldies but goodies.

I am a 16 year old year student from Australia and am interested in attending school in the U.S. on a basketball scholarship. What do I do?

Ask a Bird Expert

URL: http://www.upatsix.com/ask_experts/

URL: mailto:marybeth@ionet.net

Ask A Cardiologist

URL: http://www.atlcard.com/ask_md.html

Email to: atlcard@ix.netcom.com

Ask a Chemist

URL: http://www.chem.lsu.edu/form.html

Ask a Classics Expert from UCLA

URL: http://www.humnet.ucla.edu/humnet/
classics/questions.html

Ask a College Admissions Guru

URL: http://jayi.catalogue.com/jayi/ACG/
ques.html

Ask A Criminologist

URL: http://www.cas.usf.edu/criminology/
faculty.html

Ask a Diamond Expert

URL: http://www.citenet.net/vandaaz/ASK.HTML

Ask a Dinosaur Expert

URL: http://denr1.igis.uiuc.edu/isgsroot/
    dinos/rjjinput_form.html

Email to: jacobson@geoserv.isgs.uiuc.edu

Ask a Doctor

URL: http://www.rain.org/~medmall/ask/asklandon.html

Ask Dr. Math

URL: http://forum.swarthmore.edu/dr.math/dr-
    math.html

URL: mailto:dr.math@forum.swarthmore.edu

Ask Dr. Tooth

URL: http://www.dentistinfo.com/aska.htm

Ask an Equestrian

URL: http://www.netresource.com/eq/vet.html

Internet Homework
Helper Sites

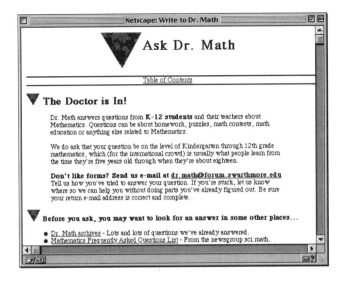

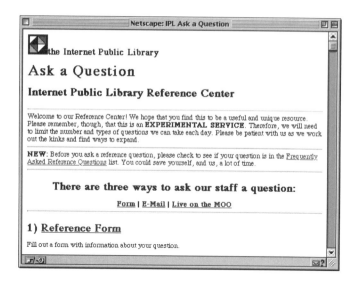

Netscape: IPL Ask a Question

■the Internet Public Library

Ask a Question

Internet Public Library Reference Center

Welcome to our Reference Center! We hope that you find this to be a useful and unique resource. Please remember, though, that this is an **EXPERIMENTAL SERVICE**. Therefore, we will need to limit the number and types of questions we can take each day. Please be patient with us as we work out the kinks and find ways to expand.

NEW: Before you ask a reference question, please check to see if your question is in the <u>Frequently Asked Reference Questions</u> list. You could save yourself, and us, a lot of time.

There are three ways to ask our staff a question:

<u>Form</u> | <u>E-Mail</u> | <u>Live on the MOO</u>

1) <u>Reference Form</u>

Fill out a form with information about your question.

Ask ERIC Questions about Education
URL: http://ericir.sunsite.syr.edu/About/userform.html

Ask a Fashion Forecaster
URL: http://www.fashionmall.com/experts/
wolfe/doc/wolfe.htm

Ask a Fashion Writer
URL: http://www.fashionmall.com/experts
/sharon/doc/sindex.htm

Ask a Fly Fisherman
URL: http://www.flyfield.com/ask_experts.htm

Ask a Geologist
URL: http://walrus.wr.usgs.gov/docs/ask-a-ge.html
URL: mailto:ask-a-geologist@usgs.gov

Ask a Government Contractor
URL: http://www.kcilink.com/govcon/
contractor/ate/index.html

Ask a Holography Expert

URL: http://www.shadow.net/~holodi/ask.html

Ask a Reference Librarian

URL: http://ipl.sils.umich.edu/ref/QUE/

Ask a Mad Scientist

URL: http://medinfo.wustl.edu/~ysp/msn/submit.html

Ask a Meteorologist

URL: http://www.weather.com/metnet.html

URL: mailto:metnet@landmark.net

Ask a Musician

URL: http://sln.fi.edu/~helfrich/music/askexprt.html

URL: mailto:helfrich@fi.edu

Ask a New England Life in the Early 19th Century Expert

URL: http://www.osv.org/pages/askjack.htm

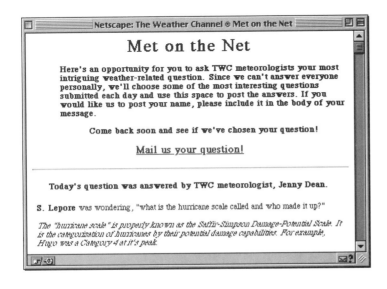

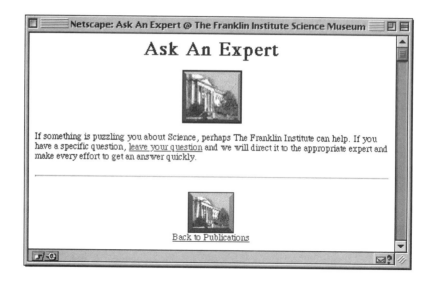

Ask a Population Geneticist

URL: http://www.ag.auburn.edu/~mwooten/form1.html

URL: mailto:mwooten@ag.auburn.edu

Ask a President Lincoln Expert

URL: http://gettysburg.welcome.com/dearmr.html

Ask a Scientist

URL: http://www.cedarnet.org/aska/scientist/index.html

Ask a Scientist from the Franklin Science Museum

URL: http://sln.fi.edu/tfi/publications/askexprt.html

Ask a Vulcanologist

URL: http://volcano.und.nodak.edu/vwdocs/ask_a.html

Ask Shamu about Marine Mammals

URL: http://www.bev.net/education/SeaWorld/
    ask_shamu/asintro.html

URL: mailto:sea.world@bev.nett

Ask a Government Contractor

URL: http://www.kcilink.com/govcon/
    contractor/ate/index.html

Ask a Pediatrician

URL: http://www.umn.edu/nlhome/g028/
    reinb002/askdr.html

URL: mailto:reinb002@gold.tc.umn.edu

Ask about Plastics

URL: http://www.harbec.com:80/askexp.htm

URL: mailto:info@harbec.com

Ask a Soy Bean Expert

URL: http://www.ag.uiuc.edu/~stratsoy/
    expert.html

Ask the Internet Public Library about Research using the Net

URL: http://www.iren.net/cfpl/forms/aal_form.html

Internet Homework
Helper Sites

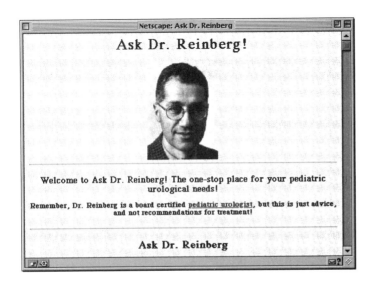

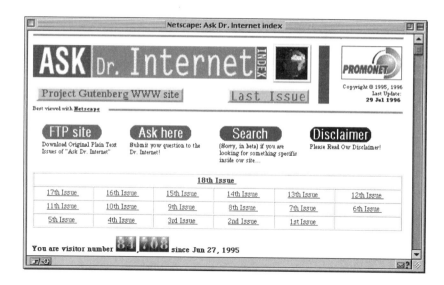

Ask Mr. Modem about the Online World

URL: http://www.intellinet.com/CustomerService/
FAQ/AskMrModem

Ask Dr. Internet

URL: http://promo.net/drnet/

Ask the World Wide Web Expert

URL: http://www.charm.net/~web/Dr.Web/

Ask a Computer Networking Expert

URL: http://www.netcreations.com/fibercorp/
ask_dave.htm

Ask a Battery Expert

URL: http://www.netcreations.com/fibercorp/
ask_jack.htm

Ask a Movie Expert

URL: http://www.movienet.com/movienet/promail.html

Ask About Housing

URL: http://www.herald.ns.ca/
homesquestions.html

Ask about Hilton Head Island

URL: http://www.aesir.com:80/HiltonHead/
Expert/Questions.html

Ask about Accounting, Finance & Taxes

URL: http://www.captive.com/experts/
af%26t.html

Business

Rutgers Accounting Web (RAW)

URL: http://www.rutgers.edu/Accounting/

RAW is an accounting information retrieval
system, available on Internet for use by accounting scholars, practitioners, educators, and
students. It provides access to an evolving
knowledge platform containing a variety of
accounting materials.

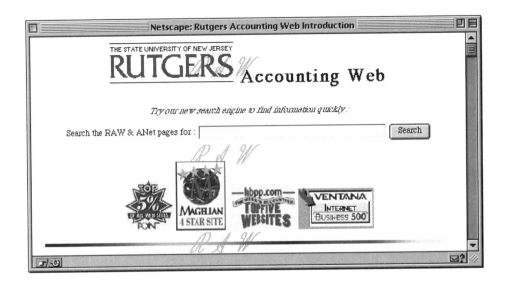

Netscape: Xenon Labs: The Universal Currency Converter(tm)

I WANT TO CONVERT...

555

```
CAD Canadian Dollars
USD American Dollars
GBP British Pounds
DEM German Marks
```

INTO

```
TTD Trinidad and Tobago Dollars
TRL Turkish Lira
VEB Venezuelan Bolivar
XEU European Currency Units
```

Perform Currency Conversion

Click here for information on the Universal Currency Converter™.

Universal Currency Converters

URL: http://www.xe.net/currency/

URL: http://bin.gnn.com/cgi-bin/gnn/currency/

These sites allow you to perform interactive foreign exchange rate conversion on the Internet. For instance, inputting $20 U.S. Dollars equaled 29 German Marks.

The Annual Report Source

URL: http://www.annualreport.com/source/

Doing a report on a company and need to access their annual reports for the past three years running? Look no further than The Annual Report Source.

Advertising & Marketing on the Internet

URL: http://www.yahoo.com/Business_and_Economy/
      Marketing/

This address links you to hundreds of online resources concerning advertising and marketing products on the Net! A must-read by all fledgling Internet entrepreneurs.

Access Business Online

URL: http://www.clickit.com/touch/home.html

Everything a business student could ever need to keep them on their competitive toes is found here, including BizWiz, a database of Web links that are strictly business. You'll even find links to business services such as financing, leasing, and loans.

Direct Marketing World

URL: http://www.dmworld.com

This free electronic directory of the direct marketing industry contains information on businesses and services, as well as full page "datacards" or information sheets on thousands of business-related mailing lists. This is a real nuts-and-bolts site where you can post your resume, create a direct marketing catalog, learn the ins-and-outs of selling in cyberspace, and tap a glossary of direct mail terms. Features today's business news from Reuters online.

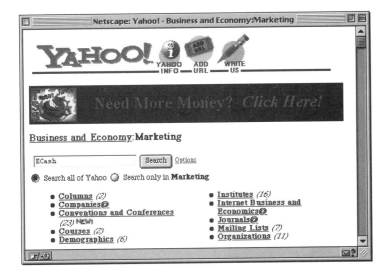

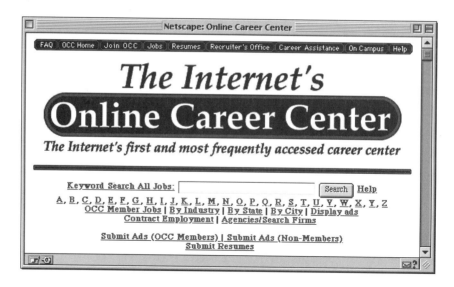

Internet Job Search Aids

URL: http://www.cob.ohio-state.edu/dept/fin/
jobs/jobssite.htm

This site offers Money magazine's list of the 50 hottest jobs in America, links to online career centers, and a bevy of recommendations that are mostly university-produced pointers on job hunting, developing skills, and preparing for an interview.

U.S. Securities and Exchange Commission

URL: http://www.sec.gov

When you visit this site, be sure and say hello to EDGAR, the Electronic Data Gathering, Analysis, and Retrieval system. It contains thousands of up-to-date financial reports from public companies across the United States. The SEC's site also provides information on the agency's structure, the laws it enforces, numerous investor guides, and links to online publications about investing.

The Money Page

URL: http://moneypage.com

This site is the most comprehensive guide to banking and financial services on the Net! Includes information about Banks, S&Ls, and Credit Unions; Investment Banking; Electronic Money, the latest news, and more.

Business Schools

URL: http://www.yahoo.com/
    Business_and_Economy/Business_Schools/

If you're in the process of looking for a college or university that offers a Business program, look no further than this Web page. It links to hundreds of business schools worldwide, many of which offer virtual tours of their campuses, financial aide information, entrance requirements, and more.

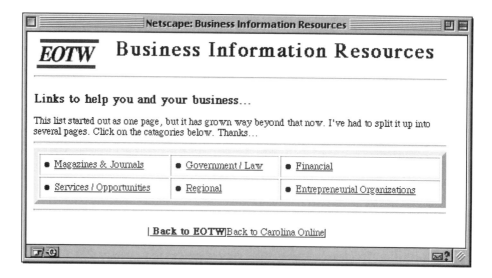

Business Information Resources
URL: http://sashimi.wwa.com/~notime/eotw/
business_info.html
Contains dozens of pointers to business information on the Net. From information on advertising online to national business directory listings,
you'll find it here!

Intellectual Property Information Mall
URL: http://www.fplc.edu/ipmall.htm
This page links to a unique collection of intellectual property resources served up by the
Franklin Pierce Law Center and others on the
Internet. It is intended to offer "one stop shopping" for intellectual property information of
interest to students and professionals at all
levels.

Consumer Information Center
URL: http://www.pueblo.gsa.gov
You've seen the TV commercials, now view and
download the publications online, free! The

Consumer Information Catalog lists over 200 free and low cost publications covering health, business, home, and money matters, and more—many of which can be downloaded right from this site.

Consumer World

URL: http://www.consumerworld.org

Consumer World has gathered over 1100 of the most useful consumer resources on the Internet. Whether you want to check an airfare, find an ATM machine anywhere in the world, file a consumer complaint with a state agency, read 100s of consumer booklets, research a law, look up the wholesale price of a car, locate a Better Business Bureau, listen (literally) to the latest news, contact a company's customer service department, check stock quotes or CD rates, or clip electronic coupons, you can do it in Consumer World.

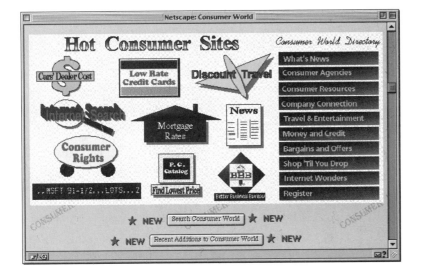

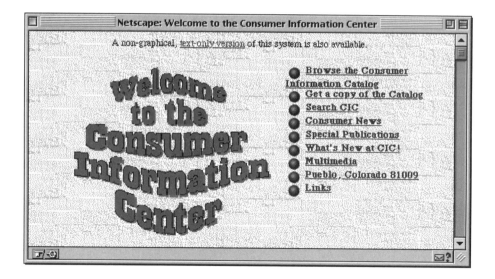

Mailing Lists

Accounting News

URL: mailto:listproc@scu.edu.au

Type **subscribe ANews-L <Your Name>** in the body of your message

Provides a news channel for accounting related stories. A must for all business students taking accounting classes to stay up to date on the latest innovations in this field.

Customer Support using the Internet

URL: mailto:majordomo@lists.infoboard.com

Type **subscribe** in the body of your message

Perfect for business students interested in finding out how to support customers, employees, and business partners by implementing Internet based solutions (Web sites, mailing lists, etc.)

Usenet Newsgroups

URL: news:alt.business

URL: news:clari.biz.industry.agriculture

URL: news:clari.biz.industry.automotive

URL: news:clari.biz.industry.manufacturing

URL: news:clari.biz.market.news

URL: news:clari.biz.market.report

URL: news:clari.biz.top

URL: news:clari.biz.world_trade

College Prep & Vocational Education

Adventures in Education

URL: http://www.tgslc.org

This site contains tips on applying for financial aid, finding the college of your dreams, and saving for your education.

CareerMosaic

URL: http://www.careermosaic.com

Post your resume and search out job leads in thousands of major industries!

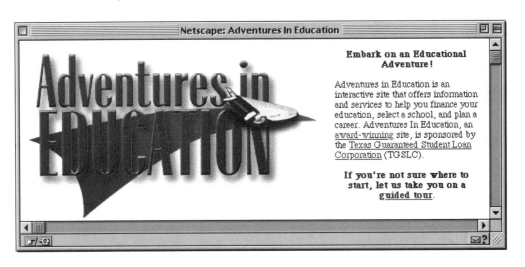

Netscape: Adventures In Education

Embark on an Educational Adventure!

Adventures in Education is an interactive site that offers information and services to help you finance your education, select a school, and plan a career. Adventures In Education, an award-winning site, is sponsored by the Texas Guaranteed Student Loan Corporation (TGSLC).

If you're not sure where to start, let us take you on a guided tour.

How you can structure your high-school career to give yourself the best chance at getting into the college or university of your choice. Plus: A look behind the scenes as admissions officers consider a new crop of hopeful applicants.
A special report by The Seattle Times.
The College Admissions Game

College Admissions Game

URL: http://www.seatimes.com/educate.html

How you can structure your high-school career to give yourself the best chance at getting into the college or university of your choice? Plus: A look behind the scenes as admissions officers consider a new crop of hopeful applicants, all at this killer Web site!

CollegeApps.com

URL: http://www.collegeapps.com

Is college really for you? What should you major in? This site contains a detailed questionnaire to help you decide whether college is for you, where to go, and more. Includes great information on the college application process, financial aid, and scholarships.

College Board Online

URL: http://www.collegeboard.org/

Here you'll find a broad menu of information to aid in the transition from high school to college, including a college search database, College Board test dates across the U.S., online SAT registration, and a really helpful financial aid calculator.

College Link

URL: http://www.collegelink.com

Find out more about hundreds of the finest U.S. colleges and the best way to apply using your computer! College Link offers special software that helps you apply to multiple colleges and universities while entering your application information just once. Wow!

FinAid

URL: http://www.finaid.org/fin

This is a comprehensive free resource for student financial aid information on the Web. Free scholarship search, financial aid calculators, a glossary, and bibliography of related information both online and off!

Internet Homework
Helper Sites

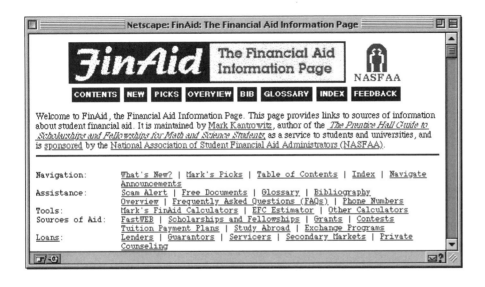

FutureScanner

URL: http://www.futurescan.com

Each online issue of *FutureScanner* focuses on a specific career and provides the information you and your friends need to determine which careers are most appealing. Find what practitioners in a given field do every day. Find out what they like, and don't like, about their work. FutureScan gives you the whole story, so you can make informed decisions about your future.

How are you going to pay for college?

URL: http://www2.nelliemae.org/nellie/
mae/whereBegin.html

This single Web page will help you answer this question—from when to send in your loan forms to who to talk to about scholarships.

The Ideas of a University

URL: http://quarles.unbc.edu/ideas/

This home page opens the door to the university campus for you, and lets you talk to instructors from many disciplines, at your own leisure. They explain to you what is involved in their subject, how you can major in it, why you might proceed to further degrees, and what jobs these degrees may lead to.

Peterson's Education Center

URL: http://www.petersons.com/resources/
    finance.html

Lots of great information on financing your college career from one of the experts in the field.

The Student Guide

URL: http://www.ed.gov/prog_info/SFA/
    StudentGuide/

This site contains complete information to financial aide offered to college and university students by the federal government. From Stafford Loans to PLUS Loans, it's all here.

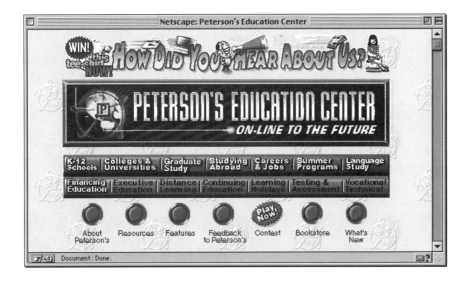

Netscape: Bay State School of Appliances Home Page

Bay State School of Appliances

Start Learning NOW For the Future!

Bay State School of Appliances is a private Vocational Technical School, accredited by the Accrediting Commission of Career Schools and Colleges of Technology and Licensed by The Massachusetts Department of Education. Bay State School of Appliances is also a member of the Massachusetts Association of Private Career Schools. The programs offered at Bay State maintain a strong emphasis on "Hands On" training, along with theory.

At Bay State you can train to be a:

COMPUTER SERVICE TECHNICIAN

Vocational Schools

URL: http://www.yahoo.com/Education/
       Vocational_Schools/

Contains hundreds of links to vocational institutions, from the American Motorcycle Institute to the Wisconsin School of Electronics.

Mailing Lists

Colleges and High Schools Cooperative Learning Group

A mailing list helping to bridge the gap between high school and college students and enable both groups to work together.

URL: mailto:COLRN-L@ADMIN.HUMBERC.ON.CA

Type **subscribe COLRN-L <Your Name>** in the body of your message

Academic and Scholarship Information for
High School Students
URL: mailto:CSTEP@LISTSERV.SYR.EDU
Type **subscribe CSTEP <Your Name>** in the body
of your message

Usenet Newsgroups

URL: news:alt.college.us
URL: news:soc.college.admissions
URL: news:soc.college.financial-aid
URL: news:soc.college.grad

Commercial Online Services Homework Helpers

Academic Assistance Center
America Online offers access to a ton of homework helpers here, including homework assistance by subject area, a killer tutoring center,

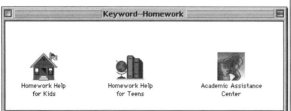

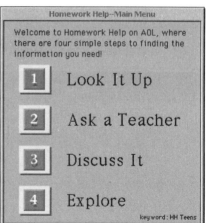

Homework Help--Main Menu

Welcome to Homework Help on AOL, where there are four simple steps to finding the information you need!

1 Look It Up

2 Ask a Teacher

3 Discuss It

4 Explore

keyword: HH Teens

Keyword--Homework

Homework Help for Kids

Homework Help for Teens

Academic Assistance Center

and information about academic contests you can enter.

America Online Ketword: AAC

America Online Homework Help

Access online encyclopedias, special homework message boards for teens, and ask a teacher via AOL's famous teacher pager service.

America Online Keyword: Homework

American Heritage

This real world magazine about the history of the U.S. is now available online.

Prodigy Jumpword: Choice

America Online's Internet Browser

America Online Keyword: Web

Bosnia Updates

Find out the latest concerning Balkan Operation Joint Endeavor.

America Online Keyword: Bosnia

College Board Online

America Online Keyword: College Board

Compton's Encyclopedia Online

Access Compton's in a whole new way—online!

America Online Keyword: encyclopedia

CompuServe: GO ENCYCLOPEDIA

Prodigy Jumpword: encyclopedia

Computer Basics

Get up to speed on the basics of how computers work, and how to make them work for you!

Prodigy Jumpword: computer basics

Education Software

Looking for a calculator program to help with your algebra homework, or a free program to organize your assignments? Look no further then the software databases in AOL's Education Forum.

America Online Keyword: Education

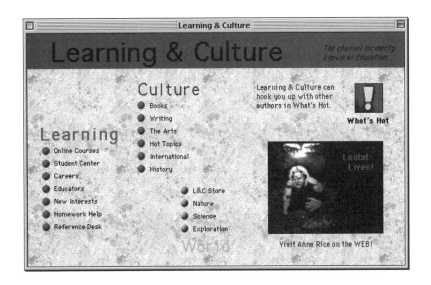

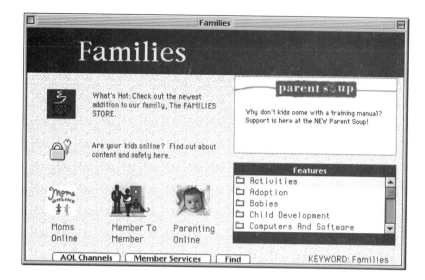

European Forum

Although the messages are sometimes in English and sometimes in French or German, this lively area in CompuServe will link you directly to people living across the European Continent!
CompuServe: GO EURFOR

Family Forum

Extensive electronic resources of interest to any student in a home economics or health class!
America Online Keyword: pin
CompuServe: GO MYFAMILY
Prodigy Jumpword: homelife bb

Health Topics

Health information and library available on Prodigy.
Prodigy Jumpword: report

International Issues Forum

Offers in-depth coverage of international news events, and hosts several active discussion groups which are frequented by people from around the world.

America Online Keyword: Issues

Library of Congress Online

Contains more than dozen online exhibits from the real world Library of Congress—online!

America Online Keyword: Library

Living History Forum

How did men and women dress in 15th Century Scotland? Find out here! Members of the Society for Creative Anachronisms are more than willing to answer your history questions here.

CompuServe: GO LIVING

Martin Luther King, Jr.

Read MLK's writings, speeches, and a history of his life and work in the civil rights movement.

America Online Keyword: MLK

```
KING HOLIDAY A Hero is Remembered
```

📁 ACLU:The King Legacy Collection	Chat
📁 NEW YORK TIMES:1963 March on Washington	Message Boards
📁 ATLANTIC MONTHLY:Flashback - Martin Luther King	
📁 Martin Luther King, Jr. Speech Collection	Go to Top News

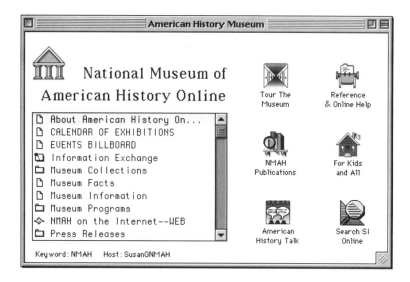

National Museum of American History

America Online Ketword: American History

Newspapers & Magazines Online

Need to find information for a current events assignment? Access online newspapers and magazines from countries around the world.

America Online Keyword: Newstand

America Online Keyword: Today's News

America Online Keyword: @times

Prodigy Jumpword: news

Newsweek

Get this week's complete issue on Prodigy.

Prodigy Jumpword: newsweek

Nova

This award-winning science TV show from PBS has made the move online.

Prodigy Jumpword: explore

Political Science Discussions

America Online Keyword: Political Science

Prodigy Homework Helper

Access a complete virtual reference library online to help you get your assignments done quickly.

Prodigy Jumpword: refrnce

Prodigy's Internet Browser

Prodigy Jumpword: Web

Reference Desk

Access online encyclopedias, dictionaries, and subject-specific reference guides.

America Online Keyword: Reference

America Online Keyword: Reference Help

CompuServe: GO REFERENCE

Smithsonian Museum Online

America Online Keyword: Smithsonian

Internet Homework
Helper Sites

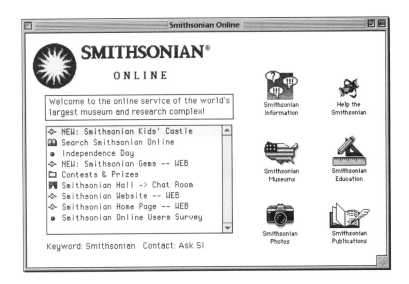

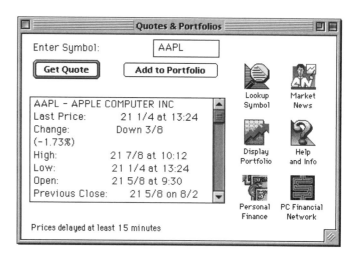

Stocks and Bonds

Create your own stock portfolio with funny money and track its progress over time, read the latest about the stock and bond markets, and get up-to-the-minute stock quotes.

America Online Keyword: Stock

Student Forum

Contains discussion groups and chat rooms devoted to more than a dozen academic interests—from Art to Science.

CompuServe: GO STUDENT

Teacher Pager

Sign on the America Online and activate the teacher pager to summon a teacher to help with your homework. Teacher's are on call to help you with your English, Languages, Math, Science, and Social Sciences assignments.

America Online Keyword: Teacher Pager

Time magazine

Get this week's complete issue on AOL.

America Online Keyword: Time

Weather Reports

View satellite images and the latest weather
reports from around the world.

America Online Keyword: Weather

CompuServe: GO WEATHER

Prodigy Jumpword: a-z us weather

U.S. News & World Report

Get this week's complete issue on CompuServe.

CompuServe: GO USNEWS

English & Literature

Classics Archive

URL: http://the-tech.mit.edu/Classics/

The Classics Archive is an award-winning
searchable collection of 400 classical Greek and
Roman texts (in English translation) complete
with user-provided commentary, provided by the
faculty at MIT. The original electronic sources
for the works (in plain text) are also available.

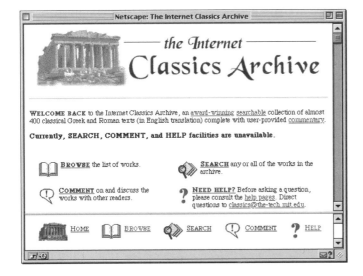

Cool Word of the Day

URL: http://www.dsu.edu/projects/word_of_day/
    word.html

Expand your vocabulary or test your knowledge with this fun page, sponsored by Dakota State University.

English as a Second Language

URL: http://www.lang.uiuc.edu/r-li5/esl/

ESL learners who want to enhance their English skills with the help of the Web can use the writing lab or the Exchange featuring online stories (with errors) and writing instructions. Visit LinguaTec for a course for foreign-born professionals who want to become more proficient in business culture. This site also has a jobs locator page.

English Server

URL: http://english-server.hss.cmu.edu

This site contains more than 18,500 files in all areas of the arts and humanities, and boasts over 200,000 readers per week. It contains writings and research of interest to any student of literature, and includes pieces related to fiction, non-fiction, history, cultural theory, Cyber (Internet) literature, and more.

Electric Library

URL: http://www.elibrary.com

This for-pay site allows you to research images and text from brand-name publishers. With over one billion words and over 21,000 images, the Electric Library can answer your most essential questions. First time visitors can sign up for a free two-week trial period and conduct 100 searches.

Internet Homework
Helper Sites
10

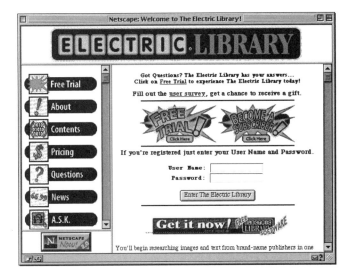

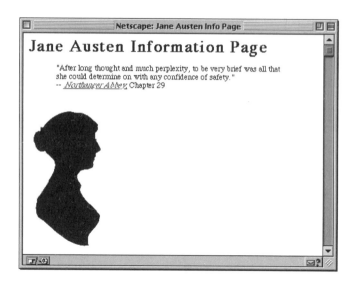

Jane Austen Home Page

URL: http://uts.cc.utexas.edu/~churchh/
janeinfo.html

A great source for info on the popular English writer who lived from 1775 to 1817. Her novels and other writings are all here, as well as lots of other interesting information about her and her times.

Lingua Center Grammar Safari

URL: http://deil.lang.uiuc.edu/web.pages/
grammarsafari.html

When bagging big game, you go to the jungle. When you want to snare grammar structures, you turn to the text. That's what this site does with the millions of articles on the Internet. You can search for conjunctions, gerunds, infinitives, dangling prepositions, and more in documents on the World Wide Web Crawler. Enter search requests at the Electronic Newsstand and find the grammatical structures you need.

Online Books Page

URL: http://www.cs.cmu.edu/Web/books.html

It's hard to believe "Little Red Riding Hood" was the object of censorship but that is some of what students will learn from this site, which is also a great resource of more than 1,000 online books. There is also an index of common repositories of online books and other documents which students can search by author or title. Plus there are specialty and foreign-language repositories for foreign-language materials in German, Swedish, and Italian.

Science Fiction Study Guides

URL: http://www.wsu.edu:8080/~brians/
      science_fiction/Science_Fiction_Guides.html

Contains more than a dozen study guides for students of this cutting-edge genre of literature. Includes listings for H.G. Wells, Ursula LeGuin, Philip K. Dick, and William Gibson (who coined the term cyberspace in 1984.)

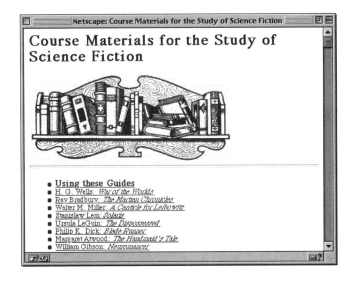

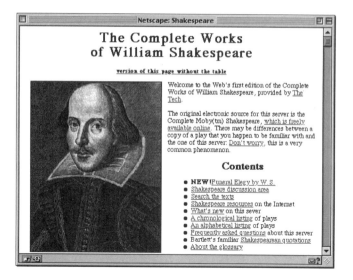

Strunk's Elements of Style

URL: http://www.columbia.edu/acis/bartleby/
strunk/

Your English teacher's favorite writing resource guide is now online! This book is intended for use in English courses in which the practice of composition is combined with the study of literature. It aims to give in brief space the principal requirements of plain English style.

The Complete Works of William Shakespeare

URL: http://the-tech.mit.edu/Shakespeare/

Hamlet may have asked "To be, or not to be?" but Shakespeare decided to be on the Internet with a complete set of his works. This is a good reference site that allows you to search for other Shakespeare links, chronological listings of his plays and a list of Bartlett's familiar Shakespearean quotes.

Nando Times

URL: http://www2.nando.net/nt/nando.cgi

The best way to learn proper usage of the written word is through reading. This site allows the user to do that with comprehensive stories gathered from 32 services and compiled in news, features, columns, and graphics menus. Read Andy Rooney and *Dick Tracy*. Get business advice and tips on car repair. This service is continually updated with up-to-the minute information. If you subscribe for an annual $12 fee, you may access searchable archives.

Responses to the Holocaust

URL: http://jefferson.village.virginia.edu/
holocaust/response.html

This site contains a hypermedia source book for the humanities centering on the Nazi genocide in Europe. You'll find a timeline of the event, extensive writings by the survivors, photographs, and more.

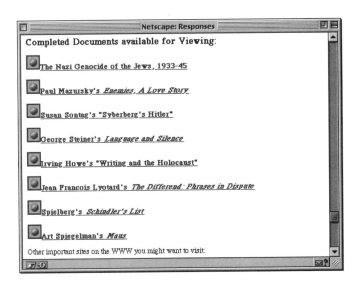

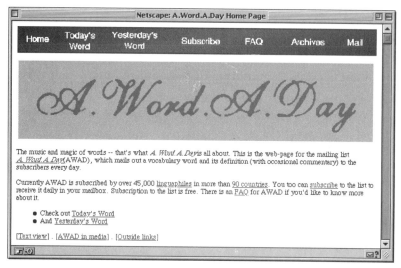

Mailing Lists

A Word A Day

The music and magic of words—that's what A.Word.A.Day is all about. This is a mailing list from a wordserver which mails out an English vocabulary word and its definition (with occasional commentary) daily.

URL: mailto:wsmith@wordsmith.org

Type **subscribe <Your Full Name>** in the subject line of your message

Students of American Literature

Discussion among students of American Literature.

URL: mailto:AML-LIT@CFRVM.CFR.USF.EDU

Type **subscribe AML-LIT <Your Name>** in the body of your message

Usenet Newsgroups

URL: news:alt.appalachian.literature

URL: news:alt.folklore.urban

URL: news:humanities.lit.authors.shakespeare

URL: news:tnn.literature

Foreign Languages

Online dictionaries

URL: http://www.bucknell.edu/~rbeard/
diction.html

Online dictionaries covering more than 25 languages—from Algerian to Welsh, and everything in between!

Diario de Yucatan

URL: http://www.yucatan.com.mx/diariox.htm

Mayans were an ancient Indian people who were one of the first cultures to develop arts and sciences, a system of hieroglyphics, and a well-ordered social class system. Hosted by El Diario, a Yucatan publication, this site highlights other features of the area and includes top news stories in Spanish, financial and entertainment news, and classified ads. Some pages are in English.

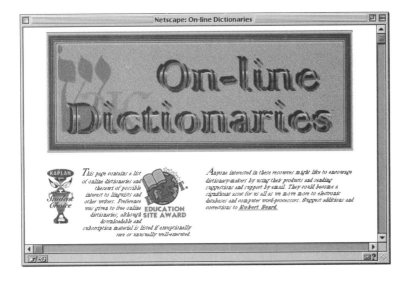

A website 'con sabor'

Latino Link

URL: http://www.latinolink.com/

This bilingual site contains stories, columns, and photographs by Latino journalists as well as a job bank. The accent is on Mexico and Puerto Rico, but the site also addresses issues that affect Latinos in the United States, such as myths and misconceptions about Latinos as well as entertainment and art categories that feature Latin artists.

The Human Languages Page

URL: http://www.willamette.edu~tjones/
    Language-Page.html

Studying a foreign language? Interested in other languages? Here's a great resource for more than 550 languages from A to Z, with dictionaries and sound files for pronunciations.

MundoHispano

URL: http://web.syr.edu/~lmturbee/mundo.html

MundoHispano is a MOO, that is a Multi-user's domain that is Object-Oriented (MOO). It's a community of native Spanish speakers from Spain, Columbia, Peru, and Costa Rica. Students can interview other MOOers, gather information, hunt for vocabulary or idioms, build rooms in response to an in-class reading and MOOmail correspondences. It is helpful to use a client program to sort out the text.

Mailing List

Foreign Languages Across Curriculum

If your school uses intensive scheduling or cross-curriculum teaching, you'll find this list a big help in completing your assignments; includes both foreign language and other subject areas.

URL: mailto:FLAC-L@BROWNVM.BROWN.EDU

Type **subscribe FLAC-L <Your Name>** in the body of your message

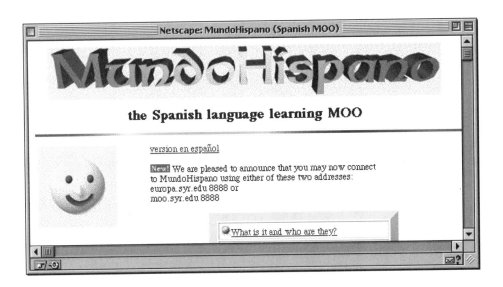

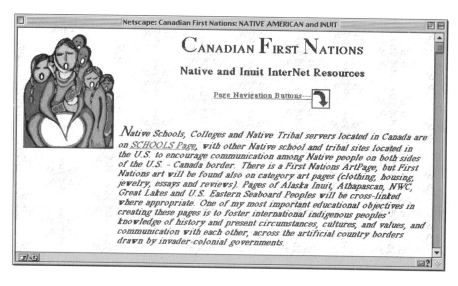

Usenet Newsgroups

URL: news:k12.lang.art

URL: news:k12.lang.esp-eng

URL: news:k12.lang.francais

URL: news:k12.lang.russian

URL: news:misc.education.language.english

Geography & Travel

Native & Inuit Internet Resources

URL: http://indy4.fdl.cc.mn.us/~isk/canada/canada.html

For comprehensive information on Native peoples of Canada, Alaska, and the Arctic, this site offers maps and geography; First Nation art; galleries and museums; Canada's School Net; a disk-imaging library; and Native business pages filled with educational information. Take the interactive Canadian geography quiz that makes a game of learning. Or click on Stories and read about Geow-lud-mo-sis-eg, magical little beings similar to leprechauns who appear to certain people at certain times in certain places in many Native communities.

CityNet

URL: http://www.city.net

Staunton is a sleepy little town in Virginia, and you'd never guess it was the 1856 birthplace of Woodrow Wilson. That's one of the little details students will discover when they use this comprehensive international guide to communities around the world. Updated every day, it's won numerous awards for its information on more than 1,153 cities and 578 destinations categorized by regions and maps.

The Arctic Circle

URL: http://www.lib.uconn.edu/ArcticCircle/

Who lives in the Arctic Circle? How does industry impact the Circumpolar North's environment? This virtual classroom explores such issues. Composed of a collection of case studies, the settings range from isolated northern villages to urban executive suites of multinational

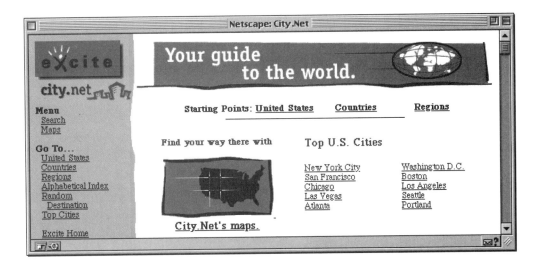

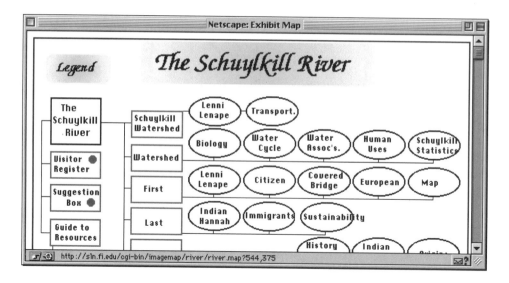

corporations. Participants will explore important relationships between human societies and the natural environment. Or click on the Canadian Heritage Information Network and find a list of organizations, government departments, and agencies, primarily in Canada, which are engaged in heritage activities.

The Schuylkill River

URL: http://sln.fi.edu/river/schuylkill.html

If you can't get to the Schuylkill River in Philadelphia, this site is the next best thing to being there. Navigate the "Ganshowahanna," as the Leni Lenape Indians called the river, with a click on the map that begins an exploration of the many topics related to its origin and watersheds. Learn about Indians, early settlers, and trappers who used the river for navigation and a source of food. This site is a model for classrooms around the world where students can research and document local watersheds, savannas, or cities. A Guide to Resources includes suggestions for educational activities, a list of online resources, and a bibliography of related materials.

Serbia

URL: http://www.yugoslavia.com

Most people never heard of this area of the world until blood started spilling during a civil war. But this site goes beyond the gory nightly news headlines and reveals a picture of the people concentrating on everyday activities, recipes, and poetry. Students will find information about famous Serbian Nikola Tesla, who invented devices and discovered many concepts important to our modern society. Click on Beograd, the Serbian name of the capital city we know as Belgrade, and hyperlink to information that reveals its ancient history.

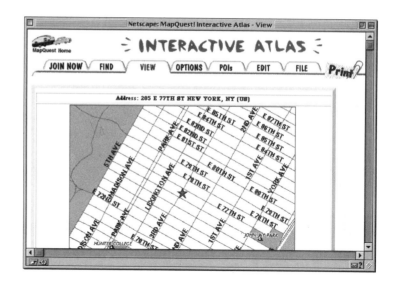

Welcome to Slovakia

URL: http://www.tuzco.sk/

Ahoj! That's Slovakian for hello—just one of the cultural tidbits students will learn from this site. This site represents the eastern half of the former Czechoslovakia. Students will find population data, a picture of the new country's flag, and information on the Slovenska Koruna (Slovak crown). Plus, there is travel information and daily news from The Slovakia online multimedia magazine. Nice graphics and a university-sponsored clickable map make this a fun and interesting site.

MapQuest

URL: http://www.mapquest.com

MapQuest is several types of maps rolled into one. There's the interactive atlas which is a street guide to the continental U.S. The coolest part is TripQuest, where you type in a destination, and the site plots a route for you to follow by car.

CIA The World Factbook

URL: http://www.odci.gov/cia/publications/
 95fact/index.html

This gives you all the up-to-date information and more than you can get out of an encyclopedia on every country in the world. It has more than the typical facts of climate and population, but also ethnic divisions and how many FM radio stations the country has!

Virtual Tourist II

URL: http://www.vtourist.com/vt/

The Virtual Tourist II is a map-based guide to local and regional information on the WWW, operating in close association with City.Net. It is an excellent service for tourism, geography education, and community services.

Internet Homework
Helper Sites

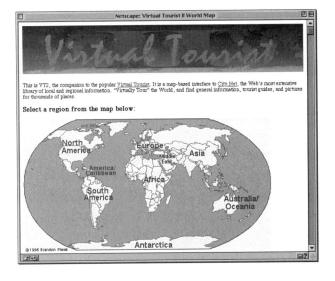

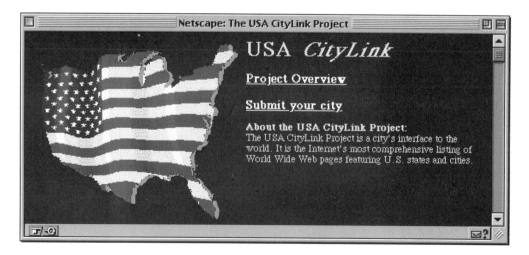

The Perry-Castaneda Library Map Collection

URL: http://www.lib.utexas.edu/Libs/PCL/
Map_collection/Map_collection.html

Many types of electronic maps to look at, as if you had your own atlas in front of you.

USA CityLink

URL: http://www.neosoft.com/citylink/

Provides in-depth information on hundreds of U.S. cities and states.

National Park Service

URL: http://www.nps.gov

A great place to explore national parks across the U.S., with pictures and maps. Plan your summer vacation or research a school project. Links to the states. Click the name of the park!

Los Angeles River Virtual Tour

URL: http://www.lalc.k12.ca.us/laep/smart/river/
tour/index.html

Take a fascinating tour of how an urban area gets its drinking water, with great text and photos and superb links to the plants, wildlife, and people along the river.

Mailing Lists

Geographic Resources Center Forum

In existence to help students track down links to geography resources on the Internet.
URL: mailto:majordomo@geog.hkbu.edu.hk
Type **subscribe GRC <Your Name>** in the body of your message

Usenet Newsgroup

URL: news:bit.listserv.geograph

Health

Emergency Medical Services Home Page
URL: http://galaxy. TradeWave.com/editors/
    fritz-nordengren/ems.html
Complete EMS page with emergency first aid information of use to any high school student, as well as lots of links to a variety of related sites.

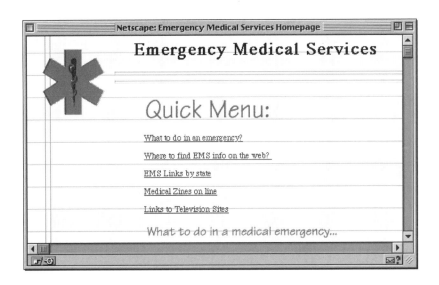

Action On Smoking and Health (ASH)

URL: http://ash.org/ash/

This Web site is maintained by Action on Smoking and Health (ASH), a national organization devoted solely to the problems of smoking and to protecting nonsmokers' rights.

Guide To Women's Health Issues

URL: http://asa.ugl.lib.umich.edu:80/chdocs/
    womenhealth/womens_health.html

In-depth guide to those health issues specific to women. Deals with issues important to high-school age women, such as self-image and building self-esteem.

USA Today Children's Health

URL: http://web.usatoday.com/life/health/
     lh015.htm

Children's health page of this popular national
newspaper, updated regularly, a sort of cursory
look at current trends in children's and teens'
health issues.

Ask the Dietician

URL: http://www.hoptechno.com/rdindex.htm

Dietician Joanne Larsen M.S., R.D., answers
questions on any number of health topics. She's
waiting to hear from you!

International Food Information Council Home
Page

URL: http://ificinfo.health.org

Comprehensive site with information on possibly every food and nutrition topic imaginable.

Netscape: NUTRITION ADVOCATE

NUTRITION ADVOCATE

News of the Cornell-China Project

Dear Reader,

I have been a researcher, lecturer, and policy advisor in the field of diet and cancer for nearly 30 years. Since 1963, primarily from an academic position, I have seen the many faces of establishment science and have been both rewarded and distressed by what I have witnessed. I have seen a vast increase in consumer nutrition information and, regrettably, an almost equal increase in consumer confusion. One week we hear that eating meat increases our risk of colon cancer, the next week the exact opposite. One news report states that dietary fat is not related to breast cancer, another says it is. It seems to me that public confusion has grown far beyond acceptable limits.

Nutrition Advocate

URL: http://envirolink.org/arrs/advocate/
 nut1.htm

Electronic periodical written by a number of medical doctors and PhDs with fairly substantial (i.e., more so than *USA Today*) articles dealing with current issues of health and nutrition.

Depression Guide

URL: http://users.aol.com/DebDeren/depress.htm

An informative guide to clinical depression, written by a person diagnosed with this ailment, thereby giving a first-hand perspective.

Melissa's Therapy FAQ

URL: http://abulafia.st.hmc.edu/~mmiles/faq.html

An in-depth look at the often misunderstood subject of therapy, from the perspective of a "client."

The Heart: A Virtual Exploration

URL: http://sln2.fi.edu/biosci/heart.html

An exhaustive look at the human heart with a great deal of information on keeping the heart healthy and some photos that may not be for those with weak stomachs.

CPR—You CAN Do It!

URL: http://weber.u.washington.edu/~gingy/
    cpr.html

The CPR homepage, while it still stresses the importance of taking a course, it gives all of the necessary information to perform CPR and even allows viewers to download the long or short version of an instructional video.

American Red Cross Home Page

URL: http://www.redcross.org

The official Red Cross page, complete information about the organization, including how to help.

The following is shown within the browser window:

sptimes.com THE TIMES PUBLISHING COMPANY **Index page**

The **Florida International Museum** opened its doors in January 1995 with its premier exhibition, Treasures of the Czars. Over **600,000** visitors came to the downtown St. Petersburg museum to see the Romanov artifacts. This virtual tour was constructed to promote that exhibition. We have left this site up under exclusive contract with the Moscow Kremlin Museums, owners of the exhibition.

TREASURES OF THE CZARS
FLORIDA INTERNATIONAL MUSEUM

American Dental Association Online

URL: http://www.ada.org/index.html

Full information about the ADA including in-depth information on personal dental hygiene.

Usenet Newsgroups

URL: news:sci.med.aids

URL: news:misc.health.aids

URL: news:misc.health.diabetes

URL: news:sci.med.diseases.cancer

URL: news:sci.research

History

Treasures of the Czars

URL: http://www.times.st-pete.fl.us/Treasures/
    Default.html

Visit this interesting exhibit of the Czars of Russia at the Florida International Museum. Be sure to also visit the museum's link to its "Splendors of Ancient Egypt" exhibit.

Encyclopedia of Women's History

URL: http://www.teleport.com/~megaines/
women.html

What began as a way for students to participate in Women's History Month in March 1995 has evolved into a Web site featuring descriptions of women throughout history with charming spins that only children could give. (Nuclear physicist Lisa Meitner is described as someone who "helped Albert innestin with the Adom bomb.") The site contains hyperlinks to other women's history sites and the U.S. Census' statistics on women. This page contains entries from students in grades 3 through 12 and, for some students, English is a second language.

Enter Evolution

URL: http://ucmp1.berkeley.edu/history/evolution.html

Evolution is as much a history of an organism as it is a science. Learn the history of the earth through the study of geology and see how it relates to the evolution of plants and animals.

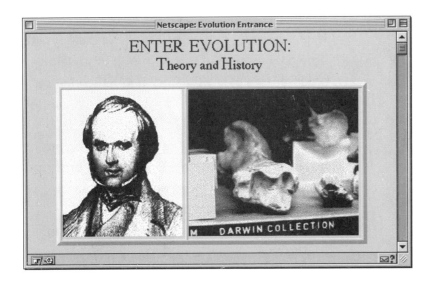

ENTER EVOLUTION:
Theory and History

DARWIN COLLECTION

The main body of this hypertext comes from An outline of American History, but all links to original sources or articles about details have been prepared for this project in HTML by a number of contributors. This project will continue to grow as long as we will find new texts, and as long as volunteers will provide new articles. If you want to contribute, read this. If you would like to sponsor this project, here is the information you need.

Through this site you can take a trip in geological time. Visit the Pleistocene era, for example; search for plant and animal fossils; meet such creatures as Heterodontosaurus, one of the earliest Ornithischian dinosaurs; scan a glossary of biological terms; and hyperlink to the Academy of Natural Sciences.

From Revolution to Reconstruction

URL: http://grid.let.rug.nl/~welling/usa/
revolution.html

Here's a handy outline of American history with links to appropriate subject matter and details often glossed over in history books. Read about the Civil War and click on Abraham Lincoln to read his first inaugural and Gettysburg addresses. Read about Christopher Columbus as a "red-haired, handsome man" before browsing his letter to the king and queen of Spain in 1494. This site covers the colonial period through the post–Civil War era of expansion and reform.

Perseus Project of Tufts University

URL: http://www.perseus.tufts.edu

Meet Sophocles, Euripides, Odysseus, Achilles, and other famous Greeks in this multimedia library of archaic and classical Greek. The Perseus Project introduces beginners to the antiquities and provides a research tool for experts. Named for the Hellenic hero who explored the world to its most distant corners, this library contains art, coins, sculptures, and buildings plus links to sites in art and archeology.

Selections from the African-American Mosaic

URL: http://lcweb.loc.gov/exhibits/
African.American/intro.html

This first resource guide to the library's African-American collections covers nearly 500 years of the black experience in the Western hemisphere. Meet Paul Cuffee, a successful Quaker ship-owner of African-American and Native American ancestry under the Beginning of Colonization heading. The exhibit is also covers abolition, the migration of blacks from the

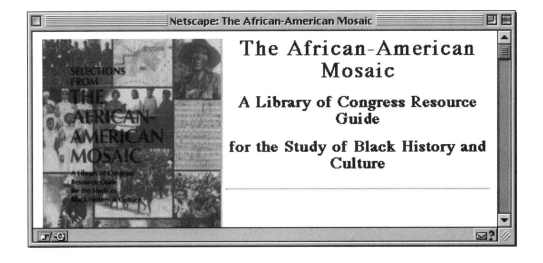

South, and the Work Projects Administration, which generated written and oral histories, plays, posters, and photographs relating to African-American history.

Titanic Home Page

URL: http://gil.ipswichcity.qld.gov.au/~dalgarry/
main.html

Meet the real life woman named in the Broadway musical and film *The Unsinkable Molly Brown* on this page published by a 13 year old. Learn about Molly and other Titanic survivors, the details of the Titanic, why it was considered "unsinkable," and why it sank.

United Nations Home Page

URL: http://www.un.org/index.html

Students can visit the virtual United Nations and its headquarters on an 18-acre site in Manhattan to learn about the special U.N. stamps, that can only be mailed from the building, and the U.N.'s history, such as the fact the name was

devised by Franklin D. Roosevelt and membership has grown from its original 51 in 1945 to its
current 185. The site features supplemental
educational materials on global issues appropriate for three different age levels.

U.S. Postal Service

URL: http://www.usps.gov

In the more than two centuries since Benjamin
Franklin was named the first postmaster general
in 1775, the postal system has helped bind this
nation together, support the growth of com-
merce, and ensure a free flow of ideas and
information. This site describes the postal system's part in American history and provides
information on stamps and the criteria for how
stamps are suggested, chosen and designed. You
can also find nine-digit zip codes, view wanted
posters, and find information on auctions of
unclaimed loose-in-the-mail items.

Internet Homework
Helper Sites

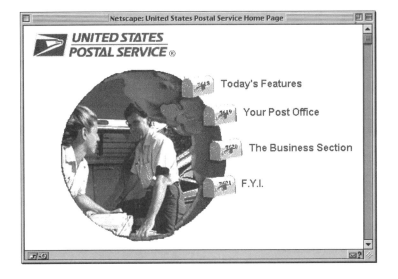

Encyclopedia Mystica

URL: http://www.bart.nl/~micha/

From Greek mythology to folklore and legends, here is a great source of information.

The City of Hiroshima

URL: http://www.city.hiroshima.jp

This site gives the history of Hiroshima, extraordinary photographs of the damage due to the atomic blast and the city's commitment to peace.

The Library of Congress

URL: http://www.loc.gov

Everything you ever wanted to know about U.S. government, from the president to the Congress, the CIA, and the Department of Agriculture. See the "Explore the Internet" link, too.

NASA Historical Archives

URL: http://www.ksc.nasa.gov/history/
     history.html

A virtual history book of U.S. space flight, from unmanned satellites to mission-by-mission descriptions of the Space Shuttles. Incredible historical links to related sites.

Exploring Ancient World Cultures

URL: http://cedar.evansville.edu/~wcweb/wc101/

This site covers eight ancient world cultures: the Near East, India, Egypt, China, Greece, the Roman Empire, the Islamic World, and Medieval Europe. It even explains why we need to know about ancient cultures!

Life of the Prairie

URL: http://www.gps.com/life/life.htm

this site connects a couple strong subjects on prairie living: women homesteaders, Jessamine's diary from 1863 through 1877, a collection of pioneer photographs and more.

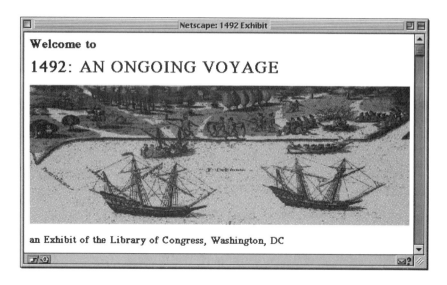

Ancient World Web

URL: http://atlantic.evsc.virginia.edu/julia/
    AncientWorld.html

Designed to search by subject or region, or the overall Meta Index, anything having to do with the ancient world.

The American Civil War Homepage

URL: http://funnelweb.utcc.utk.edu/~hoemann/
    cwarhp.html

This Web site gathers together in one place hypertext links to the most useful online electronic files about the American Civil War (1861-1865). It contains letters, a timeline, specifics on battles, and even some rosters of combatants!

1492: An Ongoing Voyage

URL: http://sunsite.unc.edu/expo/1492.exhibit/
    Intro.html

Contains a detailed history of the exploration of the "New World" by Christopher Columbus.

This exhibition examines the first sustained contacts between American people and European explorers, conquerors, and settlers from 1492 to 1600.

Mailing Lists

History of the U.S. Civil War

Join the discussion about the history of the Civil War via this active mailing list.

URL: emailto:H-CIVWAR@MSU.EDU

Type **subscribe H-CIVWAR** in the body of your message

History of Russia

Thousands of schools offer Russian History courses, and students have come to rely on this mailing list for help in conducting research on the subject.

URL: mailto:H-RUSSIA@MSU.EDU

Type **subscribe H-RUSSIA** in the body of your message

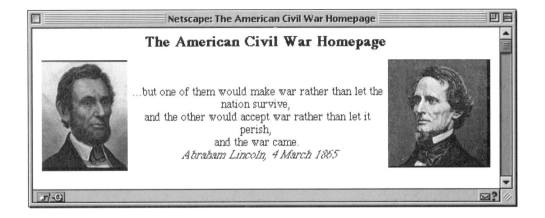

Usenet Newsgroups

URL: news:alt.history.american.ap-exam

URL: news:alt.living.history

URL: news:bit.listserv.history

URL: news:clari.living.history

URL: news:soc.history

URL: news:soc.history.war.misc

URL: news:soc.history.war.us-civil-war

URL: news:soc.history.war.us-revolution

URL: news:soc.history.war.vietnam

URL: news:soc.history.war.world-war-ii

URL: news:soc.history.what-if

Internet Stuff

Apple Computer

URL: http://www.apple.com

Apple computer home page complete with internet updates, downloadable software, and software updates, as well as special "youth central" section for kids and teens.

IBM Corporation

URL: http://www.ibm.com

Excellent information of interest to users of the
OS2 and Windows operating systems.

Internet Statistical Trends

URL: http://www.genmagic.com/internet/trends/

Complete abstracts and statistics of Internet
usage.

c\net online

URL: http://www.cnet.com

Online version of popular Internet/computer
cable TV show contains reviews of tons of software, Web sites, and in-depth features about
various facets of the Net as written by the creators of the TV show.

Hotwired

URL: http://www.hotwired.com

A quirky, hip source of up-to-date news and
views about computers and the Net.

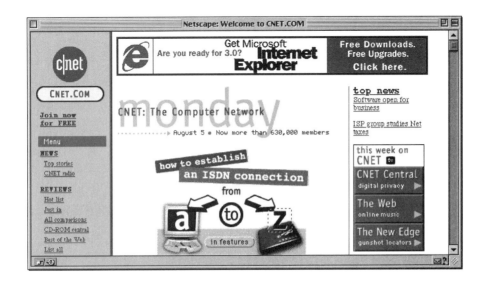

Ad Nauseam
URL: http://www.crl.com/~jnelson/nauseam/
E-zine containing Web commentary, full of reviews of the latest hardware, software, and more.

Online Access: Web Addition
URL: http://www.redflash.com/oaweb/
A comprehensive guide to Internet services.

E-mail Discussion Groups
URL: http://www.nova.edu/Inter-Links/
    listserv.html
A complete guide to email discussion groups as well as help in understanding how to subscribe and unsubscribe.

Internet Tour
URL: http://www.globalvillage.com/gcweb/tour.html
If you're new to the Net, be sure to take this tour of the Net to get your bearings.

A Beginners Guide to Effective Email

URL: http://www.webfoot.com/advice/
   email.top.html?Yahoo

This site contains a style guide for writing
effective email!

Home Page URLs

URL: http://www.valleynet.net/~kiradive/
Easily understood beginner's guide to creating
your own Web pages from the ground up, even
if you've never heard of HTML before!

Mailing Lists

IWatch Digest

IWatch Digest is your Internet Roadmap to new
and useful resources on the Net.
URL: mailto:LISTSERV@GARCIA.COM
Type **subscribe iwatch <Your Full Name>** in the
body of your message

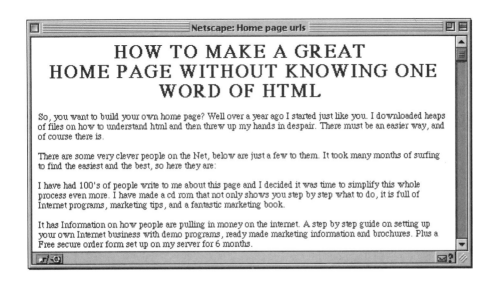

Netscape: Home page urls

HOW TO MAKE A GREAT
HOME PAGE WITHOUT KNOWING ONE
WORD OF HTML

So, you want to build your own home page? Well over a year ago I started just like you. I downloaded heaps of files on how to understand html and then threw up my hands in despair. There must be an easier way, and of course there is.

There are some very clever people on the Net, below are just a few of them. It took many months of surfing to find the easiest and the best, so here they are:

I have had 100's of people write to me about this page and I decided it was time to simplify this whole process even more. I have made a cd rom that not only shows you step by step what to do, it is full of Internet programs, marketing tips, and a fantastic marketing book.

It has Information on how people are pulling in money on the internet. A step by step guide on setting up your own Internet business with demo programs, ready made marketing information and brochures. Plus a Free secure order form set up on my server for 6 months.

Scout Report

The Scout Report is published weekly by Inter-NIC Information Services, and contains links to the latest and greatest Internet sites to come online!

URL: mailto:listserv@lists.internic.net

Type **subscribe scout-report <Your Full Name>** in the body of your message

URL: URL: http://rs.internic.net/scout/report

Usenet Newsgroups

URL: news:comp.internet.net-happenings

URL: news:alt.best.of.internet

URL: news:alt.culture.internet

URL: news:alt.folklore.internet

URL: news:alt.internet.guru

Math

Mental Math Exercises
URL: http://jjj.mega.net/BEATCALC/
Small homepage advertising a free e-mail
service which sends out regular tips and tricks
for doing math quickly without a calculator.

International Mathematical Olympiad
URL: http://camel.cecm.sfu.ca/IMO/IMO.html
Includes information about the competition, the
teams, and lists of different difficulty-level
problems used at the IMO in the last five years.

Mathematics & Problem Solving Task Centers
URL: http://www.srl.rmit.edu.au/mav/PSTC/
    index.html
Fun problems to solve for various age groups.
Features "Problem of the Month" and a number
of good links.

Internet Homework
Helper Sites

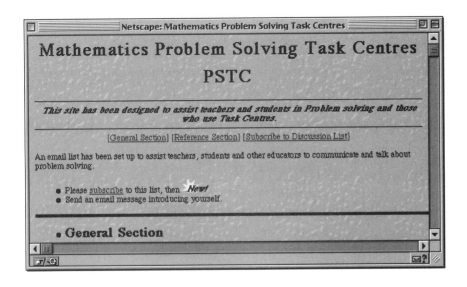

Netscape: Mathematics Problem Solving Task Centres

Mathematics Problem Solving Task Centres
PSTC

This site has been designed to assist teachers and students in Problem solving and those who use Task Centres.

[General Section] [Reference Section] [Subscribe to Discussion List]

An email list has been set up to assist teachers, students and other educators to communicate and talk about problem solving.

- Please subscribe to this list, then *New!*
- Send an email message introducing yourself.

- **General Section**

Appetizers & Lessons for Mathematics & Reason
URL: http://www.cam.org/%7Easelby/lesson.html
Contains a number of lessons in math and logic, menu laid out as an analogy to a café menu.

This is Mega-Mathematics!
URL: http://www.c3.lanl.gov/mega-math/
Colorful, mostly high-school level math site with activities, information, and games.

Frequently Asked Questions in Mathematics
URL: http://daisy.uwaterloo.ca/~alopez-o/
    math-faq/node1.html
Just what it says, a math FAQ, dealing mostly in algebra and post-algebra mathematics.

Library of Congress Vatican Exhibit, Mathematics History
URL: http://sunsite.unc.edu/expo/vatican.exhibit/
    exhibit/d-mathematics/Mathematics.html
A look at math in ancient Greece, some of the earliest Western mathematical theory.

The Prime Page: Index of Information on Prime Numbers

URL: http://www.utm.edu/research/primes/

Somewhat specific, as the name implies, this site will be more interesting to students who are interested in mathematical theory and trivia. problems for other high-school students.

Mathematical Quotation Server

URL: http://math.furman.edu/~mwoodard/
   mquot.html

A well organized collection of a wide range of quotations from famous figures dealing with mathematics.

The Math Jokes Homepage

URL: http://apk.net/~holtz/math/humor.txt

I'm embarrassed to admit how much I like this page, jokes about math as well as jokes told with a mathematical construction. (You have to see it to find out what that means.)

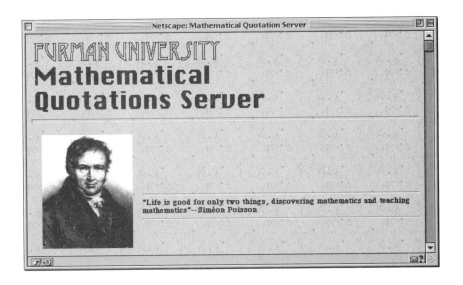

Online Calculator

URL: http://www.math.scarolina.edu/cgi-bin/
   sumcgi/calculator.pl

This Web site functions as a basic calculator, in case you don't have one handy!

MathNews

URL: http://www.undergrad.math.uwaterloo.ca/
   ~mathnews/index.html

Comprehensive college math newsletter with some learning disguised as fun.

Math Help Homebase 1995

URL: http://www.nashville.com/~Sandra.Smith/
   math.htm

Come here for help with all of your math homework!

Mailing Lists

Internet Amateur Mathematics Society

Discussions of math puzzle and problems of interest to junior high and high school students.

URL: mailto:iams-request@hh.sbay.org

Type **subscribe iams <Your Name>** in the body of your message

Usenet Newsgroups

URL: news:alt.math.undergrad

URL: news:can.schoolnet.math.sr

URL: news:geometry.pre-college

URL: news:sci.math

URL: news:sci.math.num-analysis

Reference Desk

Repositories of Primary Sources

URL: http://www.uidaho.edu/special-collections/
    Other.Repositories.html

A listing of over 800 websites located worldwide describing holdings of manuscripts, archives,

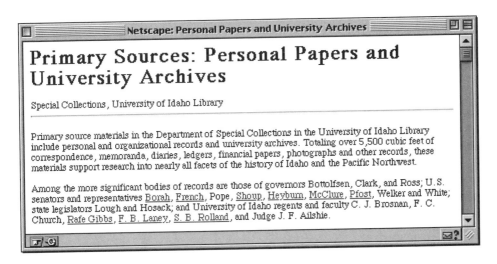

rare books, historical photographs, and other primary sources for the research scholar. All links have been tested for correctness and appropriateness.

Free Internet Encyclopedia

URL: http://www.cs.uh.edu/~clifton/
   encyclopedia.html

This is an encyclopedia composed of information available on the Internet. The MacroReference contains references to large areas of knowledge, FAQs where available, and pointers to relevant areas of the MicroReference. The MicroReference contains short bits of information and references to specific subjects, sometimes with instructions on finding the specific subject inside a general reference.

Roget's Thesaurus

URL: http://humanities.uchicago.edu/
   forms_unrest/ROGET.html

Webster's Dictionary
URL: http://c.gp.cs.cmu.edu:5103/prog/webster

Virtual Reference Desk
URL: http://infoshare1.princeton.edu:2003/
vlib/erefdesk/Eref3.html
Princeton University's reference library offers up
this concise listing to dozens of online dictionaries, encyclopedias, Internet resources, geographical resources, legal resources, and governmental
resources.

CNN Interactive
URL: http://www.cnn.com
All the news of the day, on-line and up-to-date,
from CNN News around the globe.

Time Magazine
URL: http://pathfinder.com
Site changes weekly; U.S. and international
issues of *Time* magazine as well a clickable map
to various Time Inc. links and an easy access to
congressional voting records by zip code.

Internet Homework
Helper Sites

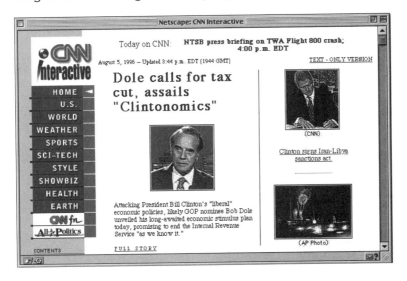

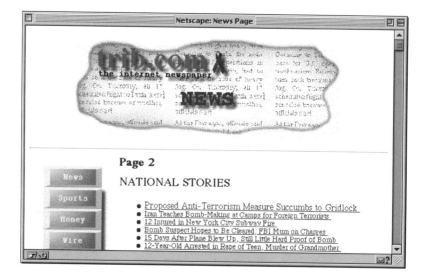

The Complete Works of William Shakespeare

URL: http://the-tech.mit.edu/Shakespeare/
works.html

Not just the works but a number of helpers for understanding them and further reference.

Wire Services

URL: http://www.trib.com/NEWS/

Links to the Reuter's and Associated Press wire services, the largest news services in the world.

Weather Page

URL: http://www.trib.com/WEATHER/

Up-to-date weather and earthquake info page for the whole world.

Utne Reader

URL: http://www.utne.com/reader/magazine.html

Left-leaning current-events magazine, reasonably advanced reading level and a large variety of subjects.

New York Times Fax

URL: http://nytimesfax.com

Free subscription to 8-page *New York Times* front-page stories and even daily crossword in down-loadable Acrobat format.

Britannica Online

URL: http://www.eb.com

The popular encyclopedia, now online. Access the site and sign up for a free 7-day trial!

Book Nook

URL: http://schoolnet2.carleton.ca/english/arts/
　　　lit/booknook/index.html

Book reviews written by and for K–12. Very cool. Students can submit as well.

Book Web

URL: http://charlotte.spiders.com/bookweb/

All kinds of information about books, all free, different categories, current publishing news.

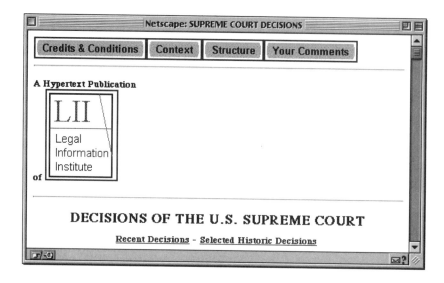

City.Net

URL: http://www.city.net

World travel guide and geography education site, information and links.

Supreme Court Decisions

URL: http://www.law.cornell.edu/supct/
supct.table.html

A complete listing of U.S. supreme court decisions, easy to access if you know the case you want to see or if you just want to browse.

The WWW Virtual Library

URL: http://www.w3.org/hypertext/DataSources/
bySubject/Overview.html

This is a very complete guide to many different subjects and sources of information available online.

Usenet Newsgroups

URL: news:alt.help.with.homework

URL: news:clari.news.briefs

URL: news:clari.world.briefs

Science

Virtual Frog Dissection

URL: http://george.lbl.gov/vfrog/

Complete illustrated process with activities.

Volcanoes Page

URL: http://www.geo.mtu.edu/volcanoes/

Educational information, basic stuff as well as
updates on currently active volcanoes around
the world.

United States Geological Service Home Page

URL: http://www.usgs.gov/

This site contains information about everything
that the USGS does as well as tons of basic
geology information.

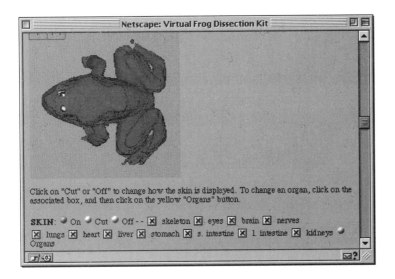

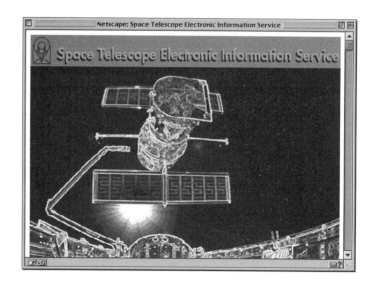

Netscape: Space Telescope Electronic Information Service

Earth and Universe
URL: http://www.eia.brad.ac.uk/btl/
An informative astronomy site with lots of audio and video.

Space Telescope Electronic Information Service
URL: http://www.stsci.edu
A guide to the operations of the Hubble Space Telescope with photos from space.

NASA Space Shuttle Web Archives
URL: http://shuttle.nasa.gov
Information about the history of the space shuttle program in general as well as more detailed stuff about recent and upcoming missions.

The Tree of Life Home Page
URL: http://phylogeny.arizona.edu/tree/phylogeny.html
Easy-to-use introduction to phylogenetic biology.

WebElements

URL: http://www.shef.ac.uk/chemistry/web-elements/

The complete Periodic Table of the Elements—now on the Web! Includes complete information about every element, and a history of how it was discovered or first created.

Saturn Ring Plane Crossings

URL: http://newproducts.jpl.nasa.gov/saturn/

A single site dedicated to an a rare positioning of the planet Saturn which allows for better study of that planet.

Butterfly World

URL: http://www.introweb.com/butterfly/

All about butterflies with a nice layout and great pictures.

History of Science, Technology & Medicine

URL: http://www.asap.unimelb.edu.au/hstm/
hstm_ove.htm

Biographies, subject histories, and links to museums and other science history sites.

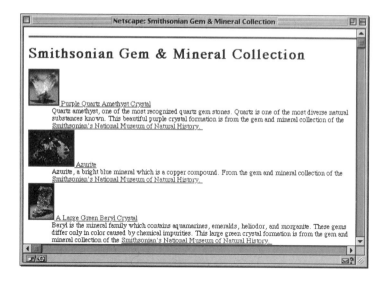

Smithsonian Gem & Mineral Collection

URL: http://galaxy.einet.net/images/gems/
gems-icons.html

A beautiful colorful look at rare stones and crystals.

The Virtual Prof.'s Physics Shop

URL: http://ici1.integratedconcepts.com/virtualprof/

Helpful information for college and advanced high-school physics students.

The Heart: A Virtual Exploration

URL: URL: http://sln.fi.edu/biosci/

An interactive and searchable site about the detailed inner workings of the human heart, complete with animations, sounds, on-line activities, and more. Be sure to check the links to the museum!

Mailing Lists

Earth Biosphere Discussions

This list is broadly interdisciplinary (whatever that means!), but the main focus is on ecology and the biosphere.

URL: mailto:LISTSERV@UBVM.CC.BUFFALO.EDU

Type **subscribe biosph-l <Your Full Name>** in the body of your message

Rocks & Fossils

List members share experiences and pointers to online information about rocks, minerals, fossils, paleontology, archeology, and prehistoric anthropology.

URL: mailto:majordomo@world.std.com

Type **subscribe rocks-and-fossils** in the body of your message

Internet Homework
Helper Sites

Women's Studies Resources

The women's studies database, created in September 1992, serves those people interested in the women's studies profession and in general women's issues. The database contains collections of <u>conference</u> announcements, <u>calls for papers</u>, and <u>employment</u> opportunities, as well as a <u>picture gallery</u>, and a significant number of <u>government documents</u>, and much more. If you have questions or comments, please contact the database coordinator at <u>megan@info.umd.edu</u>

● <u>Frequently Asked Questions</u>
    Frequently asked questions about the women's studies directory.
● <u>Search Women's Studies</u> (?)
    A keyword search of all files in the women's studies directory.

Usenet Newsgroups

URL: news:can.schoolnet.phys.sr

URL: news:sci.answers

URL: news:sci.astro.hubble

URL: news:sci.bio.ecology

URL: news:sci.chem

URL: news:sci.energy

URL: news:sci.geo.earthquakes

URL: news:sci.geo.meteorology

Social Studies and Humanities

Women's Studies Resources

URL: http://www.inform.umd.edu:8080/EdRes/
     Topic/WomensStudies

This is the most comprehensive guide to feminism and women's studies on the Web with links and its own articles/essays. Good for people who are curious or already know what they are looking for.

Project DIANA

URL: http://www.law.uc.edu/Diana/

A complete up-to-date guide to human-rights issues around the world.

The ANTHAP Home Page

URL: http://www.acs.oakland.edu/~dow/
anthap.html

Contains an excellent overview of anthropology, material ranges from a "What is Anthropology?" to in-depth theoretical papers.

Self Help and Psychology Magazine

URL: http://www.well.com/user/selfhelp/

An easy-to-read guide to psychology.

Guide to Philosophy

URL: http://www.und.ida.liu.se/~y92bjoch/
indexet.html

An introduction to the subject with biographies of well-known philosophers and links to related sites.

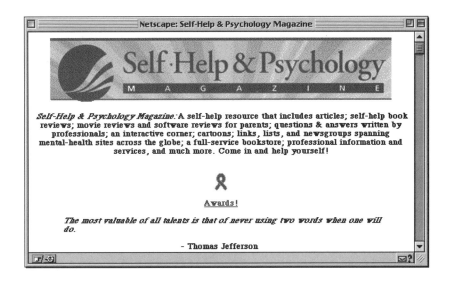

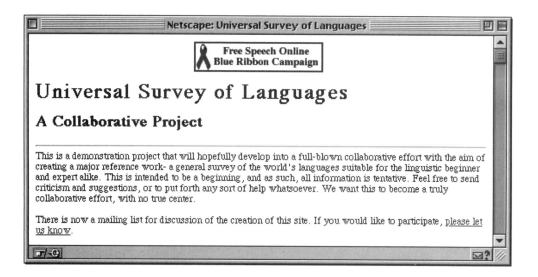

Everything Postmodern

URL: http://helios.augustana.edu:80/~gmb/
postmodern/

A good complement to the "Guide to Philosophy," this page is all one needs to start to understand modern philosophical theory. Somewhat advanced reading but not incomprehensible, it does contain good introductory stuff.

Universal Survey of Languages

URL: http://www.teleport.com/~napoleon/

A guide to languages around the world, both real and invented, with examples and not-too-complex text on linguistic theory, etc.

Ethnologue Database

URL: http://www-ala.doc.ic.ac.uk/~rap/
Ethnologue/

A completely statistical guide to possibly every language spoken around the would, USA section contains eye-opening statistics about Native American languages.

Archaeology Magazine

URL: http://www.he.net/~archaeol/index.html

Not the entire magazine , but enough information for anyone interested in current archaeology issues and links to other related pages.

The African-American Mosaic

URL: http://lcweb.loc.gov/exhibits/
    African.American/intro.html

An overview to the Library of Congress exhibit of the same name.

The Media History Project

URL: http://spot.colorado.edu/~rossk/history/
    histhome.html

A complete guide to the history of media and communications.

FedWorld

URL: http://www.fedworld.gov

A comprehensive guide to U.S. government information and online links to more than 150 federal agencies and departments.

U.S. Census Data

URL: http://www.census.gov

Complete data from the 1990 U.S. Census can be found here.

Mailing Lists

Bosnia Reports

Weekly news reports from Bosnia-Herzegovina, as well as occasional other postings.

URL: mailto:majordomo@world.std.com

Type **subscribe nebosnia-list** in the body of your message

Holocaust Research List

The Holocaust Research List is devoted to Holocaust research, and the refutation of those who deny the event.

URL: mailto:server@nizkor.almanac.bc.ca

Type **subscribe nizkor <Your Full Name>** in the body of your message

NativeNet

Provides information and discussion concerning issues relating to indigenous people around the world, and current threats to their cultures and habitats (e.g. rain forests).

URL: http://www.fdl.cc.mn.us/natnet/

Usenet Newsgroups

URL: news:soc.culture.native

URL: news:alt.culture.us.1970s

URL: news:alt.culture.china

URL: news:soc.culture.indian

URL: news:soc.culture.iraq

Study Break!

The Internet Movie Database

URL: http://www.msstate.edu/Movies/

An online guide to films from around the world with links to many other movie resources.

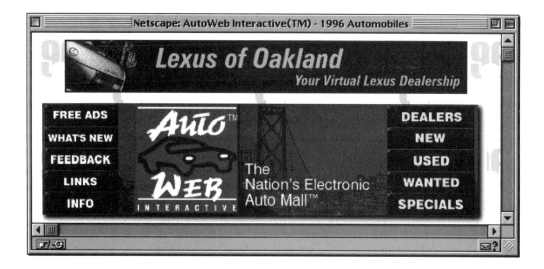

The Internet Pizza Server

URL: http://www.ecst.csuchico.edu/~pizza/

A quirky little site, but fun. Warning: Virtual pizzas do not help if you're really hungry!

Autoweb

URL: http://www.autoweb.com/autos/96/

If you're interested in new or used cars, this is the place to go, or at least the place to start.

The Dog WWW Homepage

URL: http://www.sdsmt.edu/other/dogs/dogs.html

Lots of fun for lovers of canines, information about many different breeds, getting a puppy, and links to other dog sites.

Feline Information Page

URL: http://www.best.com/~sirlou/cat.shtml

It would be unfair to include a dog page without a cat page!

Adventure Sports Online

URL: http://www.adventuresports.com

A guide to all kinds of outdoor sports.

NBA.com

URL: http://www.nba.com

The official home page of the National Basketball Association.

Team NFL

URL: http://www.nfl.com

The official home page of the National Football League.

Women's Sports Page

URL: http://fiat.gslis.utexas.edu/~lewisa/womsprt.html

Overlooked, underfunded, maginalized—women's sports receive some much-needed attention on this page.

Internet Homework
Helper Sites

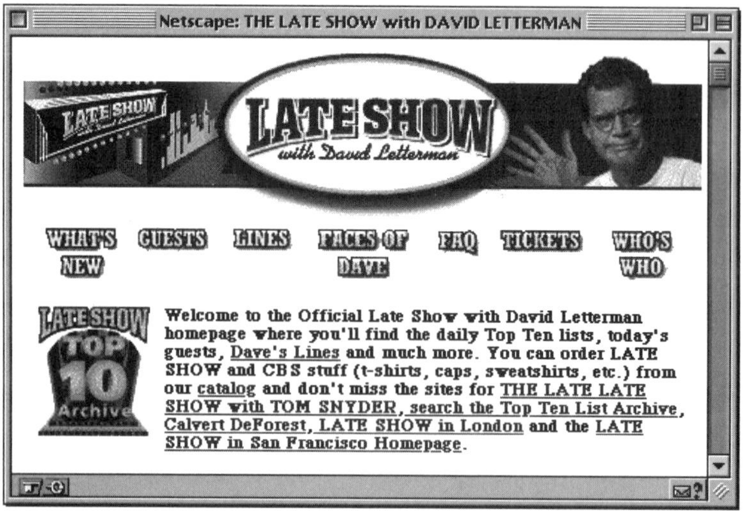

Scifi Channel: The Dominion

URL: http://www.scifi.com/

The science fiction fan has many resources on the web, and this is as good a starting place as any.

SonicNet

URL: http://www.sonicnet.com

A comprehensive guide to “alternative” music.

Jazz Online

URL: http://www.jazzonln.com

The jazz fan’s refuge on the web.

The Late Show With David Letterman

URL: http://www.cbs.com/lateshow/lateshow.html

The official “Late Show” home page.

The Ultimate Tolkien Page

URL: http://adria.fesb.hr/~rozga/Tolkien.html

Loads of stuff about one of the greatest story tellers of the English language.

Mailing Lists

Generation X

Discussion of Generation X (Generally defined as 17–28 year old people with no defined purpose in life) values and ideals.

URL: mailto:listserv@age.cuc.ab.ca

Type **subscribe <Your Email Address>** in the body of your message

Skate-Talk

Skateboarding related discussion for students of all ages!

URL: mailto:listserver@tumyeto.com

Type **subscribe skate-talk in** body of your message

URL: http://skateboard.com/skate/

Usenet Newsgroups

URL: news:alt.humor.best-of-usenet

URL: news:alt.humor.puns

URL: news:rec.humor

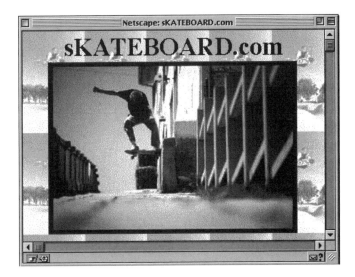

Search Engines & Directories

Saavy Search
Enter your keywords one time and search five engines simultaneously
URL:http://guaraldi.cs.colostate.edu:2000/form

ResearchIt!
Access to dozens of online research and reference tools
http://www.iTools.com/research-it/

Electric Library
Retrieve information from over 900 news and refernce sources
www.k12.elibrary.com/classroom

DejaNews
Research thousands of newsgroups in seconds
URL:http://www.dejanews

WebCrawler
URL: http://www.webcrawler.com

LISZT
Find just the right mailing list out of 55,000 that
can help you.
URL:http://www.liszt.com

Internet Public Library
Search the world's largest online "library"
URL:http://www.ipl.org

Yahoo
A terrific directory and a powerful search
engine.
URL: http://www.yahoo.com

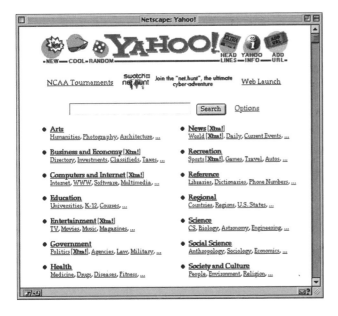

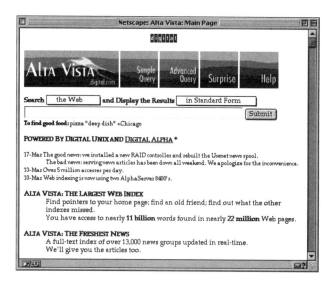

AltaVista
Many call it the fastest web search engine - over 50 million web pages
URL: http://altavista.digital.com

Excite
Excite offers many search engine options to customize your search
URL: http://www.excite.com

Inktomi
Unique set of customized search options
URL: http://www.inktomi.com

Magellan
URL: http://www.mckinley.com

Online basics for students

Whether you're a Net veteran or new
to the online world, you'll find tons of great info
in this appendix. In it, you'll learn:

* A brief history of the Internet.
* Netiquette rules.
* How to get online.
* How to use email, file transfer protocol (ftp),
gopher sites, Usenet newsgroups,
Internet Relay Chat, and the World Wide Web.

Where the Net came from, how to get hooked up, and how to use its navigation tools

The Internet is still very much evolving as a worldwide communications system, and millions of junior high and high school students around the world are logging on every month for the first time—both from home and at school.

Before you grab your digital surfboard and hang ten online, you'll need to learn the ropes. That's where this appendix comes in. Here you'll find everything you need to know to get up and running on the Internet. Even if you've only spent a few minutes in front of a computer at school or home, you'll find this information easy to read and understand. Your parents would also be interested in reading this appendix because it contains some important information on choosing an Internet connection for your household.

This appendix will take you through the history of the Internet, give you some basic information on how to get connected to it (which you'll want to show to your parents if you don't have access to the Internet just yet), and tell you how to use its navigation tools—email, the World Wide Web, gopher, file transfer (ftp), telnet, Usenet newsgroups, and Internet Relay Chat.

Keep in mind that there's a lot of information crammed into this section! You may want to read the rest of this book first, try out the key concepts on your computer, and then return here to get more detailed information.

The Internet's beginnings

You mean a bunch of computer geeks with bell bottoms made this thing?
Yes indeed! The Internet was created by a group of American techno-gurus in the late '60s, and their hard work has changed the planet. But everyday people like us weren't able to surf the Net until 1990 or so. That wasn't all that long ago!

When you look at the stats, it's plain to see that the Internet's use has exploded faster than the printed word, faster than recorded sound, and even faster than movies and television. The Internet is said to grow *10 percent per month* in terms of both the total number of users and computers connected to it. That means about four million new users and thousands of new computers connect to the Net every 30 days. Yikes!

Consider some of these startling Internet statistics:

• There are 30 million Internet users across the planet. (This number is widely debated, but hey, we've been on the Net long enough to know that it's got to be darn close!)

- 160 nations have full Internet access; only Africa is largely unconnected.
- Schools in more than 45 U.S. states are connected to the Internet in some fashion.
- About 10,000 primary, elementary, and secondary schools were estimated to be connected to the Net in the spring of 1996.

Unlike pogs and Power Rangers,™ the Internet is certainly *not* a fad. The Net will, no doubt, change dramatically between now and the turn of the century as things like rapid growth, increasing commercialism (businesses are connecting to the Net like crazy), and government intervention work their way into the system.

Many threats to its existence, including attempts at government regulation and near-overcrowding, are certain to develop. But an equal number of opportunities will emerge as well, and that's what should be important to you as you embark on your first Internet surfing sessions.

Journey into the virtual frontier

The Internet, the final frontier! The Net is:

- Creating new and exciting opportunities for learning in exciting, innovative ways.
- Making it possible for mere mortal school kids to collaborate with fellow students from all over the known universe in real time, face-to-face.

- Allowing students worldwide to create and imagine virtual worlds.
- Opening new, fresh frontiers of human interaction never before available—as we boldly go where we've never gone before! (Mr. Data, access the Internet and get me the latest Romulan status reports!)

Seriously though, the Internet is an incredible place, but you may be wondering, "Why all the hoopla?" Put simply, the Net makes it possible for you to access millions of sources of information. Millions of people share information on the Internet every day, too, and hundreds of thousands of organizations offer services and information for free online. Entirely new sources of information have appeared this month alone that cannot be found anywhere else. Up-and-coming Internauts, such as yourself, quickly discover how exhilarating it all can be during their first journeys into cyberspace.

Online Basics for Students

So, just what is the Internet?

It's hard to define the Internet in a few sentences. Technically, the "Net" refers to the interconnected, spiderweb-like system of millions of computers linked together around the world. To put it in more simple terms, when you connect to the Internet with a computer and a device called a modem you're instantly able to access all of the people and organizations who also connect their computers to the Net—anywhere in the world. Modems enable computers to communicate through phone and data lines, and that's how people from the far reaches of the world get linked together every time they sign on to the Net.

What does the Net look like?

Millions of computers spread out across the world are linked together. When you access the Internet with your computer, your PC becomes yet another link in this growing community. That means you have the ability to instantly access other computers in connected countries—no matter where they are in the world. The map below gives you an idea of how widely the Internet is used around the world.

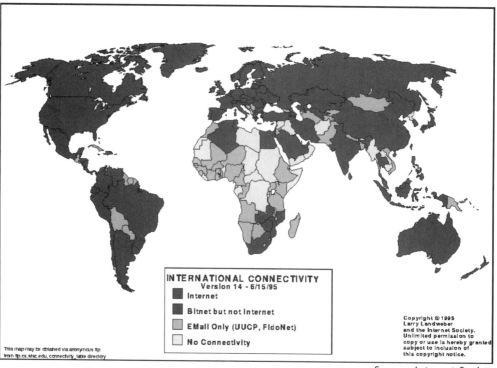

Source: Internet Society

How did the Internet start?

The Internet was started by the U.S. military's Advanced Research Projects Agency (ARPA) in the mid 1960s. At that time, the Net was designed to be a communications network for government researchers spread out across the nation. Universities and laboratories doing research-and-development projects for the government were granted access to the Internet, known then as the ARPANet. That way, researchers could stay in contact with each other and work together to complete projects. Since the Internet was funded mostly by government money, for almost three decades it was used exclusively by government, research, and higher education personnel. But that changed slowly in the 1980s as more and more people became aware of this incredible communications tool.

When the government cut much of its funding for the Internet in the early 1990s, policies controlling use of the Internet were relaxed, and it was opened up to commercial use. Suddenly it seemed everyone wanted to get online!

A new kind of business arose to meet this need—the *Internet Service Provider* (ISP). By the end of 1991, ISP businesses offered low-cost Internet access to individuals, businesses, and schools. At about the same time, commercial online services like America Online, Prodigy, and even CompuServe opened gateways to the Internet, which instantly gave nearly eight million people access to the Net!

Online Basics for Students

Internet Timeline

To fully understand how the Internet came into being, here's a detailed Internet Timeline as compiled by Robert Hobbes Zakon. You can get a copy of the latest timeline via email.

URL: mailto:info@classroom.net

On the first line of your message (called the body), type **send timeline** in all lowercase letters. After you send in this message, you'll get the entire timeline within two minutes, right to your emailbox. Wow! Welcome to the Internet!

1957

USSR launches Sputnik, the first satellite. In response, the United States forms the Advanced Research Projects Agency (ARPA) within the Department of Defense to establish a U.S. lead in science and technology.

1962

The first theoretical paper is published by a U.S. scientist dealing with the creation of a communications network using a revolutionary new computer networking technology. This leads to the first discussion of an *"Inter-net*working*"* of computers connecting the nation's research centers and colleges.

1969

ARPANet is commissioned by the Defense Department to begin research into computer networking. Later, the first portions of the experimental system go online at UCLA, the Stanford Research Institute, and the University of Utah.

1971

Twenty-three computers are now connected to the early Internet and can exchange information between each other in experimental ways.

1972

The first email program is created to send messages across the network and thus holds the title as the first official Internet communications tool.

1973

First international connections to the ARPANet go online in Norway and England.

1979

Usenet newsgroups are established between Duke and the University of North Carolina. (Today, these online message boards number more than 13,000 and cover topics from aardvarks to zoology.)

1982

Something called *transmission control protocol and Internet Protocol* (TCP/IP) is approved as the communication standard for ARPANet. This leads to the first definition of an "Internet" as a connected set of networks using the protocol, which remains in use today.

1983

Desktop computers become widely available to the public at somewhat affordable prices. (Back then, $1,000 bought you a "computer" running at a super-fast 8 MHz with a cassette tape drive! Most computers today run at 33–225 MHz.)

1984

The number of computers on ARPANet breaks 1,000.

1986

The National Science Foundation creates a new part of the ARPANet that allows for nongovernmental online traffic (NSFNet). Later that year, the first nongovernment citizens begin to hook up to the ARPANet.

1987

The number of computers on ARPANet breaks 10,000.

1988

The first K–12 schools in the United States connect to the system, mostly to utilize email.

1989

The number of computers on ARPANet breaks 100,000. First email relay begins between a commercial online service (CompuServe), and the ARPANet goes live.

1990

ARPANet ceases to exist. *The network is now officially referred to as the Internet.*

1992

The World Wide Web is created by a research facility (surprise, surprise) in Switzerland. The number of computers on the Internet breaks 1,000,000. First audio multicast (March) and video multicast (November).

1993

The White House comes online just after the National Information Infrastructure (NII) Act is passed.

Stephen King is the first author to publish a short story via the Internet (September).

Businesses and media start to take an interest in the Internet as the number of users climbs above 10 million.

The service traffic on the World Wide Web grows at a **300,000** percentage annual growth.

1994

The U.S. Senate and House of Representatives bring information servers online.

The first flower shop (Grant's Florist in the United States) begins taking orders via the Internet. Shopping malls, advertising, and mass marketing find their way online.

The total number of computers hooked to the Internet: 2,864,000. The number of countries reachable by email: 140. Total Internet users by the end of the year: 14 million.

1996-1997

YOU get connected to the Internet!

:-)

Online Basics for Students

The Internet community

According to recent estimates, more than 10,000 new Internet services and information sources come online each month. Earlier, I said that four million computers connect to the Net every month. That's true—but not all of the four million machines contain information you can access.

Think about that for a minute. There are ten thousand new things to see and do online every month. Man, how do you stay on top of it all!? Internet search tools, of course, which is what this book is all about!

Almost all of these resources—including documents, software, and databases—are free. That's because the Internet's atmosphere is one of sharing information and helping people around the world solve problems. Such problems include that algebra homework you have to turn in by next week! The philosophy of the Internet community is that information should be shared with anyone who's interested, and the battle cry of the Internet community is "Information wants to be free." Actually, that was the same battle cry of those techno-geeks who created the Internet in the '60s, but it's still heard on the Net today.

While this is beginning to change as more and more "pay-per-use" commercial services spring up on the Net, many new users still experience an almost giddy feeling of camaraderie when they become part of this enormous yet personal global community.

Rules of online behavior
You mean I have to follow rules online, too?

Sorry, but yes! With all the chaotic activity online, a sense of order is necessary on the Information Superhighway. Just as we have speed limits and rules of the road that govern our driving, so we must follow some basic rules of the Internet. Otherwise, chaos would reign, and the Internet wouldn't be such a positive force as it is. While there is no Internet police force, per se, to serve and to protect the inhabitants of the Net, communication within this global community is informally regulated by a code of conduct called Netiquette. (Get it? Etiquette with an N attached to the front of it.)

Be cool or be flamed

For the most part, the atmosphere on the Net is congenial and open, but you must realize the responsibility that comes along with the privilege of having access to this worldwide treasure trove of information. Users who violate Netiquette with thoughtless or inappropriate behavior often get *flamed* by angry users—they quickly receive dozens or even hundreds of nasty email messages that clog up their mailboxes as punishment.

The Ten Commandments of Computer Ethics

1. Thou shalt not use a computer to harm other people.
2. Thou shalt not interfere with other people's computer work.
3. Thou shalt not snoop around in other people's files.
4. Thou shalt not use a computer to steal.
5. Thou shalt not use a computer to bear false witness.
6. Thou shalt not use or copy software for which you have not paid.
7. Thou shalt not use other people's computer resources without authorization.
8. Thou shalt not appropriate other people's intellectual output.
9. Thou shalt think about the social consequences of the program you write.
10. Thou shalt use a computer in ways that show consideration and respect.

Source: Computer Ethics Institute

Also realize that what you access or send over the Net directly affects other computer networks and the people who run them. Many of the rules of the Net have to do with the amount and kind of data that's transferred across the Internet. The purpose of the Net is to share information, but our computers and networks can only handle so much. Violating netiquette often means sending more "junk" over the Net than is actually necessary. As a result, each of these networks has its own set of rules that users must follow. System operators could take away your "right" to access their resources for repeatedly violating their rules.

Most sites have things called Acceptable Use Policies that forbid putting unlawful materials on their systems (like pirated software); abusive language or behavior or *flame baiting* (for exam-

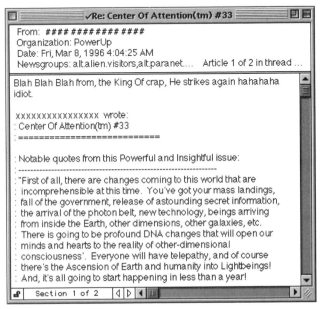

```
☐ ▧▧▧▧▧  √Re: Center Of Attention(tm) #33 ▧▧▧▧▧  ◲▤
From: #### ######### ####
Organization: PowerUp
Date: Fri, Mar 8, 1996 4:04:25 AM
Newsgroups: alt.alien.visitors,alt.paranet....   Article 1 of 2 in thread ...
─────────────────────────────────────────────────────
Blah Blah Blah from, the King Of crap, He strikes again hahahaha
idiot.

xxxxxxxxxxxxxxxx  wrote:
: Center Of Attention(tm) #33
: ===========================
:
: Notable quotes from this Powerful and Insightful issue:
: ----------------------------------------------------------------
:"First of all, there are changes coming to this world that are
: incomprehensible at this time. You've got your mass landings,
: fall of the government, release of astounding secret information,
: the arrival of the photon belt, new technology, beings arriving
: from inside the Earth, other dimensions, other galaxies, etc.
: There is going to be profound DNA changes that will open our
: minds and hearts to the reality of other-dimensional
: consciousness'. Everyone will have telepathy, and of course
: there's the Ascension of Earth and humanity into Lightbeings!
: And, it's all going to start happening in less than a year!
 ⌐|  Section 1 of 2   ◁▷ ◂▥▥       ▸
```

If someone doesn't agree with your post to a newsgroup, you may be publicly insulted. A message like this one can be considered flame bait.

ple, posting crude comments that bait others to fight back); and transmitting messages or programs designed to slow-down or incapacitate another's computer or sending network viruses.

Before using the services at any site, look for text documents that contain guidelines and policies. They're usually found in the main directories and are labeled something like AUP or policy.txt.

So, to sum up, here are the main rules of Netiquette:

- Treat other online users as you would like to be treated.

- Be forgiving of other users' mistakes online; you were once (or are) an Internet "newbie" (someone new to the Net), too!

- Know where you are in cyberspace; what may be allowed in one place online may be strictly *verboten* in another.

- Lurk before you leap; read what others have written before you post your comments.

- Share your knowledge with others; when you learn something new pass it along to someone else who can benefit.

- Respect other people's privacy; don't snoop around where you don't belong.

Is it easy to get on the Internet?

Yes! New user-friendly Internet browser software and lower online access costs make it easier and cheaper than ever before to surf the Internet. Most of the software (like the popular Netscape browser) is plug-and-play. That means you can plug them into your computer and start playing online within a matter of minutes. No matter how you connect to the Internet, you'll be able to use this great plug-and-play software to track down online information quickly!

The costs of hooking up

Going online doesn't have to be expensive. Your total online costs for *one year* most likely will be less than $300. If you already have a computer, all you'll need is:

Online Basics for Students

- A modem (about $100 for a fast 28.8 model), which connects your PC to a phone line.
- A telephone line (about $14 to $20 per month).
- A subscription to a commercial online service, such as America Online or Prodigy, or a direct Internet account with a local Internet Service Provider. Commercial services cost about $10 per month, with a $2 per hour usage charge. A local ISP will charge you between $15 and $30 per month for unlimited, direct Internet access.

If you do need to buy a computer, the price of an IBM-compatible Pentium machine, with a

75-megahertz processor and 540-megabyte hard disk drive (which is the minimal configuration) is less than $1,400, including a high-resolution color monitor and a modem. Complete Power Macintosh computer systems are now available in the $1,300 dollar price range as well and are used by millions of Internet surfers everyday.

How do I get connected to the Internet?

You can get connected to the Internet in two ways:

1. Via a commercial online service like America Online or Prodigy.
2. Direct Internet access through an Internet Service Provider (ISP).

Commercial Online Services

Commercial services are big companies that pay big bucks to have other companies (like *Time* magazine and *The New York Times*) put killer content on their service. That's why they charge you a pretty big fee to access their information every month.

The main commercial services are America Online (AOL) and Prodigy, but there are also other choices such as CompuServe, Microsoft Network, Pipeline, and Delphi. At a base level, each of the services lets you connect to the online communities they've created and send email to other members and over the Internet. Beyond these basic offerings, most of them also allow you to surf the Net (albeit pretty darn slowly) using their own Internet browser software.

As far as your homework goes, almost all the commercial services have extensive news and information that they receive from companies with whom they have agreements (magazines, newspapers, dictionary and encyclopedia companies, entertainment companies,and so forth). Most of the information from commercial services is included in their flat monthly fee, but some charge additional hourly costs. Some of the services even have homework helper services. In a moment, we'll go over the advantages and disadvantages of the commercial services.

If you decide you want to use a commercial service, contact them ASAP. They'll be glad to give you the free software you need to connect to them. Often they'll waive the first month's fee (usually about $10) and give you 10 or 15 hours of connect time for free for the first month to get you started.

However, we strongly recommend you consider getting connecting to the Internet through an Internet provider. If your parents already have an America Online or Prodigy account, though, go ahead and use it. You can get comfortable using the Net and then switch if you can persuade them.

Commercial Online Services Contact Info

Okay, so they don't provide high-speed access to the Internet. But commercial online services like America Online and Prodigy provide access to lots of great homework resources you can't find on the Internet. Most commercial services have customer support personnel who will help you if you have problems, too.

America Online
(800) 827-6364
Monthly fee: $9.95 (includes five hours free)
Hourly fee: $1.95
URL: http://www.aol.com

CompuServe
(800) 848-8199
Monthly fee: $8.95
Hourly fee: $3
URL: http://www.compuserve.com

EarthLink Network®
(800) 876-3151
Monthly fee: $19.95 (unlimited hours)
Hourly fee: none
URL: http://www.earthlink.net

Microsoft Network
Monthly Fee: $4.95 (includes three hours free)
Hourly fee: $2.50
URL: http://www.msn.com

NetCom

(800) 501-8649

Monthly fee: $19.95 (unlimited hours)

Hourly fee: none

URL: http://www.netcom.com

Prodigy

(800) PRODIGY

Monthly fee: $9.95 (includes five hours free usage) or $30 for 30 hours

Hourly fee: $1.95

URL: http://www.prodigy.com

Internet Service Providers

All Internet service providers (ISPs) connect you directly to the Internet. No fuss, no muss! There are no extra services like those provided by the commercial services, but, typically, there are no hourly charges either. The exact name of the direct, graphical Internet connection they'll hook you up with is sometimes called a direct SLIP/PPP Internet connection. Be sure to get this kind of graphical connection.

ISPs usually charge a flat monthly fee, regardless of how long you spend on the Internet. That means for between $15 and $30 a month, you can surf the Net to your heart's content and not rack up any hourly fees. This is certainly the most cost-effective way to go.

Keep in mind that most ISPs provide really fast connections to the Net. That means you can surf the Net more efficiently and find the information you need in much less time than if you did it through a commercial service. ISPs usually provide the software you'll need to do basic email and Internet browsing, too. Be sure to ask what software they provide. Think twice before signing up with an ISP that doesn't give you Internet access software or won't tell you how to get it once you join. In reality, a web browser like Netscape Navigator or Microsoft Internet Explorer are all you'll need to surf the Net!

Some ISP's are well-run companies, dedicated to providing you with the service you need. They ensure that you will always be able to connect and have support personnel who will help you. Other ISPs may provide little or no support, and you may get a busy signal when you try to connect, especially during their prime times. This is usually in the early evening just when you're trying to get down to doing your homework.

Before you choose an ISP, it's a good idea to talk to some of their current customers to find out what their experiences have been. If possible, ask a few of your online friends what company they use!

Finding Internet Service Providers (ISPs)

Since there isn't a central "Internet headquarters" to call for Internet service (I've always wondered why not), you'll need to arrange an Internet connection through an Internet provider on your own. Depending on where your parents work, they may be able to let you access the Internet through a connection they get for free from their employer. It couldn't hurt to ask!

You can keep long-distance charges low by locating an ISP in your local calling area or choosing one that offers low-cost, dial-up access through a local phone number. Call a few local computer stores to track down the phone numbers of local ISPs, or look in the Yellow Pages under either Internet or Computers. *(Remember that the CD-ROM in the back of the book contains EarthLink Network TotalAccess™ software, with Netscape Navigator.™ EarthLink is one of the largest national ISPs.)*

◄—————— ⮘BONUS!⮚

Online Basics for Students

National Internet Service Providers

If you can't find a local ISP, don't despair. Here is a list of companies that can provide connections to the Internet anywhere in the United States. Their fees vary, so give them a call and ask 'em for the best deal on a graphical (SLIP/PPP) Internet connection via a local phone number in your area.

By the way, those things with the letters "URL" in front of them are World Wide Web addresses. Don't worry about knowing how to use those until we get to the Web section.

Phone numbers and URLs of some National
Internet Service Providers

EarthLink Network®
(800) 395-8425
URL: http://www.earthlink.net

Free.org
(715) 743-1700
URL: http://www.ferryboard.com

Global Enterprise Services, Inc.
(800) 358-4437, extension 7325
URL: http://www.jvnc.net

HoloNet
(510) 704-0160
URL: http://www.holonet.net

IBM Global Network
(800) 775-5808
URL: http://www.ibm.com/globalnetwork/

NovaLink Interactive Networks
(800) 274-2814
URL: http://www.trey.com

NetCom
(800) 353-6600
URL: http://www.netcom.com

PSI (Performance Systems International)

(800) 82-PSI-82

URL: http://www.psi.com

Portal Information Network

(800) 433-6444

URL: http://www.portal.com

Lists of ISPs on the Net

If you're already on the Internet and would like to look up ISP listings for a friend, visit the Web sites below.

ISP Directory

URL: http://www.commerce.net/directories/
    products/isp

The LIST

URL: http://www.thelist.com

Network USA ISP Catalog

URL: http://www.netusa.net/ISP

Net Access Worldwide List

URL: http://www.best.be/iap

FreeNets & Community Networks

URL: http://herald.usask.ca/~scottp/free.html

Go! Online

URL: http://www.jumppoint.com

Internet service providers versus commercial online services

Or, David vs. Goliath!

A commercial service is like a very large shopping mall that includes a museum, library, post office, newsstands, amusement park, and a room full of phones you can use to chat with people.Commercial services are constantly adding new areas in order to compete with the other commercial services and with the Internet.

Unlike most malls, though, you have to pay a monthly fee to get in. After you're in, you may have to pay more to go into a few areas. Also, if you stay more than a few hours a month, then you may have to pay an extra fee for each additional hour. (Hey, this could get expensive!) With all of their drawbacks, though, there are several distinct advantages to commercial online services.

Commercial Services: Advantages

• Commercial services are inexpensive if all you want to do is send electronic mail and use a few free services. In this case, you pay only the basic monthly fee, which may be only about ten dollars a month, but you'll have to watch your connect time. You may want to just connect, quickly get your mail, and then get off line to read it at your leisure.

• Commercial services attempt to keep you safe from people or information that might offend you. Some have parental access controls, and they all have Acceptable Use Policies (AUPs) by which everyone must abide. (Refer to the section on Netiquette earlier in this chapter for more about this.) If someone violates an AUP, he or she can be removed from the service, which helps keep people's behavior somewhat civilized.

- Each commercial service provides sources of information that aren't generally available on the Internet or on the other commercial services. For example, you can access information from *Scientific American* magazine on America Online, but not on any of the other commercial services, and (unfortunately) not on the Internet.

- You can use email to correspond with anyone on the Internet.

Online Basics for Students

- With most commercial services, you can go out into the Internet, leaving the relative safety of the mall. Many of the commercial services limit your access to some parts of the Internet, though.

- Commercial services are typically well-organized, so you can find the information you want. They have support personnel to help you if you get lost and are usually quite responsive to your needs. (As better search aids are available on the Internet, this is becoming a less significant advantage for commercial services.)

If a commercial service is a mall, the Internet is the entire world! There are places you can't go (government files, commercial services if you aren't a member, some company and university files), but you have the freedom to go anywhere else you want. The Louvre, the Library of Congress, all the information in the world is at your fingertips—all via the Internet!

Below is a list of some of the disadvantages of commercial services when you compare them to ISPs.

Commercial Services: Disadvantages

• Commercial services can be expensive. An ISP, in comparison, typically charges around $20 a month for unlimited access. If you use a commercial service that charges $10 a month plus $2 an hour for time over 10 hours, you spend $20 if you connect for 20 hours a month (about five hours a week). If you connect for 80 hours (about 20 hours a week, which is possible if several family members each are doing research or homework, playing games, or surfing the Net), your monthly bill could be around $150.

• Because many commercial services are just starting to provide Internet access, their Internet browser (software for surfing the Net) may not be of the highest quality. That is changing (America Online recently announced that their five million users can use Netscape through the service to browse the Net), but currently some browsers are unable to show many of the Web pages on the World Wide Web.

- Some of the limitations that commercial services have may prevent you from seeing information you want. The Internet is international, so there is information on the Internet from all points of view. Some commercial services may limit your access to some of that information, which could be a problem if you are doing certain kinds of research. (AIDS research, especially.)

- Commercial services are slower than direct Internet access through an ISP. Many of the commercial services have grown so quickly that they do not have the equipment to provide quick service to millions of people. America Online is a perfect example of this nagging problem. (Here's the scenario: New artwork downloading, please hold! Please hold! Arghhh! It can make you crazy!) As the services mature, this may become less of a problem.

- The World Wide Web is almost always faster when you surf it through an ISP than through a commercial service. With a commercial service, you connect to them and then they connect you to the Internet. With an ISP, however, you are connected directly to the Internet.

Online Basics for Students

Internet navigational tools

No matter how you get on the Internet, you'll use these tools to get around!

There are really only six main Internet navigation tools you'll use to help you with your homework, and your Internet browser software can access them all—email, the World Wide Web, Usenet Newsgroups, gopher, file transfer (ftp), telnet, and Internet relay chat (IRC). Okay, so this stuff sounds a little technical. Not to worry! We'll take you through each tool and explain its uses to you so you'll have a better understanding of how to use it to complete your assignments.

We'll tell you about each Internet navigation tool as they're accessed through the Netscape Internet browser software. Then, on the same page, we'll show you how it looks to access the same information on the Net via America Online and Prodigy's built-in Internet browsers. Internet browsers have become the "Swiss Army knives" of the Internet in that they allow you to do everything from send and receive email to access Usenet newsgroups—oh yeah, and access the incredible World Wide Web!

Email

It only makes sense to start with the world's most popular Internet tool—email. Ask any Internet surfer, and chances are he or she got started by experimenting with electronic mail.

For lots of reasons, email is a valuable communication tool in and of itself.

• Your messages can be carefully composed in the comfort of your living room at home or at school, then delivered to an Internet user in less than 30 seconds—worldwide!

• Unlike postal or "snail mail," messages can be delivered at anytime, and aren't affected by weekends, holidays, or the post office.

• Incoming email messages can be immediately saved to a disk, printed, forwarded to others, or simply deleted. If only junk mail was this easy to handle!

• An email message—unlike a telephone call—is totally independent of time zones and free of long distance charges!

• Messages can be zapped out to dozens, even thousands of people at once.

• Millions of people who aren't even "on the Internet" can still send and receive email. Anybody with a commercial online account on America Online, Prodigy, or another commercial service can receive any of your email messages and send one to you. In fact, many public libraries, universities, and the U.S. Postal Service are experimenting with public email terminals that will allow even people who don't own computers to send and receive electronic messages.

As a learning tool, however, email is simply invaluable. It allows you to send messages to people in all corners of the globe. You can communicate or do projects with students and teachers in other nations, send questions to geologists in California, or ask the president about his foreign policy.

Thousands of students already use email to share school info, learn foreign languages, swap school newspapers, and learn about distant cities, cultures, and climates. So can you!

Sending a message using an email program is as simple as filling in some basic *header* information and writing the actual message.

1. The **To:** field, where you place the recipient's address; that is, the person who you want to send the message to.
2. The **From:** field, where you place your own address so the recipient can send you a message in return.
3. The **Subject:** line, which contains a brief description of the message.
4. The **Cc:** or *carbon copy* field, where you put another online users' email address to send them a copy.
5. The **Attach** feature is where you can indicate which files you want to send along with the message, if any. This feature allows you to piggy-back word processor files, graphics, sounds, etc. to your email.
6. Type your message here in the **message body**, then send it on its way!

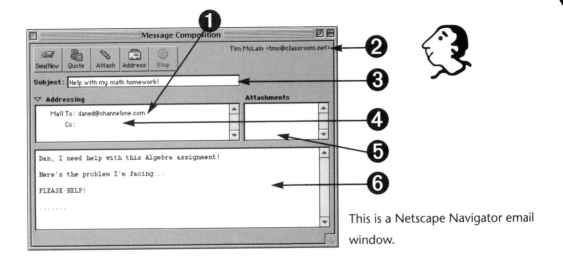

This is a Netscape Navigator email window.

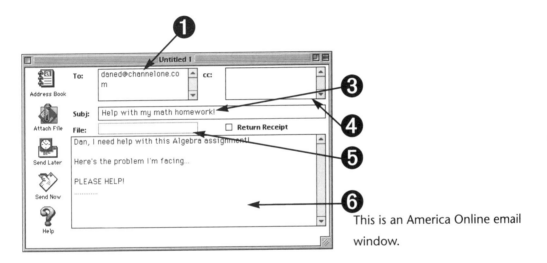

This is an America Online email window.

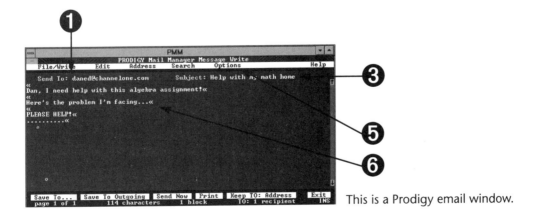

This is a Prodigy email window.

Here's what a basic email message looks like after you receive it.

This is an email from a college student sending out a survey about Irish history.

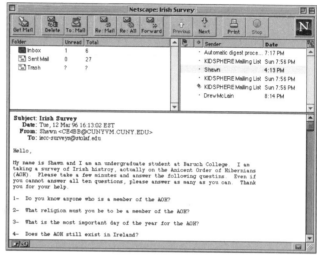

When you come across an email address of someone you want to send email to, enter it into your Internet browser in this fashion.

mailto:johndoe@internet.edu

By putting mailto: in front of the email address, your browser recognizes it as the email address of someone you want to send email to! A blank email message will appear and allow you to fill it out and send it on its way.

How do I get an email address?

When you sign up for an account with an Internet Service Provider or a commercial online service, you'll receive an email address. An example would be jstudent@supernet.com. Most people get to pick the first part or *username*, provided someone else on the service hasn't already chosen the same name. In this case, your username would be jstudent. The @ ("at") sign indicates that everything that follows provides information about the company through which you access the online world. This address depends on where you get your Internet service—jstudent apparently accesses the Net through a commercial (.com) Internet Service Provider called *supernet*.

What else can email do?

Although a majority of the messages transmitted around the Internet consist of text, email messages can actually take several forms. With today's email software, you can transmit graphics, sound, and even video to other schools and students. These multimedia files, when sent along with (or "piggy-backed" to) an email message, are known as *attachments*.

Now, the learning potential email provides becomes even more apparent. You could exchange computer images of your school building with another class in Australia. Art students could send computerized works back and forth for critiques. The uses of email are truly endless.

What can be attached to your email

You can attach both *text* and *binary* files to your email messages. Text files include anything you've created in a word processor and then saved in what's called plain ASCII text. (Some word processors call this "text only".) You can tell something is a text file by its .txt extension. The various kinds of binary files include sound and video clips, graphics of all kinds, HyperCard or HyperStudio stacks, and programs of any kind or size. In reality, anything you can store on your hard drive can be attached to an email message!

Keep in mind that a Macintosh program (for instance, a hard-drive utility) won't do a friend any good if she runs a Windows computer. And vice versa. She also won't be able to view a .gif (graphic) file you've sent her if she doesn't have a program that can open these kind of images. The bottom line is that the recipient of your attachments must have the same type of computer or program to be able to use any files you send.

How commercial online services handle attachments

America Online and Prodigy both allow you to send and receive email attachments, no matter whether your colleagues use a rival online service or have a direct Internet account. In some cases, however, users of other commercial services (such as GEnie) are very limited in terms of who they can send attachments to and receive them from. Here's a rundown of how the most popular online services handle email attachments.

America Online

AOL users have the most flexibility when it comes to attachments. Not only can they send and receive email attachments to each other directly through the service, they can also send attachments to their friends who have direct Internet accounts. AOL users can even receive attachments from their Internet friends. There is also no limit on the size of the attachments users send or receive.

When AOL users receive a file attachment via Internet mail, it is stored in their emailbox until they sign on. Once they sign on, they're able to retrieve the attachment. For example, if an Internet user sends an AOL member a file created in Microsoft Word, that member can download it immediately and then use Word to read it.

Prodigy

Just like America Online, Prodigy users can send and receive attachments to and from both other Prodigy members and Internet users. There is also no limit on the size of the file that can be sent or received.

But keep in mind . . .

All of these commercial services charge by the hour. Thus, if an Internet friend sends you a really large document, it could take as long as half an hour to download it if you're using a slow modem.

Online Basics
for Students

Mailing Lists

A mailing list is a kind of email-based message board. They're an excellent way to find and share information, all via email.

A mailing list is a public forum on a particular topic. Think of mailing lists as online group discussions which let you pose questions to experts in hundreds of fields. Think how that alone could help you with your homework!

Subscribers to mailing lists can contribute messages of their own or read articles submitted by other members. Subscribing to a mailing list means you instantly get each article as it's *posted.* (A posted message is sent to each subscriber to the mailing list.) There are more than 4,000 of these discussion lists on just about every topic imaginable.

There are two kinds of mailing lists—moderated and unmoderated. On a moderated list, the owner controls communication on the list. He or she reviews messages that are sent in before posting them to other members. Messages

Here's a message about a new mailing list you may want to sign up for, called WAYCOOL.

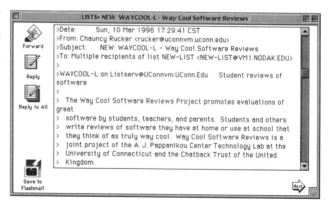

containing inappropriate, offensive, or irrele-
vant material are screened out. Unmoderated
lists publish almost anything submitted—the
good, the bad, and the ugly.

How do you know what's appropriate for a
particular list? As soon as you subscribe, most
mailing lists will send you guidelines for using
the list. Since these "Welcome to the mailing
list" messages usually contain info on how to
unsubscribe to the list, it's important to keep the
instructions for each list you subscribe to.

Subscribing to a list is as simple as sending an
email message to the list owner or their auto-
mated mailing-list processor. To subscribe to
most mailing lists, send an email message to the
list administrator's address, something like
listserv@computer.edu. In the message body, type
subscribe. Shortly afterwards you'll receive a
welcome message with instructions on how to
participate in the ongoing discussion.

Online Basics for Students

When you subscribe to a mailing list,
you'll get a welcome message like
this one in return. Be sure to save or
print this message for future reference. You never know when you'll
want to unsubscribe yourself from
the list.

How to track down lists of mailing lists

To obtain listings, use these online addresses.

Lists of lists via email

URL: mailto:listserv@vm.nodak.edu

Type get list of lists in the body of your message

URL: mailto:listserv@cunyvm.cuny.edu

Type list global/keyword in the body of your message. Be sure to replace the keyword with a subject area like *biology* or *history.* This automated system will return a list of mailing lists that fit the keyword you give it.

- Publicly Accessible Mailing Lists Archive
  URL: http://www.neosoft.com/internet/paml
- Tile.Net Index of discussion groups
  URL: http://www.csn.net/tile/listserv/
- Interest-Groups File
  URL: ftp://nisc.sri.com

Go to the *netinfo* subdirectory and retrieve the *interest-groups* file.

World Wide Web

It only makes sense to follow up our discussion of email, the world's most popular Internet tool, with the world's *second*-most-popular Internet tool—the World Wide Web. The Web is one of the newest, most exciting Internet tools.

Since 1993, the Web has grown incredibly. According to recent estimates, Web traffic increased by over 300,000 percent per year. That's because Net surfers can point-and-click their way through the Internet's text, graphics, sounds, and video that, thanks to the Web, can now all be viewed on the screen at the same time.

So actually, the Web can be seen as a CD ROM-like interface on Internet information. Cool! This combination of online media has sparked a paradigm shift on the Net, driving its exploding growth and making it easy for students world-wide to navigate its rich information resources.

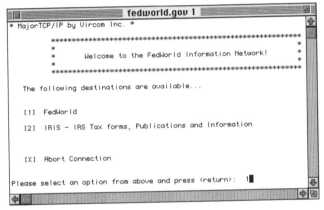

Before the World Wide Web, all Internet information was text-based. Users had to memorize cryptic commands to get around online and access information. Quite frankly, it looked pretty boring.

The Web now allows all of the text, graphics, sounds, and video clips housed on the Internet to be viewed at the same time, through a colorful, CD ROM-like interface that users navigate with a mouse.

Online Basics for Students

A

Netscape Navigator makes it easy to surf the Net

Hands down, the most popular online navigation tool used by students worldwide is the Netscape Internet browser. A recent survey of Internet use by K–12 schools with direct connections showed that Netscape is used by nearly 80 percent of students in Net-connected schools. In contrast, Mosaic, the first program to make the World Wide Web accessible to the masses in 1993, is now used by less than 5 percent of schools.

What accounts for Netscape's widespread popularity? Quite simply, it's the most powerful and easiest to use Internet navigator currently available. Internet newcomers learn how to use the software quickly and with little help. (In fact, comprehensive instructions are available with a click of the Handbook button available at the top of any Netscape window.)

Netscape 3.0 ups the ante

The first version of Netscape (1.0) took the Internet by storm in the fall of 1994. Recently, a new version of the software, Netscape 3.0, was released. It offers a host of improvements and new features, which makes it even easier to use and more powerful than any other browser in existence.

Netscape allows Internet users to access virtually every Internet site in existence, including: gopher sites, ftp sites, Usenet newsgroups, and World Wide Web sites.

Netscape 3.0 even allows you to send and receive email. Internet veterans will especially appreciate the straightforward way Netscape handles email attachments, which, until now, only the most robust email programs like Eudora could handle.

For students, this means that the only Internet navigation software you may ever need for your Internet-connected computer is Netscape 3.0. The only Internet sites Netscape cannot access directly are telnet sites. Netscape even looks and operates the same on Macintosh and Windows computers.

How to get your copy

Use any of the addresses listed below. Be sure to look for a subdirectory marked 3.0 or something similar. Versions for Macintosh, Windows 3.x, Windows 95, and UNIX computers are available.

Ftp to: ftp3.netscape.com

Ftp to: ftp4.netscape.com

Ftp to: ftp5.netscape.com

Ftp to: ftp6.netscape.com

Ftp to: ftp7.netscape.com

Ftp to: ftp8.netscape.com

URL: http://home.netscape.com/comprod/mirror/

Online Basics for Students

Microsoft Internet Explorer
Microsoft is racing to beat Netscape Navigator's lead in Web browser popularity and features. You can try it for yourself; download it for free, at:

URL: http://www.microsoft.com

What's on the Web?

The Web consists of millions of "pages" or screens of text and graphics that have built-in links to other pages on the Internet. To navigate the Web, you need *Internet browser software* that basically allows you to point-and-click your way through tons of information and multimedia materials. Netscape, as I said, is by far the most popular and powerful of these browsers. America Online and Prodigy offer their own Internet browsers as well, which look and act pretty much the same as Netscape, though they're far less powerful or speedy online.

Web pages, like other online sites and materials, have their own type of Internet address. Here's an example using NASA's Web address, and what that site looks like on the Internet.

This is NASA's Web page.
URL: http://www.nasa.gov

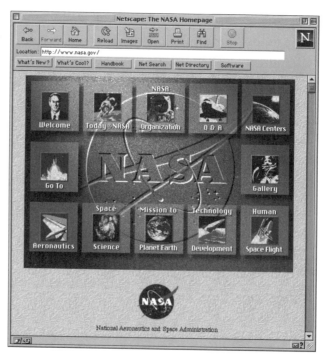

The http:// portion of NASA's address stands for something called *hypertext transmission protocol,* the method by which Web pages are sent (transmitted) over the Internet. All Web pages—which are really just files stored on an Internet computer's hard drive—have these letters in front of their online addresses. So whenever you see an article about the Internet and it contains some kind of online address starting with http:// you know it's a Web site!

The Web gets its name from the fact that Web pages and computers are interconnected in spiderweb-like fashion by *hypertext* and *hyperlinks.* These are simply words or pictures (icons) within a page that you can click your cursor on to instantly travel to some other Web document. It doesn't matter where on the Net the computer is located, and you don't have to *know* the address. Just point-and-click with your mouse, and your software does the rest.

What sort of stuff can you find on Web pages? Well, you might access the *home page* (that is, the main menu of a Web site) at Harvard University. It contains information about the university, a picture of the campus, a short video of the Harvard rowing team, a sound clip with a message from the president, and a virtual tour of the campus.

Educational resources abound on the Web, and many are perfect to use in completing your homework assignments. You can find complete, hyperlinked texts of classic novels; short video clips of physics projects; sound clips of Mozart; or detailed graphics of insects. With the Web you can pay a virtual visit to the White House or tour museums or even other nations. Students from hundreds of schools are learning how to create and mount their own Web pages, which is an easier task than many would imagine. These students command a global audience for their projects, school newspapers, and other work.

As you can imagine, the great thing about the Web is it's multimedia capabilities. Full-color graphics, video, and sound clips are just as easy to access as text. And, like other Internet tools, the Web is entirely searchable. Users can enter the address for—or link to—numerous locations to begin keyword searches. (Man, is this stuff awesome or what?)

A quick aside: How do Web browsers know where to find WWW resources? They work on the basis of *Uniform Resource Locators,* called *URLs* for short. The Web uses URLs to indicate the location of information on the Internet. In essence, it's possible to represent almost any file or computer on the internet using a URL.

The first portion of a URL represents the Internet navigational software used to access a piece of information. The middle portion is usually the address of the computer where the data or computer is located. The final portion may be the name of an individual file. A URL is always in the form of a single, unbroken line containing no spaces.

Thus, hyperlinks not only connect to other documents on the Web, but also allow you to use other Internet services. Internet browsers are also powerful ftp, gopher, and Usenet news-group navigators.

When you find something interesting or valu-able, you can save it to a disk or hard drive, print it, or make a *bookmark* or *hotlist* entry for the site. With millions of Web pages on the Internet, you'll need this feature to help you find your way back to the things you've accessed!

Where to find it

Here are some examples of URLs that can be accessed with a WWW browser.

This will connect you to the Electronic Frontier Foundation's Web server. The http:// prefix means this is a Web site.
http://www.eff.org

This will access the company's public hard drive via ftp and down-load (retrieve) the file "Incite95.txt" directly to your computer.
ftp://ftp.classroom.net/wentworth/Classroom-Connect/Incite95.txt

This will open a gopher, or menu-based Internet session.
gopher://wiretap.spies.com

This will open a telnet, or interactive session.
telnet://pac.carl.org

This will send an email message to this Internet user.
mailto:user@computer.edu

This will allow you to read and send posts to this Usenet newsgroup.
news:alt.hypertext

The Web and the Internet—aren't they the same thing?

It's important to recognize that the World Wide Web is *not* the Internet. The Web merely uses the Internet to transmit online information between computers. Of course, the Web wouldn't be possible without the Internet. But it's important that you don't get the two confused.

Where did the Web come from?

The Web's history can be traced back to 1992, when a team of researchers in Europe began developing a new way to share their research via the Internet. Sound familiar? The Internet itself began in a strikingly similar way!

The researchers had grown tired of sending their graphical data and research to each other in text-only form, and wanted a new way to graphically present their information online to each other in real-time.

Their work came to fruition with the release of Mosaic, a free program distributed across the Internet to anyone who wanted it. Mosaic allowed users to access the World Wide Web and the graphical documents stored on it. While the first documents were put on the Web by researchers, like many tools on the Internet, users began to find new uses for Web technology. Today there are millions of Web documents online, housed in computers at every corner of the globe!

What does the Web look like through the commercial services?

We used the NASA home page as our example earlier. Here's what the same site looks like through the America Online and Prodigy browsers.

This is the America Online web browser.

This is the Prodigy web browser.

Express yourself online

One cardinal rule for communicating to the public on the Internet is *keep it short*. That doesn't leave much room for sharing anything other than relevant information— "just the facts ma'am." So is the Net totally without personality, emotion, or humor? As if!

There are several ways to communicate your attitudes. Two primary means are *smileys* (also called emoticons) and *signature files,* used in any activities involving mass communication, including mailing list or newsgroup postings. Of course, if you're exchanging personal messages with a teacher from your high school, you can be as verbose as you wish (unless he or she is your English teacher).

Smileys or emoticons are made up of basic keyboard characters that, when viewed sideways, resemble facial expressions. Here are some of the more common ones and their meanings; with a little imagination, you could come up with dozens more.

:-)	A basic smile, used to express happiness or sarcasm
}:-)	A smile with a furrowed brow (as in, why am I really smiling here? I don't really mean it!?)
;-)	A flirtatious smile or "inside joke" expression
:-(	A frown
B-)	Wearing glasses

Signature files are like customized business cards you attach to newsgroup or mailing list posts and email messages. The only real rule about signature files is that they shouldn't be too long—four to six lines is the norm.

This is a nice, basic signature file.

To be sure you get a response to all of your calls for help with your homework assignment, a signature should contain your name and email address. Never put your home phone number in your signature file! For personal or "fun" uses, a signature file can contain your favorite quote or musical lyric, even a one-line poem.

Numerous abbreviations or acronyms are commonly used on the Internet, including:

CUL	See you later
FAQ	Frequently Asked Question
FYI	For your information
FYA	For your amusement
IMHO	In my humble opinion
IOW	In other words
OTOH	On the other hand
TIA	Thanks in advance

It's impossible to pick up on all of them right away—it's one trick experienced "Net Heads" use to detect Internet novices. It'll only take a little time on the Net, though, to gain command of this unique Cyberspace pseudo-language.

Online Basics for Students

Why are Web browsers sometimes called "killer" applications?

To many Internet users, their Web browser software has come to replace all other Internet navigational software—they've all been "killed" in favor of this all-in-one Internet browser program. Thanks to software like Netscape, there's no longer a need to load up separate and distinct programs for browsing the Internet. They can handle gopher, ftp, email, and more, all via a single program.

Information about the Web, on the Web!

Check out the following Internet sites to find out more about the Web.

Entering the World Wide Web: A Guide to Cyberspace
URL: http://www.hcc.hawaii.edu/guide/www.guide.html

Starting Points for Web Navigation
URL: http://www.ncsa.uiuc.edu/SDG/Software/Mosaic/

StartingPoints/NetworkStartingPoints.html
The World Wide Web's Original Home in Switzerland
URL: http://www.w3.org/hypertext/WWW/LineMode/Defaults/default.html

World Wide Web Frequently Asked Questions (FAQ) File
URL: http://sunsite.unc.edu/boutell/faq/www_faq.html

World Wide Web Starter Kit Online
URL: http://www.state.ut.us/webinfo/

Usenet Newsgroups

You can think of Usenet news, or newsgroups, as giant, worldwide bulletin boards. An estimated ten million people from around the globe can read and post to any of more than 13,000 newsgroups covering an incredible range of topics. Usenet news is available to Internet users, many computer bulletin board subscribers, and members of most commercial online services, including America Online and Prodigy.

Usenet Newsgroups follow the same principle as email and mailing lists, except that instead of receiving material in your mailbox all day long you access a complete online listing or bulletin board of posts made by other people. Newsgroups are circulated around the world to tens of thousands of computer sites known as news servers, which are paid for by your Internet Service Provider or commercial online service. Any individual user of those news servers can choose to read any article—what the message postings are called—from any one of the newsgroup topics, and then post a reply. That reply is then circulated to every other news server in the world. Not every site receives all postings, and some newsgroups are regional, circulating only throughout a particular geographic area.

It's easy to find the newsgroups you need because they are arranged in alphabetical order by words that describe their topics. For example, the newsgroup comp.systems.amiga is dedicated to Amiga computer systems, while comp.systems.mac refers to Apple Macintosh computers. There's a listing of Newsgroup classifications on page 342. Two Usenet newsgroups you'll want to check out first are alt.help.with.homework and alt.help.with.homework.compsci. By their names you can guess what goes on there!

The facing page shows what Newsgroups look like when using Netscape, America Online, and Prodigy. They're all showing a sample posting from the sci.astro.hubble newsgroup, a forum devoted to discussing what the Hubble Space Telescope does everyday. Today, it revealed the surface of Pluto for the first time!

What newsgroups are available to you depends on the "newsfeed" your Internet service provider carries—the concept is similar to cable television. Some groups are found on almost every news server; others are limited to regional areas.

As with mailing lists, most newsgroups post a general information document highlighting what's accepted and what's not. In some groups anything is acceptable—including calls for help with your homework—while others have stringent requirements. Newsgroups are where the majority of Net flaming occurs (which was mentioned in the Netiquette section earlier in the appendix.) Thus, it's best to monitor a newsgroup or "lurk" for a while to get a feel for its atmosphere and what sort of conduct is accepted.

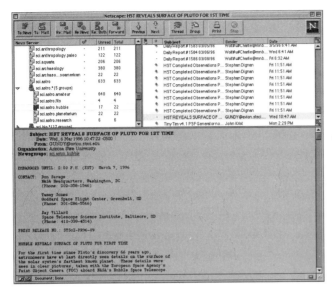

This is an example of Netscape News.

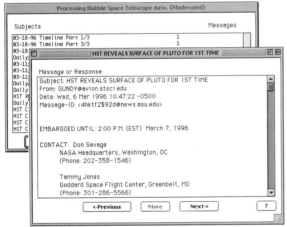

This is an example of America Online News.

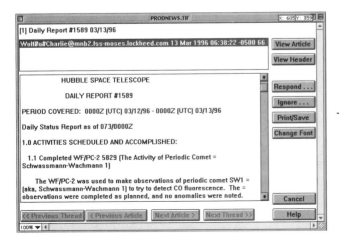

This is an example of Prodigy News.

Newsgroup classifications	
Type	**Description**
alt.	Alt groups are generally defined as alternatives to the mainstream groups listed below; they're easier to create, so the door is open to all sorts of off-the-wall, strange, or downright chaotic discussions.
comp.	These newsgroups are primarily about computers and are frequented by computer professionals and hobbyists.
k12.	These groups host discussions related to K–12 students, educators, and the subjects they teach and study.
sci.	Discussions in the sci. groups focus on the sciences, ranging from biology to nuclear physics.
misc.	Newsgroups classified as misc. are usually ones that don't fit into any other category.
soc.	These newsgroups deal with social science issues.
talk.	The talk. newsgroups usually feature lots of continuing debates or flame wars on a variety of topics.
news.	These newsgroups have to do with the Usenet news network itself.
rec.	This stands for recreational. An example is rec.hobby.sewing.

Gopher

Gopher makes it easy to find, access, and retrieve files from all over the Net. It allows you to "go for" online information contained in easy-to-read menus. Gopher sites were the first easy-to-navigate Internet information sources, thanks to their menu systems. Less than three years after gopher's invention, however, the Web came along and stole its thunder! That's why you don't see too many new gopher sites coming online these days.

When you come across a gopher address such as ericir.syr.edu for the Educational Resources Information Center, or ERIC, enter it into your Internet browser in this fashion:

gopher://ericir.syr.edu

When you put gopher:// in front of the gopher address, Netscape will recognize it as, well, a gopher site address and connects you with it right away.

You use your mouse to navigate the menus in gopher sites, which lead to text files, programs, or even pictures. When you find something interesting or valuable, you can save it to a disk or hard drive, print it, or make a *bookmark* for the site.

With tens of thousands of sites to visit on more than 6,000 gopher servers around the world, it's easy to get lost in cyberspace. When you're at a gopher site that you may want to return to, select the bookmark option and give the site a descriptive name. Then, you can just jump back to that site—without even knowing its Internet address—at any time. Sounds a lot like the hotlist or bookmark feature of Internet browsers, doesn't it?

Here's what the main screen of the popular gopher site, ERIC, looks like using Netscape, America Online, and Prodigy.

This is a gopher site on Netscape.

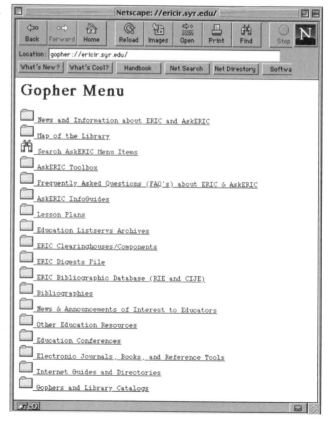

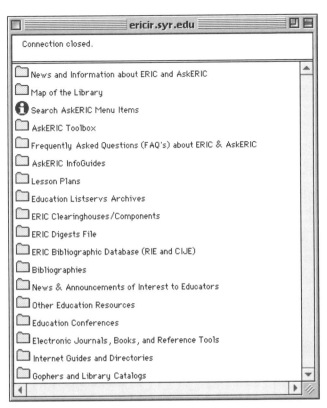

This is a gopher site on America Online.

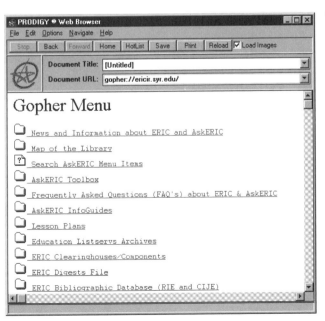

This is a gopher site on Prodigy

File Transfer Protocol

Another widely used Internet navigation tool is *file transfer protocol,* or ftp. This tool lets you transfer documents or files from Internet computers around the world directly to your desktop. Actually, ftp lets you access these computers'hard drives and then take files from them. (You'll feel like a hacker every time you access one of these sites!)

Thousands of Internet sites give you access via ftp so you can retrieve files without special passwords. These locations are known as *anonymous ftp sites.* This means that you can access them by using *anonymous* as your login name and your email address as your password.

The figures below and on the next page show what ftp looks like using Prodigy, AOL, and Netscape. Clicking on a file on this site will download (retrieve) it right to your hard drive!

Prodigy ftp: Clicking on a file on this site will download (retrieve) it right to your hard drive.

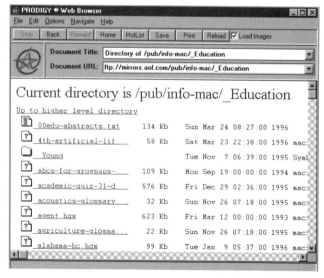

America Online ftp: Clicking on a file on this site will download (retrieve) it right to your hard drive!

Netscape ftp: Clicking on a file on this site will download (retrieve) it right to your hard drive!

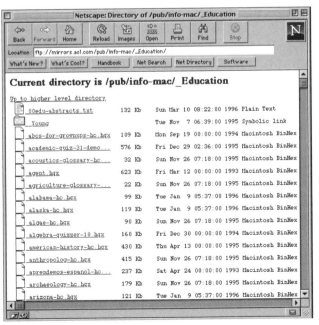

Since you're using an Internet browser to access ftp sites, you won't have to type any of this to get in. The program takes care of this for you without you even seeing it! America Online's public ftp site on the Net, for example, contains thousands of files—from programs to free documents! When you come across an ftp address (like AOL's), enter it into your Netscape browser in this fashion:

ftp://mirrors.aol.com

By putting ftp:// in front of the gopher address, your browser recognizes it as an ftp site address and connects you with it right away!

You must know a site's exact Internet address before you can ftp to it. Once you connect to a site, you'll see a directory of contents similar to File Manager in Windows or a Macintosh directory. Click on menu folders to navigate through the remote computer's contents and retrieve files to your own computer.

Here are four helpful hints for navigating ftp sites:

1. At many sites you'll see a directory called *pub* (for public) when you first log in. Most files made available to the Net community are usually stored in these *pub* directories. You'll want to click on that subdirectory to see what's there and to find your way to the file you want.

2. If the site is a large one, you'll often find a file called *index01.txt* or something similar. It's usually a good idea to download that file

first, since it will give you more information and descriptions of available files. This can save you lots of online search time!

3. Remember that not all files are the same. *Text files* contain only text and usually end in .txt or have the word *text* in the file name. Software programs, graphics, or picture files are called *binary files.* Netscape will handle both kinds of files seamlessly, but it's still important to know that these two types of files exist.

4. If you have trouble connecting to a site, it may be because the maximum number of permitted users are already logged in. Wait a few minutes and try again. Many sites are run by colleges, universities, businesses, or government organizations that use their computers for work. Be courteous and logon during off-hours—that is, after 6 P.M. in your time zone. Most sites provide specific guidelines for usage. Look for welcome messages or readme.txt files.

Telnet

Telnet brings a huge amount of computing power to your little PC! With telnet you can connect to a computer in the next room or halfway around the world—and use it as if you were sitting at its keyboard. Once you login to a telnet computer, you gain access to all of the programs, databases, and resources stored on that computer and made available to the public. For example, you could telnet to the U.S. Geographic Names Database computer and, following its simple instructions, select menus that'll lead you to information about geographic coordinates, state populations, elevation, and even zip codes.

Some telnet sites are restricted, (you can be sure you're not allowed into any Pentagon computer!), but thousands allow the public to login and see what's there. Each telnet site is different, with different menus, content, instructions, and navigating capabilities.

When you come across a telnet address (like FedWorld's below), enter it into your Netscape browser in this fashion:

telnet://fedworld.gov

By putting telnet:// in front of the telnet address, Netscape recognizes it as a telnet site address and connects you with it right away.

In order to use telnet via Netscape, you'll need to have a separate telnet program installed on your computer. Ask your Internet provider for the address of their nearest site containing telnet

Connect to the FedWorld telnet site, and you'll soon be presented with a main menu.

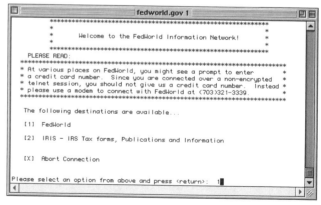

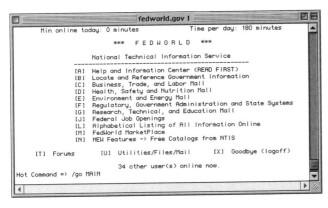

```
┌──────────────────── fedworld.gov 1 ──────────────────┐
│ Min online today: 0 minutes        Time per day: 180 minutes │
│                                                        │
│              ***  F E D W O R L D  ***                 │
│                                                        │
│          National Technical Information Service        │
│       ------------------------------------------       │
│       [A]  Help and Information Center (READ FIRST)    │
│       [B]  Locate and Reference Government Information  │
│       [C]  Business, Trade, and Labor Mall             │
│       [D]  Health, Safety and Nutrition Mall           │
│       [E]  Environment and Energy Mall                 │
│       [F]  Regulatory, Government Administration and State Systems │
│       [G]  Research, Technical, and Education Mall     │
│       [J]  Federal Job Openings                        │
│       [L]  Alphabetical Listing of All Information Online │
│       [M]  FedWorld MarketPlace                        │
│       [N]  NEW Features -> Free Catalogs from NTIS     │
│                                                        │
│   [T]  Forums      [U]  Utilities/Files/Mail    [X]  Goodbye (logoff) │
│                                                        │
│                  34 other user(s) online now.          │
│ Hot Command => /go MAIN                                │
└────────────────────────────────────────────────────────┘
```

From there you can navigate to the other menus, directories, and actual programs as if the FedWorld computer were your own.

software for your computer. At this time, America Online and Prodigy do not offer access to Telnet sites.

Telnet merely involves entering the address of the remote computer, assuming it allows public access. Of course, not all computers permit such access. Some telnet sites require pre-authorized accounts of special passwords, but most of the ones you'll want to visit will indicate the required password and login sequence on-screen when you first log on.

You'll probably start your Internet travels prepared with a list of sites to visit, so you'll already know the required passwords. As you build your own roster of favorite telnet sites, make sure to note the login and password requirements. For many sites open to the public, logging in as *Guest* and using *Guest* as the password will work.

It's also helpful to jot down the commands used for navigating a particular site. Telnet menus are text-based, so you must enter keys or numbers to get around—for example, Page Down to scroll down the screen, or Q or X to quit or exit. These commands are usually shown at the bottom of each screen, or you can type Help or ? to get a list.

Internet Relay Chat

There's a way to get information even faster than communicating via email or newsgroups. Internet relay chat (IRC) is the online world's version of citizen's band radio. By using IRC software, you can access individual IRC servers and engage in real-time "conversations" with users from around the world who are logged into the same server. (America Online and Prodigy offer online chat rooms as well, but you'll only find other members of each service hanging out there. You need to use IRC to talk to people from around the world!)

Using IRC you can:

• Communicate in real-time with experts and other students anywhere in the world.
• Conduct online conferences or seminars with other teachers and schools.
• Locate and query experts in a particular field.
• Develop interpersonal skills while learning about the Internet.

The specific kinds of projects you can conduct via IRC are limited only by your imagination. Chat in Spanish with a class in Portugal, and you'll get immediate feedback and insight into the language you just couldn't get from a textbook. Keep in touch with friends who have moved away, or see how a classmate in Germany is doing in her foreign exchange placement.

Conversations taking place on an Internet Relay Chat channel aren't influenced by a speaker's race, religion, sex, or physical abilities: You truly are what you type. And it's all very inexpensive, especially if you consider how much long distance charges would cost to achieve the same goals. IRC data are zapped around the world via Internet computer networks, so the only costs are Internet service provider costs—your normal hourly or monthly rate.

You can access IRC in one of two ways. If your provider carries IRC on its server, then you can use programs like Homer (Macintosh) or WINIRC (Windows) to get your computer logged on to a particular channel; otherwise, you'll have to telnet to a computer offering access to IRC. Either way, you have to know a few commands to get around and start talking to other Internauts. First, start your IRC program, either by typing IRC at the prompt (if you have a text-based Internet account) or clicking on the appropriate icon (if you have graphical access). If you have to telnet to a remote site, follow on-screen instructions for using that host's IRC application. IRC software automatically searches for the nearest available server. If the first one is too busy, it keeps looking until it can log you in to a less-crowded server. Then you'll want a list of channels, which serve to organize the thousands of people online at once (actually, almost 15,000 people can simultaneously use Internet relay chat).

Type /**LIST** to get a list of open channels. Once you find the channel you want, simply type /**JOIN** <**channel name**> to get in on the conversation. You'll probably get some type of message welcoming you to the group. From this point on, anything preceded with a forward slash is a command; anything typed *without* a slash becomes a public message. Now it's just a matter of learning some simple commands to customize your communications. For example, you can send a message to just one person on the channel, or block out messages from certain users. You can also start or open a new channel by typing /**JOIN** followed by a name that doesn't already exist on the list. Whoever opens a new channel becomes the *channel operator* (op, for short) by default. Ops have complete control over the channel they open: They can make it private, remove users, give other members "ops" rights, or entirely shut down the channel. See pages 356–358 for a comprehensive listing of IRC commands, servers, telnet sites, help files, and other resources.

IRC presents interesting possibilities for helping you do your homework, but there are many inappropriate chat areas. IRC channels are home to the same kinds of inappropriate material often found in unmoderated newsgroup postings. Except for the channel operator, there's really not much in place to control offensive behavior. You must be aware that using IRC requires you to take some responsibility, much as you're expected to show maturity and constraint when using the telephone.

Above all, never give out any information on the Net that you wouldn't give out to strangers on the street, including home phone numbers and addresses, computer or security alarm passwords, or other sensitive personal information. You really shouldn't give anyone your full name, either.

A sample IRC session

There are a few steps and commands you need to know before you connect to a server and start chatting. See pages 356 and 357 for a list of some basic IRC commands. Note that many of the commands can be accessed using the pull-down menus or clickable buttons on most new IRC software. Remember—anything you type while in a channel will appear on the screens of every other user unless you type a forward slash (/) first.

1. Start your IRC software and enter the name of a server, such as *poe.acc.virginia.edu*. See below for a list of servers. Soon a console or main window will appear.
2. Type **/list** or select "List" from a pulldown menu. Another new window called the listing window will appear.

3. Wait for all the channel names to download, then type **/join #<the channel's name>**. To join an IRC channel called Trekkies, you'd type **/join #Trekkies.**

4. If you type **/join #** followed by a channel name not already on the list, you will create your own channel and become the *channel operator* (see "Operator Commands" below).

5. Another window will open. Soon, lines of text will start scrolling down your screen. This is the actual discussion. Again, if you type a message and hit Enter *without* a slash first, the message will appear in the channel.

6. From any point in your IRC session you can return to the console window and type **/help** to get a list of all the commands.

Basic IRC Commands

Command	Definition
/help	Lists all commands
/list -min10	Lists channels with at least 10 users
/list -max10	Lists channels with no more than 10 users
/join #Sports	Join the Sports channel
/who #sports	Lists who's in Sports channel
/whois JDoe	Gives details about user JDoe
/msg JDoe	Send a private message to JDoe
/nick JDoe	Change your online nickname to JDoe
/ignore ObNox1	Ignores all messages from ObNox1
/query JDoe	Opens a private channel with JDoe, no matter what channel he or she is on at the time
/quit, /bye, or /exit	End the IRC session

IRC Operator Commands

Command	Definition
/kick JDoe	Kicks JDoe off the channel
/+i	Channel becomes invitation only
/+m	Channel is moderated—only operator can talk
/L20	Maximum users is 20
/o JDoe	Give JDoe operator rights

IRC Servers (use port 6677)

merlin.acf-lab.alaska.edu   organ.ctr.columbia.edu

nova.unix.portal.com   hobbes.catt.ncsu.edu

irc.colorado.edu   irc.csos.orst.edu

irc.math.ufl.edu   irc.duq.edu

irc.uiuc.edu   irc.bga.com

sluaxa.slu.edu   irc.math.byu.edu

irc-2.mit.edu   irc.virginia.edu

A final word

Some of the stuff we talked about in this appendix may seem a little difficult at first, but, with a little effort, you'll find that you can really get a lot out of the Internet. If you've basically used it only as a form of entertainment in the past, now is the time to reevaluate it as a tool that can actually help you become more successful in school. If you're completely new to the Net, take a deep breath and begin practicing some of the exercises and tips in this book. Ask your parents and teachers for help, and you'll be surfing like a pro in no time!

Look it up!

Here you'll find definitions
for all those strange words
and confusing acronyms scattered
throughout the book.

Acceptable Use Policy (AUP)	A legally binding document signed by online users which regulates the rules of Internet use at a school, business, or home.
Archie	A program that locates files that are freely available on anonymous ftp sites across the Internet. To use Archie, telnet to one of these sites and login as archie.
Boolean Searching	The process of adding the words **and, or, not**, two parenthesis, or an asterisk (*) between and around the keywords in your searches. These words and characters are known as Boolean operators.
Browser	See Web Browser
Bulletin Board Service (BBS)	A forum for users to browse and exchange information. BBSs are accessible by telephone via a personal computer and a modem. Many BBSs are small operations run by a single person that allow only several users to logon at the same time. Some are much larger and allow hundreds of users to login simultaneously to use the system. Huge, commercial examples are America Online and Prodigy.
Commercial online service	A company that, for a fee, allows computer users to dial in via modem to access its information and services, which now includes indirect access to the Internet. Examples are America Online and Prodigy.

Database A computer holding large amounts of information that can be searched by an Internet user. A storehouse of information on the Net.

Dialup Internet connection Lets a user dial into an Internet Service Provider using a modem and telephone line to access the Internet.

Directory A list of files or other directories on a computer at an Internet site.

Download/upload To download is to transfer (retrieve) a file from another computer to the user's computer. To upload is to send a file to another computer.

Email Allows users to send and receive messages to each other over the Internet and through commercial online services like America Online and Prodigy.

Emoticons Smileys and other character art used to express feelings in email communication.

Flame To send a harsh, critical email message to another user, usually someone who has violated the rules of netiquette by spamming.

Frequently Asked Questions (FAQ) FAQ files answer Frequently Asked Questions on thousands of Internet-related topics. They're freely available at many locations on the Net. This ftp site holds every FAQ on the Net. URL: ftp://rtfm.mit.edu/pub/usenet/news.answers/

Ftp site A publicly available Internet file transfer site. Ftp sites look like ftp://mirrors.aol.com/pub/ through an Internet browser.

Gopher A menu-based system for browsing Internet information. Gopher sites look like gopher://eri-cir.syr.edu through an Internet browser.

Graphical user interface Software designed to allow the user to execute commands by pointing and clicking on icons or text to navigate the Internet.

Hacker A computer user who illegally visits networked computers to look around or cause harm.

Home page The first Web page a user sees when visiting a World Wide Web site. Akin to a table of contents or main menu to a Web site.

Hotlist A personal list of favorite Web addresses, organized in a single list. All Web browsers allow users to create hotlists so users can return to their favorite Web sites. Also known as Bookmarks.

HTML (Hypertext Markup Language) Programming "language" of the World Wide Web. HTML turns a text document into a hyperlinked World Wide Web page.

Hyperlink A highlighted word or graphic in a Web document that, when clicked upon, takes the user to a related piece of information on the Internet.

Hypertext	The mechanism that allows Internet users to browse through information on the Web. Web pages are created with hypertext (HTML), and contain links to other Web documents or resources located on Internet computers.
Infobot (or mailbot)	An email address that automatically returns information requested by the user. Akin to a real world faxback service.
Internaut	Anyone who uses the Internet.
Internet	The global "network of networks" that connects more than four million computers in 160 countries. The Internet is the virtual "space" in which users send and receive email, login to remote computers (telnet), browse databases of information (gopher, World Wide Web), and send and receive programs (ftp) contained on these computers.
Internet account	Purchased through an Internet service provider, the account assigns a password and email address to an individual or group.
Internet browser	See **Web browser**
Internet Relay Chat (IRC)	Interactive, real-time discussions between Internauts using text messages. Users logon via telnet to designated Internet computers and join discussions already in progress, or create conversations of their own.

Internet server   A computer that stores data that can be accessed via the Internet.

Internet Service Provider (ISP)   Any organization that provides access to the Internet. Many ISPs also offer technical assistance to schools looking to become Internet information providers by placing their school's information online.

Internet site   A computer connected to the Internet containing information that can be accessed using an Internet navigation tool.

Keyword   A word or words that are used to search for various topics on the Internet's search engines. See also **Boolean operator.**

Knowbot   Software that searches Internet "white pages," lists of users at large institutions, to find a person's name and address.

Logon   To sign on to a computer system.

Mailing lists   There are more than 4,000 topic-oriented, email-based discussion groups that can be read and posted to. Internet users subscribe to the lists they want to read and receive messages via email.

Menu   A list of online information that leads to documents or other menus.

Modem   An electronic device that attaches to a computer and links that computer to the online world via a phone line. Modems are available for any computer, can be internal or external, and come in several speeds, known as the baud rate. The higher the baud rate, the faster the modem. The most popular modem was 14,000 baud, but 28,800 baud modems are now the standard. Most Internet service providers allow you to dial into their systems at 14,400 or even 28,800 baud.

Mosaic   The original Internet browser software available from the National Center for Supercomputing Applications (NCSA) for all computer platforms. Not as advanced or fast as the Netscape browser. URL: ftp://ftp.ncsa.uiuc.edu/Mosaic/

Netiquette   The rules of conduct for Internet users. Violating netiquette could result in flaming or removal from a mailing list. Some service providers will even cancel a user's Internet account, denying him or her access to the Net, if the violation is severe enough.

Net surfer   Someone who navigates the Internet in search of information.

Netscape   Available for Mac and Windows, Netscape is the most powerful, easy-to-use Internet browser. This software is already being used by thousands of schools worldwide and has become the de facto Web browser for millions of Internet users. URL: http://home.netscape.com/comprod/mirror/

Network A group of computers that are connected in some fashion. Most school networks are known as LANs, or Local Area Networks, because they are networks linking computers in one small area. The Internet could be referred to as a WAN, or a Wide Area Network, because it connects computers in more than one local area.

Online/Offline When you are logged onto a computer through your modem, you are said to be online. When you're using your computer but are not connected to a computer through your modem, you're said to be working offline.

Posts Email messages sent to a mailing list or Usenet newsgroup to be read by subscribers or others on the Internet.

Request for Comments (RFC) Online documents that have to do with technical standards for the Internet.

Search Engine An Internet site that allows keyword searching of online information. See Chapter 3 for reviews of many of the Net's current search engines.

Serial Line Internet Protocol (SLIP) or Point to Point Protocol (PPP, a Dial-up IP) Internet connections that allow a computer to connect to the Internet using a modem and telephone line. Users then navigate the Internet using software on their own computer. This is in contrast to using a Dialup Internet Connection, where users are forced to navigate the Net using text-based sets of menus.

Signature file Return address information such as name, phone number, and email address that users put at the bottom of email messages.

Telnet Allows users to access computers and their data at thousands of places around the world, most often at libraries, universities, and government agencies.

Text-based Internet account The user must use UNIX commands to navigate the Internet.

UNIX A computer operating system commonly used on the Internet.

URL (Universal Resource Locator) The address and method used to locate a specific resource on the Internet. A URL beginning with http:// indicates that the site is a WWW resource and that a Web browser will access it.

Usenet newsgroups More than 13,000 topic-oriented message bases that can be read and posted to. Also called newsgroups.

Veronica Veronica is a computer program that helps Internauts find what they're looking for on gopher servers around the world. Instead of looking through menus, Veronica allows users to enter keywords to locate the gopher site that holds the information they want.

Virtual A computer-generated environment.

Web Browser (also known as Internet Browser or Browser) Software that allows computer users to access and navigate the contents of the Internet. Commercial online services like America Online and Prodigy have their own graphical Internet browsers. Users who access the Internet directly primarily use the Netscape Navigator and Microsoft Internet Explorer browsers to get around online.

Web Page A single Internet document containing information that can be accessed over the World Wide Web.

World Wide Web (WWW or Web) A revolutionary Internet browsing system that allows for point-and-click navigation of the Internet. The WWW is a spiderweb-like interconnection of millions of pieces of information located on computers around the world. Web documents use hypertext, which incorporates text and graphical "links" to other documents and files on Internet-connected computers.

Index

FIND IT HERE!

Look here
for a specific topic or word
you want
to find out more about.

Now for . . .

Macintosh
PowerMac
& Windows!

Does your family have the software they need for our mediacentric world?

HyperStudio

As communicating ideas in visual form becomes increasingly important in this Age of CD-ROM and Internet, simple tools to create your own interactive presentations are a necessity! HyperStudio lets you successfully combine information, graphics, movies, and sound into exciting projects. Your family can now use one program, HyperStudio, to communicate in this new style of expression! From interactive reports for history, writing, and science, to executive-level business preparations, HyperStudio is being used by more families than all the other multimedia authoring programs combined!

Beyond bringing together text, sound, graphics, and video, only HyperStudio provides its own innovative approach to multimedia communication: Mac-Windows project compatibility, the ability to create & edit QuickTime™ movies, access data on the Internet, built-in capture of images with AV Macs or the QuickTake™ camera, and the widest range of file-type compatibility for graphics and sounds.

There isn't a typical age group or user for HyperStudio any more than there is for a pencil! Regardless of one's learning style, mode of expression, or grade level, HyperStudio makes it possible for non-technical users to create interactive multimedia projects with the look and feel of CDs.

With HyperStudio YOU can:

- Create your own CD-style projects!
- Add multimedia elements in 60 seconds or less!
- Move Projects between Windows & Mac!
- Capture elements from the Internet, laser disc, CD-ROM, & Photo-CDs!
- Be successful from the very first time you use it!

FREE
Preview CD!

Call us today
and mention
Classroom Connect!

For your FREE HyperStudio CD, call:
1-800-HYPERSTUDIO
1-800-497-3778

Roger Wagner
PUBLISHING, INC.
™

HyperStudio is available from these dealers:
MacZone 1-800-248-000
MacWarehouse 1-800-255-6227

"TO SURF AND PROTECT"

Internet Access Management Utility

CyberPatrol lets parents and teachers control children's access to the Internet, providing:
- Automatic blocking of access to specified Internet sites
- CyberNOT block list—researched Internet sites that parents may find questionable
- First and only Internet filter that works with all browsers, including 32-bit browsers
- Built-in support for the SafeSurf system
- Restriction access to certain times of day
- Limit total time spent on-line
- Control local applications use

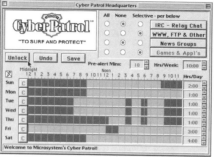

CyberPatrol's main administration screen lets parents, teachers, and others control children's use of a computer by hours of the day and by specific Internet locations.

CyberPatrol is an Internet access management utility that parents and teachers can use to control children's access to the Internet.

It allows those responsible for children to restrict access to certain times of day, limit the total time spent online in a day and block access to Internet sites deemed inappropriate. CyberPatrol also can be used to control access to the major online services and to local applications—such as games and personal financial managers.

CyberPatrol comes loaded with Microsystems Software's "CyberNOT Block List," a listing of researched Internet sites containing material that parents may find questionable. The list is divided into categories, and access can be managed down to the file directory or page level. Therefore, appropriate material at an Internet address need not be blocked simply because there is restricted material elsewhere at that address. Parents may select all or any of the categories to be blocked by content, time of day, or specific Internet site.

Parental Control

CyberPatrol allows parents to manage computer use in their own household. Cumulative duration of Internet (or applications) use can be captured and reported. In addition to providing a useful overview of computer usage, these reports can also be used to verify online provider and telephone bills.

CyberPatrol is available for Windows and Macintosh systems. CyberPatrol 3.0 for Windows provides control of children's access through Internet Applications and

web browsers, including America Online, America Online's MegaWeb Internet access service, CompuServe/Spry Mosaic, Netcruiser, Netscape, and Mosaic 2.0. CyberPatrol 3.0 also blocks sites accessed via a proxy server.

CyberPatrol 1.0 for Macintosh can block direct Internet access. This core functionality is required by the education market. Currently, the Macintosh product will intercept calls to the Macintosh TCP driver, and will block access from the popular Mac browsers and Internet applications such as Netscape, Mosaic and NewsWatcher.

CyberPatrol loads during start-up and runs in the background, controlling access to all associated applications. CyberPatrol is accessed via password, and offers two levels of parental password control. Several safeguards include controls which prevent children from disabling CyberPatrol or simply renaming blocked applications.

CyberNOT Block List

The sites on the CyberNOT Block List are reviewed by a team of professionals at Microsystems software, including parents and teachers. They use a set of criteria that categorizes Internet sites and resources according to the level of possibly objectionable content. The categories include: Violence/Profanity; Partial Nudity; Nudity; Sexual Acts/Text; Gross Depictions/Text; Racist/Ethnic; Satanic/Cult; Militant/Extremist; Drugs/Drug Culture; Alcohol, Beer, and Wine; Gambling; and Questionable/Illegal.

Parents can select the content categories they wish to block and allow access to any site on the CyberNOT List they deem appropriate. They can also deny access to sites not included on the CyberNOT List and control or block access to major online services as well as applications (games, for example).

The CyberNOT List is updated weekly and can be downloaded from the Internet using CyberPatrol.

How to Purchase

The $49 list price for CyberPatrol includes a six-month subscription to the CyberNOT Block List. **But by special arrangement with *Classroom Connect*, you can purchase CyberPatrol for only $29.95,** which includes a 12-month subscription to the CyberNOT Block List.

You can download a FREE 14-day working demo from *Classroom Connect:* **www.classroom.net/cyberpatrol.** Call Classroom Connect at (800) 638-1639.

Quantity discounts available.

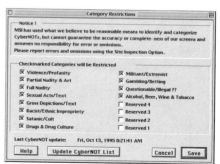

The way you do research.™
http://www.k12.elibrary.com/classroom

TM

- ◆ A complete online research library.
- ◆ Deep and broad consumer reference product.
- ◆ The best way for students and families to do research.
- ◆ Content is as safe as local public library.
- ◆ Accessible via the Internet.
- ◆ Updated daily via satellite.

Using The Electric Library, a student can pose a question in plain English and launch a comprehensive and simultaneous search through more than 150 full-text newspapers, over 900 full-text magazines, two international newswires, two thousand classic books, hundreds of maps, thousands of photographs as well as major works of literature and art.

In a matter of seconds, query results are returned to a user ranked in relevancy order, displaying reference data, file size, and grade reading level. With this easy-to-use product a researcher need only click on the document or image of interest and it is automatically downloaded. The materials can also be copied and saved into a word processing document with bibliographic information automatically transferred.

Included in The Electric Library database are materials from world renowned publishers such as Reuters, Simon and Schuster, Gannett, World Almanac, Times Mirror, and Compton's New Media. The Electric Library also incorporates a host of local, ethnic, and special interest publications.

All retrieved information can be downloaded and saved or transferred to a word processor in real time, and used for educational purposes. This includes both the text and images from The Electric Library's databases.

PARTIAL LIST OF ELECTRIC LIBRARY CONTENT

Magazines/Journals	Books/Reference Works	Newspapers/Newswires
Art Journal	3,000 Great Works of Literature	Baseball Weekly
The Economist	Monarch Notes	Jerusalem Post
Editor & Publisher	The Complete Works of	La Prensa
Inc.	Shakespeare	Los Angeles Times
Lancet	The World's Best Poetry	Magill's Survey of Cinema
Maclean's	Compton's Encyclopedia	Newsbytes News Service
Mother Jones	King James Bible	News India
National Review	Thematic Dictionary	New York Newsday
New Republic	Webster's Dictionary	Reuters
World Press Review	World Fact Book	USA Today

PRICING
Individual User: $9.95 per month
School Site License: $2,000 per year

FREE 30-DAY TRIAL!
Offer made in special arrangement with Classroom Connect

(800) 638-1639

*in*fo*nautics*

Infonautics Corporation
900 W. Valley Rd., Suite 1000
Wayne, PA 19087-1830
Voice: (800) 304-3542
Fax: (610) 971-8859
Email: k12@infonautics.com

Monstrous Media Kit
(formerly Kid's Studio)
The award-winning multimedia creativity tool for kids ages seven to seventeen.

Produce, direct and star in your own multimedia productions. CyberPuppy's Monstrous Media Kit is an all-in-one multimedia application that offers children sophisticated tools for creating their own presentations. Kids can compose brilliant pages combining photo-realistic images with paint, text, and sound, and show off their work as full-screen slide shows, movies or printed stories. Features a "Treasure Chest" of images, Cookie-Cutter Technology, QuickTime™ or Video for Windows, and Kodak PhotoCDs.

Special pricing for the CD-ROM version:
- Home or School Edition — for one user $22
- Lab Pack with 5 CDs — for up to five users $65
- Classroom Pack with 5 CDs — for up to 30 users $185
- Network Pack with 5 CDs — for up to 50 users $325
- Site License with 5 CDs — unlimited use in one school building $400

For more information, contact:
CyberPuppy Software
2248 Park Boulevard
 Palo ALto, CA 94306
Telephone: (415) 326-2449
Fax: (415) 326-6301
URL: http://www.cyberpuppy.com

Minimum Requirements, Macintosh: Mac LC or higher; CD-ROM drive; System 7; 5 MB RAM, 5MB free hard disk space;12-inch monitor with 256 colors/grays.

Minimum Requirements, Windows: 486SX; CD-ROM drive; Windows 3.1; 8MB RAM, 5 MB free hard disk space; VGA+ (640 x 480 at 256 colors)

Classroom Connect Newsletter
Send for your <u>FREE</u> <u>trial</u> <u>issue</u> today!

Walk through the crater of a live volcano, visit the White House, watch astronauts explore the universe—that's the kind of student-involving activities the Internet brings to your classroom. Each issue of the *Classroom Connect* newsletter is packed with articles you can read in minutes and immediately put to use. You'll find directions for finding free lesson plans, educational games, Internet trips, international classroom-to-classroom projects—and a host of other educational resources—all just a few keystrokes away. Whether you're an Internet veteran or a first-time user, you'll appreciate *Classroom Connect's* clear, easy-to-understand, jargon-free language.
Educator's special: $39 per year (regular $47)
Published 9 times yearly. Newsletter format. 20 pages per issue. Illustrated.

CLASSROOM CONNECT
Internet made easy in the classroom™
1866 Colonial Village Lane, Lancaster, PA 17601
Phone: **(800) 638-1639**   Fax: **(717) 393-5752**
Email: **connect@classroom.net**
URL: **http://www.classroom.net**

CLASSROOM CONNECT
FREE Trial Issue Offer

☐ Send my FREE trial issue of *Classroom Connect*. If I choose to subscribe, I'll honor your invoice for $39 for 9 monthly issues and you'll rush my FREE Bonus Gift: *The Educator's Internet Resource Handbook.* If I choose not to subscribe, I'll return the invoice marked "cancel" and keep the trial issue free of charge.

Name: _____ Title: _____

School/Organization: _____

Address: _____

City: _____

State/Province: _____ Zip/Postal Code: _ _____

Address is: ☐ School   ☐ Home

Phone: (_____)_____

Fax: (_____)_____

Email: _____

CLASSROOM CONNECT
Internet made easy in the classroom™
Classroom Connect
1866 Colonial Village Lane, Lancaster, PA 17605-0488
Phone: **(800) 638-1639**   Fax: **(717) 393-5752**
Email: **connect@classroom.net**
URL: **http://www.classroom.net**

☐ Send my FREE color catalog, plus discount coupons

0996

How to use the Internet in the K-12 classroom

The Internet Revealed
video series

This landmark videotape production quickly delivers an A-to-Z understanding of what the Internet is and how to tap its limitless educational resources. It's the one place students and teachers can turn for a thorough orientation and how-to-do-it instructions that get the beginner online. Tim McLain, nationally known writer and Websurfer for *Classroom Connect*, is your host for this lively and easy-to-understand series of four top-of-the-line, movie-quality video productions. The tapes can be viewed as a set or individually in any order.

Tape #1: The Amazing Internet gives teachers and students a taste of the tremendous global teaching and learning power. It introduces all of the communication, research and navigation tools and the phenomenal World Wide Web. Captures and holds student interest from start to finish! *Running time 17 minutes.*

Tape #2: Internet Email is the most versatile and the most commonly used communications tool. Here are clear, step-by-step directions for using the power of electronic mail to join over 4,000 global discussion lists, collaborate on international projects, and communicate with teachers, families, and students all across the globe. *Running time 27 minutes.*

Tape #3: Searching the Internet teaches hands-on navigation skills and valuable searching techniques. Learn to unlock the treasure trove of educational resources on the Internet. Includes gopher, Archie, Veronica, Jughead, principles of Boolean searching, and more. Bonus section on WebWanderer, WebCrawler, Lycos, Yahoo, and other World Wide Web search engines. *Running time 24 minutes.*

Tape #4: Discovering the World Wide Web opens the door to an inexhaustible wealth of educational information. It's an up-to-the-minute teaching and learning tool of unparalleled scope. Easy to understand, it turns viewers into World Wide Web power users. *Running time 38 minutes.*

4 VHS videotapes, ~~complete set price $150~~

EDUCATOR'S SPECIAL ! $125
Individual tapes: $40 each.

To order, detach or photocopy coupon and send to address shown. For faster service, contact:

Classroom Connect
1866 Colonial Village Lane
Lancaster, PA 17601
Phone: **(800) 638-1639** Fax: **(717) 393-5752**
Email: **connect@classroom.net**
URL: **http://www.classroom.net**

❑ **YES!** Send me **The Internet Revealed** complete 4 videotape set at **$125.**

❑ Send only the individual tapes indicated at **$40 each**:
  ❑ Tape 1: *The Amazing Internet* _____
  ❑ Tape 2: *Internet Email* _____
  ❑ Tape 3: *Searching the Internet* _____
  ❑ Tape 4: *Discovering the World Wide Web* _____
  T O T A L $_____

I may review the tapes for 10 days. If satisfied, I pay the invoice amount. If not, I return the tapes in good condition with the invoice marked "cancel." If prepaid, I'll receive a full refund immediately.

Name: _____

School: _____

Title: _____

Address: _____

City: _____ State: ___ Zip: _____

Phone: (__) _____ Fax: (__) _____

Email: _____
                                           09/96

PAYMENT OPTIONS
❑ **Payment enclosed** *(Free shipping & handling)*

❑ **Bill my credit card** *(Free shipping & handling)*
  ❑ Visa   ❑ MC   ❑ AmEx
  Card #: _____
  Exp. date: _____
  Signature: _____

❑ **School PO #:** _____

❑ **Bill me** (Shipping & handling will be added: $6 U.S., $10 elsewhere)

Internet made easy in the classroom™

Classroom Connect
1866 Colonial Village Lane
Lancaster, PA 17601
Phone: **(800) 638-1639** Fax: **(717) 393-5752**
Email: **connect@classroom.net**
URL: **http://www.classroom.net**

A visual tour of over 150 exciting educational Web sites!

Educator's World Wide Web ™

TourGuide

Find educational treasures instantly with this easy-to-use book/CD-ROM package!

Over 150 of the most valuable and fascinating educational sites have been packaged into one convenient sourcebook covering eleven subject areas. Each Web site profile includes a large reproduction of the computer screen, address information, description of the contents, ideas on how to integrate the Web site information into your curriculum, PLUS pointers to related gopher, Web, and ftp sites — giving you literally thousands of resources.

Added bonus — FREE CD-ROM

We've captured hundreds of sites on the CD-ROM — it's like having the Internet at your fingertips without even going online! Multiple active hyperlinks allow you to sample each site's contents. As an added benefit, a Web browser is included on the CD-ROM.

$39.95
Completely revised for 1996, Softcover, Over 200 pages, Illustrated, Color Section, FREE CD-ROM and Web browser.
ISBN 0-932577-16-4

Classroom Connect
1866 Colonial Village Lane, Lancaster, PA 17605-0488
Phone: **(800) 638-1639**
Fax: **(717) 393-5752**
Email: **connect@classroom.net**
URL: **http://www.classroom.net**

EDUCATOR'S WORLD WIDE WEB TOURGUIDE
—— 10-Day FREE Trial Offer ——

❏ **YES!** Please send me the
EDUCATOR'S WORLD WIDE WEB TOURGUIDE
book and CD-ROM disk with Web browser, priced at only $39.95

If I am not completely satisfied, I may return all items in good condition within 10 days for a full refund.

Name: _____ Title: _____

School/Organization: _____

Address: _____

City: _____

State/Province: _____

Zip/Postal Code: _____

Address is: ❏ School ❏ Home

Phone: (_____) _____ Fax: (_____)_____

Email:_____

PAYMENT OPTIONS:

❏ Payment enclosed

❏ Charge to my credit card
   ❏ Visa ❏ MasterCard ❏ American Express

Card #: _____

Expiration date: _____

Signature: _____

❏ School P.O. #: _____

(Add shipping & handling: U.S. $6, elsewhere $10)

Classroom Connect
1866 Colonial Village Lane, Lancaster, PA 17601
Phone: **(800) 638-1639** Fax: **(717) 393-5752**
Email: **connect@classroom.net**
URL: **http://www.classroom.net**

09/96

NEW

The Educators' Essential Internet Training System

The easiest way to teach the Internet

Everything you need to conduct a complete Internet workshop for your staff—in one easy-to-use trainer's kit.

This complete kit includes:
- step-by-step trainer's manual
- over 150 color slides on diskette
- trainer slide follow-along
- two instructional videotapes
- FREE Internet service for 30 days

- 20 easy-to-follow participants' workbooks
- blackline masters of presentation
- Internet access and navigation software
- and more!

Topics include:
- Seven best uses of the Internet in education
- Overview of the most popular ways to get on the Internet
- How to effectively use email, telnet, ftp, mailing lists, Usenet newsgroups, World Wide Web, and more!
- Critical things to remember when creating an Acceptable Use Policy — *sample AUP included*
- Shortcuts and tips busy teachers use to find lesson plans, create projects for the classroom
- Where to go and what to do to find the best educational resources on the Internet
- How to integrate the Internet into the curriculum — just the way you want it
- 50 classroom integration ideas
- Internet project list with complete contact information.

Also includes Internet lesson plans, training tips, and curriculum integration ideas!
Additional participant workbooks available.

Bonus: Complete sections designed for use with hands-on Internet training workshops.

CLASSROOM CONNECT
1866 Colonial Village Lane
Lancaster, PA 17605-0488

FOR FASTER SERVICE —
Phone: **(800) 638-1639**
Fax: **(717) 393-5752**
Email: **connect@classroom.net**
URL: **http://www.classroom.net**

---

❶ ☐ YES! Please rush the *Educators' Essential Internet Training System* to me. My special limited-time price for the complete kit is **only $199** (Reg. $249) — **a $50 savings!** I understand that if I'm not completely satisfied with the *Educators' Essential Internet Training System,* I may return the kit within 10 days for a full refund.

Name: _____ Title: _____

School/Org: _____ Street: _____

City: _____ State/Province: _____ Zip/Postal Code: _____

Address is: ☐ Home ☐ School   Phone: (___) _____

Fax: (___) _____ Email: _____

CLASSROOM CONNECT
1866 Colonial Village Lane
Lancaster, PA 17605-0488

FOR FASTER SERVICE —
Phone: **(800) 638-1639**
Fax: **(717) 393-5752**
Email: **connect@classroom.net**
URL: **http://www.classroom.net**

---

❷

Order	
_____ Training Systems (reg. $249) each $199	$ _____
_____ Additional Seminar Participant Paks	
Shipped in sets of 20 $50/set	$ _____
Subtotal	$ _____
PA residents add 6% sales tax	$ _____
Please add shipping and handling	$ _____
TOTAL	$ _____

Shipping & Handling

U.S. — $12
Canada — $22
Foreign — $37
Foreign orders allow 6–8 weeks for regular delivery. Additional charge for shipping by air.

❸ Payment Options (Payable in US funds only, drawn on US bank)

☐ My check is enclosed (Made payable to *Classroom Connect*)

☐ Charge to my credit card: ☐ VISA ☐ MasterCard ☐ AmEx

Card # : _____ Exp. Date: _____

Signature: _____

☐ P.O. # (if not attached): _____

☐ Bill me

Educator's INTERNET CD Club

New! Internet

Classroom-ready Internet™

Join the Educator's Internet CD Club today — and receive a year's worth of Internet resources on CD-ROM. No Internet access required!

iCD — for every subject area and grade level

As an iCD Club member, you'll receive four CDs during the school year. Every iCD is packed full of actual Web sites organized by subject area including: science, mathematics, language arts, world cultures, and more! You'll get great multimedia Web sites appropriate for every subject area and every grade level!

You have total control!

When you use the Educator's Internet CD Club, you can feel confident that your students will always have access to the sites you've designated. You also don't have to worry about students accessing any "inappropriate material" — because there isn't any — just pure information developed for classroom use.

Here's what you'll get:

- Actual Internet Web Sites — Six to eight different subject areas chock full of the best Web sites edited and reformatted for classroom use.
- Lesson Plans — Each subject area contains ready-to-use lesson plans.
- Activity Sheets — Gradable activity sheets for each subject area make assessment easy.
- Teaching Tips — Dozens of ideas, "mini-lessons," and added resources to further help you integrate the Educator's Internet CD Club into your classroom.
- Educator's IdeaBank — Lesson plans for any curriculum, classroom software, project ideas and other "teacher-only" resources that will help you enhance all of your educational programs.

Here's how the iCD Club works:

When you join the Educator's Internet CD Club, you'll receive four CD-ROMs — one iCD will be sent to you every 7–8 weeks during the school year. As a Charter member of the iCD Club, you'll pay the special Charter Member rate of ONLY $129 for the year (a $40 savings off the regular rate).

Plus, as an iCD member, you'll also be able to buy **subject-specific CDs** as they become available at the discount membership price of ONLY $19.95 — A 50% savings off the regular price of $39.95. Subjects include math, science, astronomy, social studies and more!

Netscape 2.0 included!

Each iCD PowerPak comes equipped with 2.0 *(for educational use only)*, the latest in Web browser technology. And we've included six multimedia player programs.

Special Bonus CD FREE, if you act now!

As a limited time offer, you'll receive absolutely FREE with your membership, the Teacher's Resource PowerPak CD — a $39.95 value! This CD is packed with "teacher only" resources and Internet teaching tips and techniques. Includes actual Internet Web sites for teachers and multimedia software. Includes 30 days FREE Internet access featuring Netscape Navigator™ software

"This is a way to get more kids to use the Net and its wealth of information, even for those who only have one or NO phone lines! It makes the Web portable."

— Barb Falkenburg
Library/Media Specialist
Edgewood, MD

"You're going to love using iCD in the classroom — brilliant multimedia resources, lesson plans, and project ideas — all classroom-ready for your immediate use."

Special Charter Membership Offer Regularly **$169**

$129 Item No. CCD00
Annual Membership includes 4 CD-ROMs
Plus FREE Teachers Resource PowerPak CD

SAVE

(800) 638-1639

24 hour Fax Line (717) 393-5752
URL: http://www.classroom.net

LICENSE AGREEMENT AND LIMITED WARRANTY

READ THE FOLLOWING TERMS AND CONDITIONS CAREFULLY BEFORE OPENING THIS SOFTWARE MEDIA PACKAGE. THIS LEGAL DOCUMENT IS AN AGREEMENT BETWEEN YOU AND PRENTICE-HALL, INC. (THE "COMPANY"). BY OPENING THIS SEALED SOFTWARE MEDIA PACKAGE, YOU ARE AGREEING TO BE BOUND BY THESE TERMS AND CONDITIONS. IF YOU DO NOT AGREE WITH THESE TERMS AND CONDITIONS, DO NOT OPEN THE SOFTWARE MEDIA PACKAGE. PROMPTLY RETURN THE UNOPENED SOFTWARE MEDIA PACKAGE AND ALL ACCOMPANYING ITEMS TO THE PLACE YOU OBTAINED THEM FOR A FULL REFUND OF ANY SUMS YOU HAVE PAID.

1.   **GRANT OF LICENSE:** In consideration of your payment of the license fee, which is part of the price you paid for this product, and your agreement to abide by the terms and conditions of this Agreement, the Company grants to you a nonexclusive right to use and display the copy of the enclosed software program (hereinafter the "SOFTWARE") on a single computer (i.e., with a single CPU) at a single location so long as you comply with the terms of this Agreement. The Company reserves all rights not expressly granted to you under this Agreement.

2.   **OWNERSHIP OF SOFTWARE:** You own only the magnetic or physical media (the enclosed SOFTWARE) on which the SOFTWARE is recorded or fixed, but the Company retains all the rights, title, and ownership to the SOFTWARE recorded on the original SOFTWARE copy(ies) and all subsequent copies of the SOFTWARE, regardless of the form or media on which the original or other copies may exist. This license is not a sale of the original SOFTWARE or any copy to you.

3.   **COPY RESTRICTIONS:** This SOFTWARE and the accompanying printed materials and user manual (the "Documentation") are the subject of copyright. You may not copy the Documentation or the SOFTWARE, except that you may make a single copy of the SOFTWARE for backup or archival purposes only. You may be held legally responsible for any copying or copyright infringement which is caused or encouraged by your failure to abide by the terms of this restriction.

4.   **USE RESTRICTIONS:** You may not network the SOFTWARE or otherwise use it on more than one computer or computer terminal at the same time. You may physically transfer the SOFTWARE from one computer to another provided that the SOFTWARE is used on only one computer at a time. You may not distribute copies of the SOFTWARE or Documentation to others. You may not reverse engineer, disassemble, decompile, modify, adapt, translate, or create derivative works based on the SOFTWARE or the Documentation without the prior written consent of the Company.

5.   **TRANSFER RESTRICTIONS:** The enclosed SOFTWARE is licensed only to you and may not be transferred to any one else without the prior written consent of the Company. Any unauthorized transfer of the SOFTWARE shall result in the immediate termination of this Agreement.

6.   **TERMINATION:** This license is effective until terminated. This license will terminate automatically without notice from the Company and become null and void if you fail to comply with any provisions or limitations of this license. Upon termination, you shall destroy the Documentation and all copies of the SOFTWARE. All provisions of this Agreement as to warranties, limitation of liability, remedies or damages, and our ownership rights shall survive termination.

7.   **MISCELLANEOUS:** This Agreement shall be construed in accordance with the laws of the United States of America and the State of New York and shall benefit the Company, its affiliates, and assignees.

8.   **LIMITED WARRANTY AND DISCLAIMER OF WARRANTY:** The Company warrants that the SOFTWARE, when properly used in accordance with the Documentation, will operate in substantial conformity with the description of the SOFTWARE set forth in the Documentation. The Company does not warrant that the SOFTWARE will meet your requirements or that the operation of the SOFTWARE will be uninterrupted or error-free. The Company warrants that the

media on which the SOFTWARE is delivered shall be free from defects in materials and workmanship under normal use for a period of thirty (30) days from the date of your purchase. Your only remedy and the Company's only obligation under these limited warranties is, at the Company's option, return of the warranted item for a refund of any amounts paid by you or replacement of the item. Any replacement of SOFTWARE or media under the warranties shall not extend the original warranty period. The limited warranty set forth above shall not apply to any SOFTWARE which the Company determines in good faith has been subject to misuse, neglect, improper installation, repair, alteration, or damage by you. EXCEPT FOR THE EXPRESSED WARRANTIES SET FORTH ABOVE, THE COMPANY DISCLAIMS ALL WARRANTIES, EXPRESS OR IMPLIED, INCLUDING WITHOUT LIMITATION, THE IMPLIED WARRANTIES OF MERCHANTABILITY AND FITNESS FOR A PARTICULAR PURPOSE. EXCEPT FOR THE EXPRESS WARRANTY SET FORTH ABOVE, THE COMPANY DOES NOT WARRANT, GUARANTEE, OR MAKE ANY REPRESENTATION REGARDING THE USE OR THE RESULTS OF THE USE OF THE SOFTWARE IN TERMS OF ITS CORRECTNESS, ACCURACY, RELIABILITY, CURRENTNESS, OR OTHERWISE.

IN NO EVENT, SHALL THE COMPANY OR ITS EMPLOYEES, AGENTS, SUPPLIERS, OR CONTRACTORS BE LIABLE FOR ANY INCIDENTAL, INDIRECT, SPECIAL, OR CONSEQUENTIAL DAMAGES ARISING OUT OF OR IN CONNECTION WITH THE LICENSE GRANTED UNDER THIS AGREEMENT, OR FOR LOSS OF USE, LOSS OF DATA, LOSS OF INCOME OR PROFIT, OR OTHER LOSSES, SUSTAINED AS A RESULT OF INJURY TO ANY PERSON, OR LOSS OF OR DAMAGE TO PROPERTY, OR CLAIMS OF THIRD PARTIES, EVEN IF THE COMPANY OR AN AUTHORIZED REPRESENTATIVE OF THE COMPANY HAS BEEN ADVISED OF THE POSSIBILITY OF SUCH DAMAGES. IN NO EVENT SHALL LIABILITY OF THE COMPANY FOR DAMAGES WITH RESPECT TO THE SOFTWARE EXCEED THE AMOUNTS ACTUALLY PAID BY YOU, IF ANY, FOR THE SOFTWARE.

SOME JURISDICTIONS DO NOT ALLOW THE LIMITATION OF IMPLIED WARRANTIES OR LIABILITY FOR INCIDENTAL, INDIRECT, SPECIAL, OR CONSEQUENTIAL DAMAGES, SO THE ABOVE LIMITATIONS MAY NOT ALWAYS APPLY. THE WARRANTIES IN THIS AGREEMENT GIVE YOU SPECIFIC LEGAL RIGHTS AND YOU MAY ALSO HAVE OTHER RIGHTS WHICH VARY IN ACCORDANCE WITH LOCAL LAW.

ACKNOWLEDGMENT

YOU ACKNOWLEDGE THAT YOU HAVE READ THIS AGREEMENT, UNDERSTAND IT, AND AGREE TO BE BOUND BY ITS TERMS AND CONDITIONS. YOU ALSO AGREE THAT THIS AGREEMENT IS THE COMPLETE AND EXCLUSIVE STATEMENT OF THE AGREEMENT BETWEEN YOU AND THE COMPANY AND SUPERSEDES ALL PROPOSALS OR PRIOR AGREEMENTS, ORAL, OR WRITTEN, AND ANY OTHER COMMUNICATIONS BETWEEN YOU AND THE COMPANY OR ANY REPRESENTATIVE OF THE COMPANY RELATING TO THE SUBJECT MATTER OF THIS AGREEMENT.

Should you have any questions concerning this Agreement or if you wish to contact the Company for any reason, please contact in writing at the address below.

Robin Short
Prentice Hall PTR
One Lake Street
Upper Saddle River, New Jersey 07458

Internet Homework Helper CD-ROM

Free software to get you up and running on the Internet right away

Here is your CD-ROM, jam-packed with free software to get you onto the Internet and using its resources in minutes! There are seven main items on the disc:

1. **Internet access software.** From EarthLink Network® this includes EarthLink Network TotalAccess™ software with Netscape Navigator.™ The software entitles you to 10 days free, unlimited dial-in Internet access with no sign-up fee.

2. ***Internet Homework Helper* HotPage.** Contains "live" Internet links to many of the best online sites listed throughout this book.

3. **HyperStudio™ multimedia software demo.** Enables you to use the multimedia files you find on the Internet to create colorful, interactive slide shows. This demo version also includes close to 200 MB of clip art, video clips, sounds, and other multimedia files.

4. **Monstrous Media Kit for Macintosh.** Multimedia authoring software that's perfect for students new to computers who want to create fun, informative interactive presentations with sounds and video.

5. **CyberPatrol™ Internet access filter software.** A highly flexible and effective means for blocking access to inappropriate online sites. The version on this CD-ROM is enabled for a full 30-day free trial.

6. **SurfWatch™ Internet access management utility.** Used by parents and teachers to control children's access to the Internet. When SurfWatch is installed on a computer, children have less chance of accidentally or deliberately being exposed to unwanted material.

7. **Electric Library™ software.** Provides an outstanding online research collection. The software on the CD-ROM is enabled for a full 30-day free trial—a whole month's access to a complete online research library.